AF528498

Modern Business Communication

Modern Business Communication

Rakesh Bijlani

ADHYAYAN
ADHYAYAN PUBLISHERS & DISTRIBUTORS
NEW DELHI (INDIA)

Published by
ADHYAYAN PUBLISHERS & DISTRIBUTORS
4378/4B, 105, J.M.D. House, Murari Lal Street
Ansari Road, Darya Ganj, New Delhi - 110002
Ph.: 011-23263018, 011-23277156, Fax: 011-23280028
Email: adhyayanpublishers@yahoo.com

Modern Business Communication

© Publishers
Edition 2011
ISBN 978-81-8435-290-0

The responsibility for facts stated, opinion expressed or conclusions reached and plagiarism, if any, in this book is entirely that of the author/editor. The publisher bears no responsibility for them whatsoever.

Printed in India

Published by Harish Chandra Yadav for Adhyayan Publishers & Distributors, Laser Typeseting at A.V. Rao and Printed at Tarun Offset Printers, Delhi

Preface

Business communication is any communication used to build partnerships, intellectual resources, to promote an idea, a product, service, or an organisation – with the objective of creating value for the business. It communication involves constant flow of information. Feedback is integral part of business communication.

Organisations these days are verly large. It involves number of people. There are various levels of hierarchy in an organisation. Greater the number of levels, the more difficult is the job of managing the organisation. Communication here plays a very important role in process of directing and controlling the people in the oragnisation. Immediate feedback can be obtained and misunderstandings if any can be avoided. There should be effective communication between superiors and subordinated in an organisation, between organisation and society at large.

Business Communication is goal oriented. The rules, regulations and policies of a company have to be communicated to people within and outside the organisation. Business Communication is regulated by certain rules and norms. In early times, business communication was limited to paper-work, telephone calls etc. But now with advent of technology, we have cell phones, video conferencing, emails, satellite communication to support business communication. Effective business communication helps in building goodwill of an organisation.

The present book is a comprehensive resource on modern business communication, designed for undergraduate, post-experience and professional management courses. Divided into seven chapters, the book emphasises not only the theoretical basis, but also the successful practice of effective business communication.

Rakesh Bijlani

Preface

Contents

1

Introduction to Business Communication

Communication is neither transmission of message nor message itself. It is the mutual exchange of understanding, originating with the receiver. Communication needs to be effective in business. Communication is essence of management. The basic functions of management (planning, organising, staffing, directing and controlling) cannot be performed well without effective communication. Business communication involves constant flow of information. Feedback is integral part of business communication. Organisations these days are very large. It involves number of people. There are various levels of hierarchy in an organisation. Greater the number of levels, the more difficult is the job of managing the organisation. Communication here plays a very important role in process of directing and controlling the people in the organisation. Immediate feedback can be obtained and misunderstandings if any can be avoided. There should be effective communication between superiors and subordinated in an organisation, between organisation and society at large (for example between management and trade unions). It is essential for success and growth of an organisation. Communication gaps should not occur in any organisation.

Business communication is goal oriented. The rules, regulations and policies of a company have to be communicated to people within and outside the organisation. Business Communication is regulated by certain rules and norms. In early times, business communication was limited to paper-work, telephone calls etc. But now with advent of technology, we have cell phones, video conferencing, emails, satellite communication to support business communication. Effective business communication helps in building goodwill of an organisation.

Business communication is somewhat different and unique rather from other type of communication since the purpose of business is to get profit. Thus to make good way for profit the communicator should develop good communication skills. Everyone knows that in the present day trends the knowledge alone won't be a fruitful one to have sustainable development. By knowing the importance of communication many organisations started training their employees in betterment of communication techniques.

Types of Business Communication

It is very important to know the type of business communication used in order to know the specific etiquettes and standards to use in a specific situation. Here are some of the communications used in business.

- *Electronic communication* comprises different modes of communication out from the traditional way. It includes e-mail, fax, teleconferencing and voicemail. This is used for external contacts and for people within the business organisation.
- *Employment communication* is a mode of communication used for employees but specifically for accepting applicants for a job. It includes application letter, follow-up communications, interview and resumes.
- *Nonverbal communication* is a mode of communication that uses body language and other means of communicating without the use of uttering words. It includes body language, expression, gestures, professional appearance, time or space.
- *Verbal communication* is a mode of communication that uses the uttering of words in communicating to external contacts and employees. It includes feedback, instructions, presentations, and telephone.
- *Written communication* is a mode of communication that requires writing in order to communicate. It includes letters, memos, proposals and reports.

It is very important that when engaging into whatever type of business communication every person in the business organisation from the top to lower rank should know the basic concepts of business communication, and how to apply them in the daily operation of the business.

Take note that a little mistake in giving out the information because of wrongfully conveying the message in any ways can cause damage to the business and worse can cost millions to the company.

Importance of Business Communication

Communication is essential for life in general but in business settings, it is critical. Communication is more than just a matter of speaking and hearing, especially within a business setting. Good communication, on the other hand, means that your message will be sent and that the people or organisations understand the message in its entirety. Further, they are much more likely to respond in a positive manner if the message was communicated effectively. A poorly communicated message will likely result in an unfavorable response.

Communication is one of the basic functions of management in any organisation and its importance can hardly be overemphasised. It is a process of transmitting information, ideas, thoughts, opinions and plans between various parts of an organisation. You cannot have human relations without communication. However, good and effective communication is required not only for good human relations but also for good and successful business.

You can use softwares like business writing software for writing effective business communication, which is required at various levels and for various aspects in an organisation such as:

Communication for Manager and Employee Relations

Effective communication of information and decision is an essential component for management-employee relations. The manager cannot get the work done from employees unless they are communicated effectively of what he wants to be done? He should also be sure of some basic facts such as how to communicate and what results can be expected from that communication. Most of management problems arise because of lack of effective communication. Chances of misunderstanding and misrepresentation can be minimised with proper communication system.

Communication for Motivation and Employee Morale

Communication is also a basic tool for motivation, which can improve morale of the employees in an organisation. Inappropriate or faulty communication among employees or between manager and his subordinates is the major cause of conflict and low morale at work. Manager should clarify to employees about what is to be done, how well are they doing and what can be done for better performance to improve their motivation. He can prepare a written statement, clearly outlining the relationship between company objectives and personal objectives and integrating the interest of the two.

Communication for increasing productivity

With effective communication, you can maintain a good human relation in the organisation and by encouraging ideas or suggestions from employees or workers and implementing them whenever possible, you can also increase production at low cost.

Communication for Employees

It is through the communication that employees submit their work reports, comments, grievances and suggestions to their seniors or management. Organisation should have effective and speedy communication policy and procedures to avoid delays, misunderstandings, confusion or distortions of facts and to establish harmony among all the concerned people and departments.

Importance of Written Communication

Communication may be made through oral or written. In oral communication, listeners can make out what speakers is trying to say, but in written communication, text matter in the message is a reflection of your thinking. So, written communication or message should be clear, purposeful and concise with correct words, to avoid any misinterpretation of your message. Written communications provides a permanent record for future use and it also gives an opportunity to employees to put up their comments or suggestions in writing.

Organisational Communication and Culture

In business, reputation and credibility need to be built up in order to get clients' trust and confidence. Having a sense of professionalism will bring a lot to the business, especially in a long term relationship with employees and clients. There is a need to make sure that every business deal is attended to promptly. Business communication encompasses not only communicating with external contacts but also with employees within the organisation. This will aid the business in being well-organised and every matter whether it is a problem, an inquiry or a sales letter will be attended to properly and promptly.

It does not mean that only a client's inquiry should be responded promptly but also feedbacks or problems arising inside and outside the business as well. This is done to have a balance within the internal and external factors, especially in relation to dealing with people, whether they are employees or other external contacts.

One of the primary reasons you are in college is to get that perfect job, to become a professional in a chosen career. As a professional, you will spend a significant portion of your time associated with one or more organisations. In the workplace today, organisations are constantly changing: structures are changing, organisational decision making is changing, and requirements for employee productivity are also changing. Indeed, one of the key variables in employee success is communication effectiveness. Much of what you have learned thus far in this text will allow you to be an effective organisational communicator.

Today's organisations require more teamwork than in past decades. The business world is expanding, and new markets are opening around the world; this globalisation requires employees to understand and adapt to a multicultural world. Communication in this multicultural world means knowing, understanding, and adapting to different communication rules across cultures. Management theorist Peter Drucker believes that contemporary organisations are now looking for "the new knowledge worker," who possesses four key characteristics:

— A college education,

— The ability to apply analytical and theoretical thinking,

— A commitment to lifelong learning, and

— Good communication skills.

Drucker suggests that the single most important characteristic of this "new knowledge worker" is his or her *ability to communicate with others who do not share the same worldview.*

Information technology is also dramatically changing the nature of the workplace. Computers and telecommunications allow us to communicate instantly across geographic boundaries. Thus, the complexity of organisational life and the rapidly changing role of technology mean more demands upon individual organisational members than ever before. Those who are successful in this changing world of work are those who develop what organisational theorist Pamela Shockley-Zalabak calls "communication competency": knowledge, skills, values, and sensitivity. Employees must possess knowledge about the organisation's communication environment. They must be sensitive to others and understand their feelings and meanings. Values reflect concern for the well-being of others in the communicating situation and an understanding of responsibility within those situations.

Organisations today depend upon creative and flexible people, workers who can solve problems working with others who may not share their points of view. To prepare for these complex organisations, communication competency is critical. Your present educational experiences provide an excellent opportunity to learn communication competency in organisations, since the school you attend is a distinct organisation that you must negotiate successfully. Many of the skills you are now developing will prepare you for the workforce. The first step in developing communication competency in organisations is understanding the cultural and systemic components of organisations.

It is critical to understand that organisations operate as distinct cultures. An organisation's culture represents the actions, practices, language, and artifacts of a group. A culture is revealed *symbolically.*

We understand a culture in numerous ways—by the way people explain the culture, by the tools used to create and maintain that culture, and by the values and beliefs that guide actions and practices. An organisation's culture results from the accumulation of learning and behaviour among a group of people and of how those individuals communicate their understanding of each other as members of the culture. Organisational culture persists through the organisation's personnel changes. As a result, communication creates and sustains culture, while simultaneously influencing how individuals communicate and interact. Many symbolic practices make up culture, including language, stories, rites and rituals, and structure.

Language

Each organisation develops its own vocabulary with which it refers to its members' activity. One of the first ways organisational members learn expressed values is through the organisation's mission statement. Have you read your university's mission statement? What does it tell you about the organisation's value system? The vocabulary or language expresses the organisation's past, present, and future values. The box Cultural Links: Organisational Cultures and Mission Statements describes the role of mission statements in organisations.

Language also reveals a great deal about such things as power relationships among members. How people are addressed provides information about their status. The level of formality or informality of language tells individuals how to act with peers, supervisors, or customers. Are supervisors in the organisation referred to by their first names or addressed as Ms. Johnson, Mr. Obama, or Dr. Singh? Whether language is formal or informal may also provide insights about how organisation members should dress or whether people are encouraged to discuss personal or social interests while at work. What special language or vocabulary have you come to understand as part of your university experience?

Stories

One way organisational members talk about their culture is through stories and myths. Organisational history is explained through corporate stories. These tell of past successes and failures, helping organisational members understand the type of risks that are acceptable. They provide members with an opportunity to recognise past and present "heroes" as well. Stories provide a critical socialisation function for new members of the organisation. They provide information about how work is done, about the appropriateness of many kinds of communication, and about the values and beliefs among organisational members. While new employees are normally provided with rule books or "standard operating procedures," stories allow new members to compare what is "written" with what is unwritten but "understood" by its members. A final function of stories is that they provide opportunities for members to feel connected to one another and to the organisation as a whole.

Rites and Rituals

The organisation's rites and rituals often symbolise the "tools" members use to create and maintain culture. Examples include the annual holiday party, the company picnic, or performance reviews. The most famous "rituals" of university life might include surviving registration, learning the maze of financial aid, and, of course, participating in graduation with all its pomp and circumstance. There are also other annual or seasonal rituals on college campuses such as homecoming parades, fund-raisers for non-profit agencies, or tailgate parties.

Structure

An organisation's structure is revealed in two ways—through the roles that individuals play and the rules and policies that govern the organisation. Thus, in order to communicate effectively within the organisation, employees must understand the roles, rules, and policies that make up the organisation's underlying support and framework.

Roles

Just as power relationships are revealed by how employees address one another, organisational structure can also be identified by individuals' titles or by the roles they play in the group. In the university system, faculty have many titles that refer to such things as their level of education, their longevity, and their level of professional standing among their peers. A lecturer or adjunct, an instructor, an assistant professor, an associate professor, or a full professor may teach one of your classes. These titles reflect the person's teaching responsibilities, his or her rank within the organisational hierarchy, and to some degree, his or her status among other faculty. There are, of course, other titles in the hierarchy, such as associate dean, dean, vice president, provost, president, chancellor, and trustee. These titles reflect an individual's job description and levels of responsibility within the university. Organisational charts that depict the relationships among the various offices and roles in your university will help you understand who's who and will give you a better sense of how communication flows within the organisation.

Rules and Policies

Another example of structure is in the rules and policies by which organisational members make decisions. Every organisation has a set of operating policies that are mandated by various authoritative figures or bodies such as the board of trustees, the president, or department heads. When you entered your college, you probably received a student handbook or code of conduct containing your school's rules and policies. Rules are more or less formal, depending upon the organisation and the type of product or service they provide. Like our earlier discussion of group rules and norms, organisational rules also may develop either implicitly or explicitly. As with groups, the more explicitly the rules are developed in the organisation and the more rules members agree upon, the more effective the organisational communication may be. Policies are formal statements about what is and is not expected of organisational members. The most common types of policies in any organisation refer to such things as pay, benefits, hiring and firing, promotion, leave, and so on.

Once individuals in organisations learn how to "read" the culture, they can interpret "what it means to work here" much more effectively. Think about the last job you had. Did you learn what was expected of you by reading the corporate manual or by observing the company's day-to-day standard operating procedures? Did you get more information from watching others and hearing stories about "heroes and villains"? When individuals can interpret cultural symbols correctly, they begin to establish the knowledge and skills needed to succeed in that organisation.

Understanding that an organisation develops its own unique cultural characteristics can assist all members in developing a greater comprehension of the organisation's "work life." Grasping the language, stories, rites, rituals, and structure can allow members to reduce uncertainty about their jobs and help them shape and adapt relationships within the organisation. As a result, individuals come to know their place within the organisational system through knowledge of its culture. The box Communication Links: Uncertainty Reduction Theory describes the ways in which new employees attempt to understand the cultural characteristics of an organisation new to them.

Communication and Organisational Systems

Understanding organisations as systems means recognising that every that organisation exists within a larger environment. A *system* is a set of parts (individuals) that are interconnected (relationships) within its environment. The larger environment provides resources to the organisation (input) and utilised the products or services the organisation creates (output). What the organisation does with these products and services is called *throughput.* To illustrate, a university system depends upon the larger environment for a variety of human, information, or fiscal resources such as students, faculty, and other employees; knowledge and information; and money from the state, benefactors, grants, and tuition fees. The university also depends upon such physical resources as electricity, computers, books, equipment, and furniture. The university system generates output through its graduates, who are potential employees, and through additional knowledge and information from research, community service endeavours, and tax dollars paid by university workers. The university processes all the resources from the environment in classrooms, meetings, research projects, and other types of activities, and this becomes the essence of "throughput" at a university. Every system is unique, just like every college or university is unique. And every individual within the organisation is connected with one another in the system.

In order to understand the way a system operates, we will discuss several characteristics, including wholeness, interdependence, openness, adaptability, and equifinality. Systems theorists Daniel Katz and Robert Kahn suggest that a systems approach focuses on problems of relationships, structure, and interdependence rather than on concrete objects in the organisation. Let's look at the relationships between the parts (individuals) of a system and the way individuals understand and process feedback to understand the system.

Wholeness

The first characteristic of a system is wholeness, or the unique configuration of the system's parts. Most organisations have different departments, offices, or individuals, but the way these elements coordinate activities constitutes the system. Restructuring the system will not threaten the wholeness of the organisation. Some universities, for example, are organised by the college structure. The university has several colleges. Each college consists of several departments. In our universities, for example, the Communication Department is a part of the College of Arts and Sciences. The chair or head of our department is responsible to the college's dean. Some larger universities, on the other hand, have an entire College of Communication that consists of several different departments such as broadcasting, film studies, journalism, communication studies, and others. Though uniquely configured, each of our institutions remains a whole organisation; it is not a loose coalition of independent, autonomous units.

Interdependence and Synergy

It is necessary to understand how the parts of the system function together in an interdependent fashion to create the whole. In a family, team, or business, the relationships among people make the group a system. Thus, systems theorists suggest, "the whole is greater than the sum of its parts." Collective energy, or synergy, increases when the parts work together. This synergy can be negative or positive. Negative synergy results from ineffective communication and misunderstanding. Positive synergy results from recognising the interdependence between system components and competent communication within the system.

Openness

Every organisation interacts differently with the environment. Environments are dynamic and changing. Today's organisations must monitor the environment and adapt to changing resources in that environment. The concept of openness refers to how the system uses feedback to adapt to changes in the larger environment. For example, changes can be economic (changes in the stock market, in number of customers, or in cost of supplies), political (changes in legislation that affect the organisation), or human (changes in technology require more worker training). Openness also means that organisations that exist in a larger system are constantly impacted by events in that larger system.

On September 11, 2001, the tragedies in New York and Washington reverberated around the world and in our schools. Many of us knew someone connected to another person working in the World Trade Centre or in the Pentagon, so the events caused shock waves on our campuses. Many faculty at our universities cancelled classes, called loved ones just to hear their voices, or talked with coworkers about their feelings. The outpouring of assistance—from raising money to donating blood— reverberated across the country and solidified our commitment to fellow Americans in need. The events of September 11 also demonstrated the incredible diversity in our American system and showed the variety of our feedback in response to tragedy. Some individuals travelled thousands of miles to assist with the rescue efforts in New York City. And while some Americans responded by reaching out to Arab Americans, others responded with hatred and violence against these individuals. We are diverse in how we give, in how we love, and in how we hate. Most of these responses are related to our individual levels of openness. In the same way, organisations respond differently to the environment depending on their respective levels of openness. For the most part, organisations that are not flexible and adaptable begin to solidify.

Adaptability through Feedback

Changes in the larger environment, then, require organisations to adapt quickly and responsibly. In order to adapt to changes, the organisation must become more pro-active in seeking out information and must adopt a flexible approach to larger environmental change. Adaptability is critical to contemporary organisations, which must constantly adopt new policies, procedures, products, and services to respond to the rapidly changing global environment. After September 11, airports around the country were closed for days, and some airlines laid off thousands of employees. Other organisations set up funding mechanisms and matched employee contributions to the "September 11th Fund," which assisted victims and their families. General Electric Corporation, for example, donated $10 million to the fund. In other words, these organisations adapted to the crisis at hand with philanthropic feedback.

Organisations must also recognise that strategies that work in one situation will not necessarily work in another. Strategies are contingent upon many environmental factors. For example, today's organisations must monitor the environment and create unique ways of adapting. A range of new jobs that focus on monitoring the environment—marketing, sales, public relations, and others—have opened up in organisations. Individuals in these jobs must have effective communication skills in order to recognise changes and to communicate those changes to others in their organisation.

Equifinality

The final characteristic of any system is equifinality. This refers to recognition that the end product (whatever output the organisation produces) can be produced in several ways. Every system has the capacity to identify and develop several ways to reach its goals. For example, think of the number of options you have when choosing an Internet provider. No matter which provider you choose, you accomplish virtually the same thing—the ability to send e-mail, surf the Net, join a chat room, and so on. Each provider, though, has *some* unique features. Another example of equifinality can be seen in the number of colleges and universities that offer communication degrees. Although there are many different ways colleges or universities might offer this degree, each may require slightly different courses or experiences within their programmes. Students achieve the same goal but travel somewhat different paths to achieve it, depending on the programme's focus.

Communication in the System

Through organisational communication, we gather, interpret, and utilise information from the environment outside the system. Communication allows the organisation to coordinate the interdependent parts within the system. Openness to feedback allows an organisation to adapt and adjust itself to environmental change. Communication and creativity within and throughout the system open a range of options in developing, modifying, marketing, and selling the organisation's products and services. Think back to the types of advertising or marketing strategies that convinced you to attend your college or university. Did admissions counsellors come to your school? Was the institution's website creative and interesting? Did you watch videos or receive a DVD? Did you receive brochures or letters? Did you go to campus and take a tour guided by a student representative? Did you speak with a faculty member? You can probably identify some key communication strategies that helped guide your decision.

Competent Business Communication

Competent organisational communication must consider its many contexts within the organisation. We communicate interpersonally with peers, supervisors, and subordinates. We also communicate with customers, clients, suppliers, and others outside the organisation. Additionally, gender and cultural differences add a level of complexity to each of these contexts. Interpersonal relationships at all levels are crucial to individual and organisational success, and they are a prerequisite for effective job performance.

Superior-Subordinate Communication

Riley and Eisenberg suggest that the key to successful communication with superiors is advocacy. Employees must understand the needs of superiors and adapt communication accordingly. One of the critical principles of effective advocacy is connecting arguments to supervisors' needs and expectations. Eisenberg and Goodall suggest the following principles to guide communication with superiors:

— *Plan a strategy*: Understand the individual and the context of your appeal.
— *Determine why the superior should listen*: Connect your appeal to something important to your boss.
— *Tailor the argument to the supervisor's style and characteristics*: Will he or she respond more favourably to statistics or a story? Adapt your evidence to his or her needs.
— *Assess the supervisor's technical knowledge*: Do not assume his or her knowledge base, know it.
— *Hone your communications skills*: Be clear and articulate in your appeals.

Communication must always be adapted to audience knowledge, expectations, values, and beliefs. Keys to successful communication to subordinates in the organisation are openness and support. Empathic listening is critical to the success of many relationships. Subordinates commonly criticise their superiors for withholding information. They need and want to know information that impacts their work. Thus, effective supervisors pass along information to subordinates and provide them with opportunities for input in discussions that impact workplace behaviour and decision making. Supportiveness in communication includes showing concern for the relationships and demonstrating respect for individuals while promoting accomplishment of tasks. Both empathic listening and genuine support from supervisors enhance employee motivation in the workplace.

Communication with Peers

Horizontal or peer communication provides social support to individuals and builds employee morale. We have discussed effective communication in work teams and its benefits in terms of decision making and relationship maintenance. Peer communication also entails talking across departments or units and with customers or suppliers. Today, focus on customer service is essential to business success. Opportunities for feedback between units in the organisation and between the organisation and its customers, coupled with rapid response to that feedback, can increase organisational effectiveness and success.

Ultimately, individuals at any level of the organisation must understand the complexity of its relationships and expectations. Communication that is clear, constant, and supportive within the variety of relational contexts enhances individual, team, and organisational effectiveness.

Using Networks and Channels Effectively

Effective organisational communication is dependent upon the appropriate use of networks and channels of communication within the organisation. Who talks to whom? Why? How? When? Where? These were some of the questions. A network links organisational members either formally or informally and describes how information travels throughout the organisation. Some formal networks are used to disseminate critical information to all employees while other networks are more informal and provide information on issues of socialisation.

Formal networks, or channels, are used most commonly when information is communicated either up (reporting the results of a particular job) or down (giving orders or advising on policy adaptation). *Informal networks* or channels are used most commonly among peers at similar levels of the organisation although sometimes the grapevine (a common name for the most pervasive informal organisational channel) is used by many individuals at all levels. The grapevine can be a positive communication channel, because it is one of the fastest ways to disseminate information. Individual members may use the grapevine to confirm information that comes from more formal channels. It assists members in interpreting and understanding information. However, the grapevine can also become a negative channel if organisational members use it as a substitute for more formal channels, such as trying to find out about critical policy or personnel changes when formal channels are lacking in information. As a result, if formal channels do not provide adequate information or allow individuals to interpret information accurately, the informal grapevine rumours replace reliable information.

Communicating Outside the Organisation

Many of you will find jobs where you will be dealing with individuals outside the organisation, such as customers, clients, suppliers, legislators, community leaders, and others. Managers today recognise that in order to ensure continued profit in the constantly changing marketplace, effective communication between the organisation and its customers and other organisations is essential. Businesses must develop and nurture long-term relationships with numerous external audiences. This is not simply a matter of economics; it is also a product of expectations. Organisations are expected to accept and enact pro-active social responsibility in their communities and in the broader global marketplace.

Organisational theorist Matthew Seeger suggests that organisations have four primary responsibilities to audiences both within and outside the organisation: philanthropic, environmental, product, and employee. Philanthropic efforts include donations of time and money to local, regional, or national charities, including arts and cultural programmes. Environmental responsibility concerns the organisation's impact on environmental resources. Product responsibility addresses product safety and conscientious use of materials in product development and production. Finally, employee responsibility includes efforts to provide a safe and motivating workplace. In the past, a common organisational philosophy was, "Let the buyer beware!" Today, however, the reverse may be true. Let the organisation beware if its products and services do not conform to customer (and other audience) expectations of social, environment, or product responsibility. Organisations, therefore, are not just about doing business but about building relationships through service and support. This is true of the "business of higher education" as well as more traditional business endeavours. The box Computer Links: Communicating Social Responsibility through a Website explains how organisations are using their websites as one of the most important channels for communicating about the ways the organisation conducts itself responsibly.

Communication Challenges in Modern Business Firms

Today's worker faces numerous challenges in the workplace. Historically workers could count on lifetime employment if they did a good job, but today that guarantee is gone. Communication in the workplace thus takes on greater importance as workers attempt to negotiate their jobs in an uncertain climate. Greater misunderstanding between and among supervisors and subordinates complicates that negotiation. The more misunderstanding occurs within an organisation, the more workers are likely to feel fear and distrust, and the less likely they may be to communicate with others.

Diverse Organisation

The workforce today looks dramatically different from that of twenty years ago. Cultural, racial, and gender diversity have never been so pronounced. For example, the number of workers over fifty-five is growing. Additionally, census data tell us that the fastest-growing ethnic population in the United States is Hispanic. As a result, the white, male-dominated workforce of yesterday is being replaced by organisations filled with individuals who look, think, and act in radically different ways.

Organisations at the turn of the twentieth century and through WWI and WWII were predominantly manufacturing based. Today, the manufacturing sector is decreasing while the service industry is exploding. Another change is workers' levels of education are much higher than ever before in history. This educated workforce demands not only pay and benefits commensurate with their levels of training and experience but also employment opportunities that are satisfying and motivating. One way to motivate workers is including them in communication and decision-making processes.

Today's educated workers also demand a more equitable balance between work and home life. Individuals want to balance their job requirements with their family's needs. In the past, all employees were expected to work the same hours, get the same benefits, and develop the same sense of loyalty to the organisation. Work was work, and employers expected no intrusions from personal or family issues. Today, however, issues of child care, elder care, and other responsibilities impact employees' lives. Organisations must also consider the number of workers with substance abuse or emotional problems. Increasingly, contemporary employers must develop counselling services to assist employees with substance abuse problems, family struggles, mental health issues, legal problems, child and parent care, or other personal issues.

Organisations that respond to these employees' needs with appropriate policies and benefits and who communicate with them in caring and sensitive ways will remain competitive in today's marketplace. Flexibility and adaptability, hallmarks of systems theory, must become the norm for contemporary organisations. Employees, too, must be flexible and adaptable to the diversity of individuals, values, and communication styles of their customers, superiors, coworkers, subordinates, and others.

Personal Relationships

Because today's workforce demands more satisfying personal relationships at work, organisations must also adapt to these new expectations. Workers today spend more than forty hours a week on the job; thus, the opportunity for enhanced social and personal relationships with coworkers is increased. Long-term relationships, both on and off the job, have the greatest potential for success when the partners are matched in such things as level of education, interests, and activities. Today we are just as likely to find these matches in our workplace as out of it.

Organisational theorists Dillard and Miller suggest that the motivation underlying romantic relationships in organisations is complex, as it involves love and ego. Employees motivated by love are looking for long-term companionship and partnership. Those motivated by ego are looking for sexual excitement and adventure. The consequences of these romantic relationships can, according to Dillard and Miller, provide improved work performance. However, negative perceptions of other employees can create problems for romantic partners. For example, if the romantic relationship ends, coworkers may continue assuming the relationship has negatively impacted the parties involved. Moving from the impersonal to the personal and to the romantic stage of a relationship with a coworker may be highly satisfying, but it could also backfire and have negative consequences both for the individuals and the organisation.

Romantic relationships are not the only types of personal relationships that we might develop through our work, however. The potential for developing deep and long-lasting friendships also exists. Sharing the trials and tribulations as well as the joys and successes of our everyday work experiences with close friends adds an additional level of satisfaction to our work experience.

Motivation

The diverse workforce consists of individuals who seek motivating and satisfying employment. But this diversity also means there is no "one-size-fits-all" motivational approach. As a result, organisations must recognise and adopt a variety of approaches to motivating workers. While communication is the common denominator in all types of motivation, the best motivational device or strategy will fail if its message and timing are not matched to individual and organisational needs. Organisational managers must seek out information from employees about what is motivating to them. Likewise, employees must be willing to communicate their needs and expectations to their supervisors. Kreps defines motivation as "the degree to which an individual is personally committed to expending effort in the accomplishment of a specified activity or goal". Eisenberg and Goodall suggest that communication can function in two ways to motivate: Managers can provide information and feedback about employee tasks, goals, and performance, and they can communicate encouragement, empathy, and concern.

Schutz suggests there are two levels of motivators important to individuals. The first level is primarily economic and includes such things as pay, benefits, and vacations. The second level is more subjective and includes motivators like inclusion in decision making and opportunities for input into policies, procedures, and products. These are motivating to us as workers because we feel a sense of ownership of our jobs, a sense of pride in our individual accomplishments, and a sense of being respected by others for our knowledge and expertise. Each of us wants to engage in work that offers us personal satisfaction and professional opportunity.

The key to motivating employees, then, is to develop opportunities for collective decision making and risk taking. Effective organisational communication also requires developing multiple channels for information to flow through the organisation and creating communication situations that encourage negotiation among participants.

ROLE OF MODERN COMMUNICATION TECHNOLOGY

There has been a sea-change in communication technologies and a corresponding sea-change in communication theory and research. The organisational communication literature traditionally focused on how variations in organisational communication were affected by variations in the size, structure, and types of organisation and how different types of organisational cultures gave rise to different types of organisational communication. The literature has now switched the causal ordering, emphasising how new forms of organisational communication can bring about new organisational structures, cultures, as well as wholly new organisational forms.

New communication technologies and possibiiities, combined with new challenges confronting organisations, are encouraging a whole new approach to organisational communication that challenges the very nature of organisations themselves. Radically new communication-enabled organisational forms are possible and are now emerging. On a less grandiose scale, new communication technologies can enable almost every aspect of organisational management and effectiveness, including change management, knowledge management, participative management, innovation, and organisational partnerships and alliances.

The most no, table advances in communication technology are groupware or computer facilitated group communication technologies. Johansen distinguishes groupware in terms of temporal and spatial contexts. These communication technologies can help traditional organisational groups work together more effectively. But, more importantly, they help dispersed individuals work as a team. The development of collaboratories, designed to help dispersed scientists conduct collaborative research and development as if they were co-located in a laboratory, may be one of the most exciting applications of the new communication technologies and computer-enabled environments. By capitalising on new communication technologies, an organisation should be able to realise a competitive advantage in its performance and in the marketplace.

Although communication technologies have opened up new opportunities, scholars and practitioners recognise that neither the theory nor the practice of organisational communication has kept up with this rapidly changing situation. Organisational communication "best practices," to the extent that they exist, are typically years out-of-date. Also the introduction of new communication technologies has caused problems as well as opportunities. Some communication technologies have led to communication overload. It is a common fallacy to assume that because communication is generally seen as a good thing, the more communication the better. Communication overload is a real problem—what is needed is better, not more, communication.

Regardless of the type of culture developed in the organisation or the nature of the relationships among employees, some form of communication technology must be utilised. While face-to-face communication is still important in today's organisation, advanced technology has made messaging faster, made access to and processing of information much easier, and made communication with others across geographical distances much more accessible. Some technology has made the office virtually obsolcte. Computer, video, and teleconferencing capabilities allow us to reach others wherever we are and whenever we want.

The Internet allows us to access information from any library in the world with a few clicks of a mouse. Organisations may use computer-assisted technology to send images and voices across time and space or use computer-assisted decision-aiding technology such as databases or programmes that provide information to decision makers. For example, Ganga and Lerner report that in 2001, 15 percent of employed people, almost 20 million workers, worked at least one full day a week at home. Of these, 3.4 million workers had a formal arrangement with their employers that allowed them to work at home. For the most part, these arrangements were possible because of increased technology.

The effects of this technology on contemporary organisations are significant. In order to acquire and keep a good job and to remain competitive, you must understands and develop expertise in many types of communication technology. For the organisation to remain competitive, it means that training must be ongoing to meet changing technology.

Technological advancements also provide opportunities for organisations to monitor and improve employee productivity. Computerised monitoring of employees is the norm in businesses today. However, managers must recognise that abuse of individual rights and privacy (also possible because of changing technology) negatively impacts corporate culture. Employee-employer rights issues are complex and continue to cause concern for employees and employers alike. As an individual beginning your career or updating your skills for a career change, you need to know how, why, and when your behaviour at work will be monitored. To counter the impact of technology that monitors your behaviour, be up-to-date on the latest advances in technology and use it wisely so as not to jeopardise your job or your unit's productivity.

References

Ashby, W. R. (1947) "Principles of the self-organizing dynamic system," *Journal of General Psychology* (37) pp. 125-128.

Autry, J. A. (2001). *The servant leader: How to build a creative team, develop great morale, and improve bottom-line performance.* Roseville, CA: Prima Publishing.

Berger, C. R., and Calabrese, R. J. (1975). Some explorations in initial interaction and beyond: Toward a developmental theory of interpersonal communication. *Human Communication Theory* 1:99-112.

Cooke-Davies, T., S. Cicmil, L. Crawford, and K. Richardson (2007) "We're not in Kansas anymore, Toto: Mapping the Strange Landscape of Complex Theory, and its Relationship to Project Management," *Project Management Journal* (28) 2, pp. 50-61.

Daft, R., & Lengel, R. (1984). Information richness: A new approach to managerial behavior and organizational design. In L. Cummings & B. Staw (Eds.), *Research in organizational behavior, Volume 6* (pp. 191-233). Homewood, IL: JAI Press.

Drucker, P. (1992). *Managing for the future: The 1990's and beyond.* New York: Truman Talley Books/Dutton.

Eisenberg, E. M., and Goodall, Jr., H. L. (1997). *Organisational communication: Balancing creativity and constraint.* 2nd ed. New York: St. Martin's Press.

Galbraith, J. R. (1977) *Organization Design.* Reading, MA, USA: Addison-Wesley.

Katz, D., and Kahn, R. (1966). *The social psychology of organisations.* New York: John Wiley & Sons.

Riley, P., and Eisenberg, E. (1991). The ACE model of management. Unpublished working papers. University of Southern California.

Schutz, W C. (1958). *FIRO: A three dimensional theory of interpersonal behaviour.* New York: Holt, Rinehart, & Winston.

Seeger, M. W (1997). *Ethics and organisational communication.* Cresskill, NJ:Hampton Press.

Shockley-Zalabak, P. (1999). *Fundamentals of organisational communication.* 4th ed. New York: Longman.

2

Theoretical Perspectives of Business Communication

Business communication—the exchange of information and ideas in an organisation—takes many forms. Communication is a necessity for every business. The style that a particular company uses is a significant part of its corporate culture. These styles range from top-down strategies to more egalitarian approaches that involve employees more fully in communicating.

Until the 1980s, a top-down style of communication prevailed in the United States and Western Europe. In this system, communications start with a senior manager who presents information to a junior manager, who then gives the information to a supervisor, who informs the line worker. Those at the end of the line had little input into decision-making. A more recent emphasis is multi-flow communication that empowers all employees. In an organisation using multi-channel or multi-flow communication, information flows in a variety of ways, from top to bottom, from bottom to top, and from side to side.

One theory of business communication includes team briefings and discussions, email exchanges, meetings and informal communications. When a company incorporates a multi-channel approach to business communication, it uses various channels to impart information. Multi-disciplinary groups are created—teams whose members can draw on their expertise in a specific area. The teams are empowered to make decisions instead of waiting for orders from above.

Upward communication, the opposite of top-down communication, encourages feedback from the lower level to higher levels. This makes it possible for managers to gather ideas from those at the grass-roots level of the organisation.

Another theory of business communication is sideways communication, in which those at the same level in the company exchange ideas.

For business communication to be successful there must be a qualified sender, regardless of where he ranks in the business hierarchy; an absence of "static" that interferes with hearing the message; and a recipient who is open to the message. When the recipient acts on the information that has been conveyed to him, the communication is considered a success.

Components of Communication

A number of early writers in the field of communication developed models of the communication process. Most of them included what were considered to be the four essential components of the process: source, message, channel/ and receiver. A model representative of those early writings is presented in Figure 1. Although the model has some major weaknesses (communication is not presented as a process)/ it does include what are generally considered the primary components of the communication process.

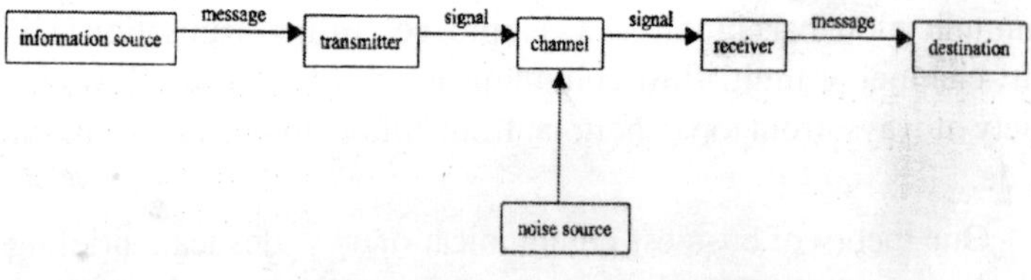

Figure 1. A simple communication Model

An expanded version of the early models is represented by the interpersonal communication model (Figure 2). As you can see/ this model allows both persons to function as sources or receivers; it also allows for the process nature of communication/ for feedback/ and for transmission of messages by either party. This model clearly presents human interaction as a process. In the organisational environment/ sources are constantly becoming receivers/ and the process is ongoing. Communication in the organisational environment is not static; it does not stop or come to a standstill.

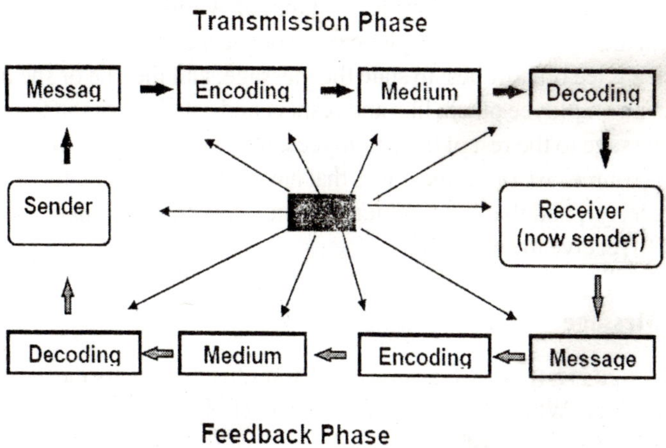

Figure 2. Interpersonal communication model

People are constantly exchanging ideas and stimulating meaning in the minds of others. Based on a combination of these models, let's take a look at the critical components in the communication process.

The Source

In the communication process, the source is the person who originates a message. In a broader view, the source could be any individual or collection of individuals—one person, a group, a dyad (twosome), or an entire organisation. It could be a group of managers wanting to explain policy changes to employees, it could be a hamburger chain attempting to influence others to buy their hamburgers, or it could be one employee explaining to another employee how to complete a certain task. Whether an organisation, group, or individual, the source has three primary functions in communication:

— determine what specific meaning is to be communicated,
— encode (translating ideas and information into messages) meaning into one or more messages, and
— transmit the message(s).

In an organisational environment, one individual may assume all three functions, but it is not uncommon to see each one performed by a different person. For example, a manager wants to communicate certain ideas to his or her employees; he or she may turn to an assistant to ask advice on how best to state the message, and then he or she may select an employee others like and respect and ask that person to carry the message to the rest of the employees. It is therefore very important that as sources we select messages that have mutual meaning for us and the receiver, and that we communicate in a way that will make others want to receive the message.

The Message

A message is any verbal or nonverbal stimulus that elicits meaning in the receiver. When communicating in any environment, most people use a combination of verbal and nonverbal stimuli to stimulate meaning in another. For simplification, we can think of verbal as employing words and nonverbal as employing other stimuli (gestures, smiles, frowns, groans, nods, yawns, touching others, and so on) to stimulate meaning. It is not uncommon for an employee or a manager to use these simultaneously when communicating with each other. It is virtually impossible to monitor all nonverbal behaviours. For example, you can more easily monitor your selection of words, but it is very difficult to monitor every facial movement, body movement, eye movement, leg movement, and so on. Sometimes our nonverbal messages will convey much more meaning than our verbal. Good managers have learned to try to interpret the meaning behind the nonverbal messages of their employees as well as the verbal messages; likewise for employees.

The Channel

A channel is a means by which a message is carried from one person to another. In live interaction, our senses (sight, sound, touch, smell, and taste) become channels. Channels can also take the form of mediated systems—television, radio, the Internet, the world wide web, film, billboards, telephones, etc. In organisations, people often become the most important channels. For example, supervisors function as channels between upper levels of management and lower-level employees. Secretaries often serve as channels between people on different levels and/or in different parts of the organisation. People serving as channels make up the informal communication network in organisations.

The Receiver

Just as the source is the person who originates a message, the receiver is the person who acquires the source's message. Like the source, the receiver can be an individual, a group, or an entire organisation. Also like the source, the receiver has three functions:

— receive the source's message,

— decode (translation of messages into ideas or information) the message into some meaning, and

— respond to the message.

Again, it is typical for one person to handle all three functions, but not uncommon for more than one person to be involved. For example, a new employee might receive the manager's message, but have an older, more-experienced employee interpret it for her or him and have another employee respond to the interpretation.

For communication to be effective, employees and managers need to consider the backgrounds and experiences of each other. This may require that we "put ourselves in the other person's shoes." A manager needs to know the employees to have effective communication with them; likewise for an employee. One of the primary reasons for problems in the organisational environment is that individuals do not understand what one another is saying because they do not communicate with each other enough to get to know one another's attitudes and feelings. Hence, many employees make major errors in communication—and so do managers. We have to be more effective sources and receivers if we want to improve communication. Even if our supervisor is an incompetent bozo, we will be more effective in communicating with "the bozo" if we go to the effort of getting to know her or him better so we are better able to adapt our messages to take her or his feelings into account.

Feedback

Feedback is the receiver's observable response(s) to a source's message. Such responses can be either of a verbal nature.

Feedback is extremely critical in all communication situations, but particularly so in interpersonal communication between manager and employee. A manager can carefully observe an employee's response to judge the success or failure of messages being sent. When feedback is negative, new messages can be constructed. Feedback is the method we use to regulate the messages we send and those that are sent: to us. Many astute managers have "advisory" groups or boards comprising selected employees whom they use as "sounding boards" for messages and information that is going to be sent to all employees. These "sounding board" groups have ideas bounced off them/ and how they respond often determines how the message is sent or whether it is even sent to other employees in the company at all.

Goals

Generally there are three major goals of communication in the organisational environment: developing interpersonal relationships, gaining compliance, and gaining understanding. Let's take a look at each of these goals and its impact on the organisation.

Most of us have the need to develop interpersonal relationships with our colleagues in organisations. It is a basic need, much like our needs for food, water, and shelter. We communicate with our colleagues with the idea that good working relationships can be formed. Whether it is in the work environment or in other environments, most of us communicate to develop interpersonal relationships with others. We want friends, colleagues, and companions we can talk with both on a formal and an informal basis.

We also communicate to gain the compliance of others. Communication directed toward gaining compliance seeks to influence others' beliefs and actions. By "gaining compliance" we mean getting another person (manager) to engage in some behaviour that is desired by the source (employee). Usually, our desire to get others to comply is influenced by the fact that we want a change of some kind. For example, the employee who wants to change her or his usual vacation time has to communicate with the supervisor in such a way that she or he will comply with the request. The employee might have to persuade the supervisor. She or he might have to promise to do extra work because it is an inconvenience to rearrange vacation schedules. Communicating to get others to comply is a way of life in contemporary organisations.

Finally, we communicate to gain understanding. We all have a need to know and understand what is going on in our environment. To know and understand, we need information. To acquire information, we must communicate with others. Much of the communication in organisations is for this purpose. People will make inquiries and ask for clarification so they can understand how and why the organisation operates as it does. Managers and employees talk to each other for many of the same reasons.

Although the three goals can be separate, it is rare when they are achieved independently. In other words, to achieve one of these goals usually requires that one or both of the other two also be achieved. Relationship development in the organisation is a good example. When we first meet a new colleague, we often need or want to know how the other person will respond to us. Hence, our desire to know more about the person and how the person will react to us in a given situation creates the need for information/ which can be acquired only by communicating with that person.

When we have gained that knowledge, we have reduced some of our uncertainty about the other person, and the goals of relationship development and gaining understanding both have been met. Often when we meet people in the work environment/ we establish a relationship and gain some understanding about them. This assists us when we want to gain a person's compliance. For example, employees who know their supervisors well and have a close relationship with them might find it easier to get the supervisor to comply with certain requests. Of course, astute supervisors are aware of this and may avoid allowing many employees to get close to them or know them too well.

Context

We conclude our discussion of the critical components of the organisational communication process by focusing on the "context" of communication. Generally, we refer to the characteristics of a situation in which communication takes place as the "context." This is an important concern for organisations because people do not communicate in exactly the same way within any two different contexts. Thus, even when we are communicating with a particular individual (for example, a manager), how and what we communicate is likely to change as the context in which we communicate changes.

There are issues we will discuss with our coworkers that we might not discuss with our supervisor. Regardless of our role in the organisation, the rules for each interaction will change when we change communication partners. We can easily draw from our own experiences how communication with close friends on the job differs from that with new members in the organisation. As our role changes (for example, we get a promotion), so do the rules for communicating with organisational members.

In conclusion, communication is a dynamic, ongoing process. We need to understand the context and the rules for a given context so we can adapt to the "real world" in which we find ourselves. Only by adapting to the context can we be more competent communicators in our organisations.

Theoretical Perspectives

The study of organisational communication is not new, but it has only recently achieved some degree of recognition as a field of academic study. It has largely grown in response to the needs and concerns of business. The first communication programmes were typically located in speech departments, but most business schools now include organisational communication as a key element of study. The study of organisational communication recognised that communication in organisations goes far beyond training managers to be effective speakers and to have good interpersonal communication skills. Moreover, it recognised that all organisations, not just business organisations, have communication needs and challenges.

The field of organisational communication is highly diverse and fragmented, as evidenced by results of literature searches on the topic, textbooks in the area, and the Harvard Business Review's compilation of its communication articles, *The Articulate Executive*. It spans communication at the micro, meso, and macro levels; formal and informal communications; and internal organisational communication practices (newsletters, presentations, strategic communications, work direction, performance reviews, meetings) as well as externally directed communications (public, media, inter-organisational). Innovation, organisational learning, knowledge management, conflict management, diversity, and communication technologies are also addressed. As a new academic discipline, organisational communication is struggling to develop and convey some sense of coherency across these many areas.

In addition to its fragmented nature, organisational communication, perhaps more than any other aspect of organisational theory and practice, has been subject to dramatic change. Before 1920, communication in small organisations was largely informal. As organisations increased in size, formal top-down communication became the main concern of organisational managers. Organisational communication in today's organisations has not only become far more complex and varied but more important to overall organisational functioning and success. While research used to focus on understanding how organisational communication varied by organisational type and structure, the emphasis has increasingly turned to understanding how new communication technologies and capabilities can help bring about new and more effective organisational forms and processes

Views of organisational communication can be categorised as those that view organisational communication as one aspect of an organisation versus those that see it as the underlying basis of the organisation itself. An example of the former is exemplified by Drenth et al., who define communication as the sending and receiving of messages by means of symbols and see organisational communication as a key element of organisational climate. The latter viewpoint is reflected by Myers and Myers who define organisational communication as "the central binding force that permits coordination among people and thus allows for organised behaviour," and Rogers and Rogers who argue that "the behaviour of individuals in organisations is best understood from a communication point of view."

In many ways, organisations have evolved in directions that make the latter view more appropriate. Changes confronting organisations and the associated changes in organisational forms have made organisational communication increasingly important to overall organisational functioning. For example:

— Work is more complex and requires greater coordination and interaction among workers

— The pace of work is faster

— Workers are more distributed

— Simultaneous, distributed work processes are more common

— Knowledge and innovation are more critical to an organisation's competitive advantage

— Communication technologies and networks are increasingly essential to an organisation's structure and strategy.

Communication is not only an essential aspect of these recent organisational changes, but effective communication can be seen as the foundation of modern organisations.

Three theoretical perspectives guide the study of communication: the technical, the contextual, and the negotiated perspectives.

Technical View of Communication

The technical view of communication is associated with information theory and usually traced back to Claude E. Shannon and Warren Weaver. Shannon, an engineer at Bell Laboratories, portrayed communication as a mechanistic system, as shown in Figure 3. The important question in information theory is "how can an information source get a message to a destination with a minimum of distortions and errors?" In applying this mechanistic approach to interpersonal communication, the question is the same, although the mechanistic system is altered to some extent and the analysis is less technical and mathematical. The technical view of communication persists as a common basis for discussions about organisational communication.

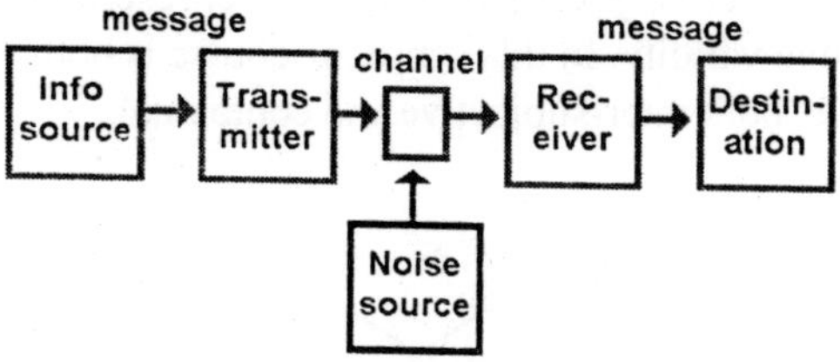

Figure 3. Information Theory: Communication as a Mechanistic System

White and Chapman introduced into this communication system both human (the person's horizon of experience, thoughts/feelings, the acts of encoding/decoding) and interpersonal feedback elements. Since that time, an array of human filters that are influenced by the person' horizon of experience (such as motive, affect, attention, knowledge, attitudes, values, and beliefs) have been specified. Although the social context affects these human filters, the larger social context is not directly addressed in these approaches.

Ccontextual Approach to Communication

The *contextual* approach to communication focuses not just on content (e.g. the accurate exchange of information or adequacy of conveying the intended meaning) but on the larger context of communication. It focuses on nonverbal cues as well as verbal content. It also looks at the relational context between the sender and receiver within the larger social/organisational/cultural context. It sees words as symbols interpreted in context. Mead and Blumer stressed communication as symbolic interaction that created meaning and one's sense of both self and society. Discourse analysis is an extension and elaboration of the contextual perspective. Rather than looking at a particular interpersonal exchange or sequences of exchanges, discourse analysis looks at an overall body of communication (including formal and informal, oral and written communication of all kinds). The goal of the analysis is to relate discourse patterns to patterns of social relations. It seeks to explicate how the creation and maintenance of social relations materialise in talk. Through discourse about itself, the organisation enacts (shapes, defines, and marks the boundaries of) itself. Discourse gives rise to objectively known collective representations that have inter-subjective validity. In this sense, discourse is both interpersonal and collective, both inter-subjective and contextual.

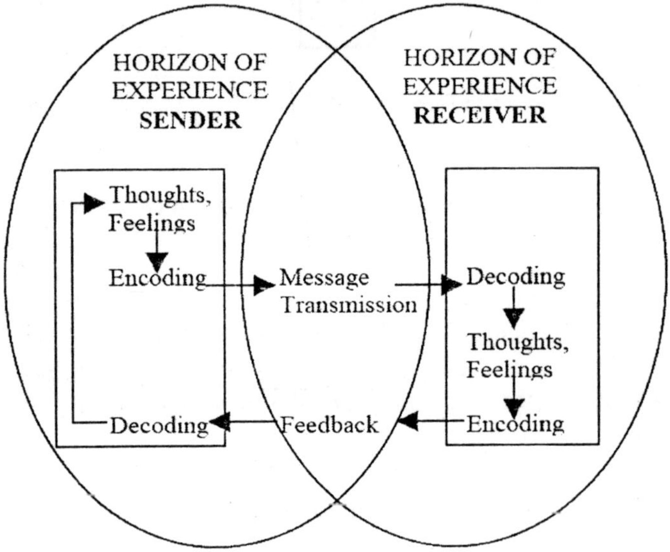

Figure 4. Technical Sender-Receiver Model of Communication

Negotiated View of Communication

Lazega goes beyond the *contextual* to the *negotiated* view of communication and meaning. Rather than examining how discourse helps create, maintain, and give meaning to social relations, he examines how the communication context itself is negotiated. For example, how *judgements of appropriateness* and *knowledge claims* (standards by which something is deemed to be technically satisfactory) come to be constructed. In this sense he elaborates on the interactive feedback component of the *technical* approach. Feedback exchanges can be viewed as a process of interpersonal negotiation. This approach can be traced back to the notion of language games and word playing introduced by the Austrian philosopher Ludwig Wittgenstein.

DISTINCTIONS OF ORGANISATIONAL COMMUNICATION

Key distinctions with respect to organisational communication involve:

— levels;

— formal versus informal;

— direction (vertical, horizontal, diagonal); and

— internal versus external focus.

Levels

Communication is frequently divided into the following levels:

— Interpersonal communication

— Group level communication

— Organisational level communication

— Inter-organisational level communication

— Mass communication.

Some authors prefer to distinguish between micro, meso, and macro levels, where micro refers to interpersonal communication; meso refers to group, organisational, and inter-organisational communication; and macro refers to all higher order communication.

Although interpersonal and group level communications reside at a lower level than organisational communication, they are major forms of communication in organisations and are prominently addressed in the organisational communication literature. Indeed, the initial focus of the organisational communication literature was the interpersonal communication skills of managers (particularly speaking and writing). As organisations became more communication-based, greater attention was directed at improving the interpersonal communication skills of all organisational members.

Many of the articles contained in the Harvard Business Review's organisational communication collection, entitled *The Articulate Executive*, address interpersonal communication and, despite the title, they do not focus exclusively on the executive. Key topics include:

— *Active, non-evaluative listening*: the skill to receive messages is as important as the skills associated with sending messages

— *Skilled incompetence*: the tendency on the part of professionals to preserve their reputations of competency by not admitting what they don't know, and on the part of most persons to duck tough issues and avoid conflict

— *The potential "flaming" effect of computer-mediated communication*: because senders are ignorant of "the social context and feel free to express themselves" and receivers don't have the advantage of nonverbal cues computed-mediated communication may result in more negatively charged communication exchanges.

Key distinctions within interpersonal communication include:

— Sending/receiving (listening)

— Oral/written/electronic (electronic can be computer mediated oral or written communication)

— Verbal/nonverbal.

Formal versus Informal Communication

In the past, the concern of managers of large bureaucratic organisations and, consequently the major focus of the organisational communication literature, was *formal, top-down communication. Informal communication*, generally associated with interpersonal, horizontal communication, was primarily seen as a potential hindrance to effective organisational performance. This is no longer the case. Ongoing, dynamic, and non-formal, if not informal, communication has become more important to ensuring the effective conduct of work in modern organisations.

Most discussions of informal communication emphasise how to manage organisational culture and climate (the context of informal communications) to prevent informal and formal communications from being in opposition. Other discussions of informal communication have focused on diversity training as a mechanism for sensitising staff to potential issues associated with informal (as well as formal) communication. Still others have emphasised conflict management as a strategy for dealing with issues that arise from informal communication and interactions between workers. More recent discussions focus on the growing dependence on dynamic computer-facilitated communications that are neither formal nor informal, such as communication within teams or within communities of practice. It may be that the formal/informal dichotomy of the past is becoming less salient as many new communication channels now exist within organisations that are neither formal nor informal.

Vertical, Horizontal, and Diagonal Communications

Communication can also be characterised as vertical, horizontal, or diagonal. Initially greater emphasis was directed at vertical organisational communication as compared to lateral communication but that is no longer the case. Diagonal communication is an even more recent emphasis in the organisational communication literature.

Vertical Communication

Vertical communication occurs between hierarchically positioned persons and can involve both *downward* and *upward* communication flows. Downward communication is more prevalent than upward communication. Larkin and Larkin suggest that *downward communication is most effective if top managers communicate directly with immediate supervisors and immediate supervisors communicate with their staff.* A wealth of evidence shows that increasing the power of immediate supervisors increases both satisfaction and performance among employees. This was first discovered by Donald Pelz and is commonly referred to as the *Pelz effect*. Pelz was attempting to find out what types of leadership styles led to employee satisfaction (informal/formal, autocratic/participative, management-oriented/frontline-oriented). He found that *what matters most is not the supervisor's leadership style but whether the supervisor has power*. One way to give supervisors power is to communicate directly with them and to have them provide input to decisions. Ensuring that supervisors are informed about organisational issues/changes before staff in general, and then allowing them to communicate these issues/changes to their staff, helps reinforce their position of power. When the supervisor is perceived as having power, employees have greater trust in the supervisor, greater desire for communication with the supervisor, and are more likely to believe that the information coming from the supervisor is accurate.

Downward Communication

Information flowing from the top of the organisational management hierarchy and telling people in the organisation what is important (mission) and what is valued (policies).

Downward communication generally provides enabling information—which allows a subordinate to do something. e.g.: Instructions on how to do a task.

Downward communication comes after upward communications have been successfully established. This type of communication is needed in an organisation to:

— Transmit vital information
— Give instructions
— Encourage 2-way discussion
— Announce decisions
— Seek cooperation
— Provide motivation
— Boost morale
— Increase efficiency
— Obtain feedback

Upward Communication

Even less is known about upward communication. One consistent finding is that employee satisfaction with upward communication tends to be lower than their satisfaction with downward communication. Larkin and Larkin found low levels of satisfaction with all the strategies commonly used to enhance upward communication, including employee surveys, suggestion programmes, employee grievance programmes, and employee participation programmes such as quality circles and team meetings. Gibson and Hodgetts note several *management-based* reasons for this lack of satisfaction, particularly that these strategies often do not involve two-way communication, are not packaged well, are poorly timed, and are apt to trigger defensiveness on the part of managers. In addition, McCelland found a number of *employee-based* reasons why upward communication tends to be poor, including:

— *Fear of reprisal*: people are afraid to speak their minds
— *Filters*: employees feel their ideas/concerns are modified as they get transmitted upward
— *Time*: managers give the impression that they don't have the time to listen to employees.

Lateral Communication

Lateral communication involves communication among persons who do not stand in hierarchical relation to one another. While recent trends to flatten organisations have enhanced the importance of lateral communications, studies on lateral communication still lag behind those on vertical communication. One fairly limited study found rather high levels of satisfaction (85 percent) with lateral communication among human resource managers, but lateral communication across managers of dissimilar functional divisions, while often cited as a major source of organisation dysfunction, has not been subject to much empirical research. It has been assumed that lateral communication at the worker level is less problematic, at least within a functional area. However, with the greater importance of teams, more attention is now being directed at communication between team members. Lateral communications between workers in different functional areas is also becoming a bigger concern as greater attention is being directed at increasing the speed of production through simultaneous, as opposed to sequential, work processes. And there is greater emphasis on communication across distributed workers and geographically separated work groups doing similar kinds of work in an attempt to promote learning and the sharing of expertise, best practices, and lessons learned.

Diagonal Communication

Diagonal communication refers to communication between managers and workers located in different functional divisions. Although both vertical and horizontal communication continue to be important, these terms no longer adequately capture communication needs and flows in most modern organisations. The concept of diagonal communication was introduced to capture the new communication challenges associated with new organisational forms, such as matrix and project-based organisations. Also, with the rise of the network organisation (both internally and externally oriented networks), communication flows can no longer be restricted to vertical, horizontal, and diagonal.

Internally versus Externally Directed Communication

The amount of literature directed at internally oriented organisational communication far exceeds that directed at externally oriented organisational communication. However, externally oriented communication is becoming a more important issue. ("Organisational Alliances, Partnerships, and Networks"), ("Participative Management and Employee and Stakeholder Involvement"), and ("Communicating Science") discuss some of the special issues associated with external communication. As organisations increase the range and centrality of their interactions with customers, suppliers, and the public preparing for and managing the communication competencies and resources of the organisation becomes ever more important.

Key Functions of Communication

Communication serves many functions in organisations. There are six functions that seem to dominate communication in the organisational context. The functions are inform, regulate, integrate, manage, persuade, and socialise.

The *informative* function of communication is fairly self-explanatory. It is the function of providing needed information to personnel so they can do their jobs in an effective and efficient manner. People need to be informed about any changes of procedure or policy that are related to their work. Sometimes this function is accomplished by people at higher levels sending information to people at lower levels/ and the reverse. At other times, people needing information must contact people who have the needed information to acquire it.

Much of the informative communication in organisations is conducted in a written format. This way, a whole group of employees can be informed with one message and at one time. On the other hand, managers may decide to call a meeting once each week (or month) which is primarily of an informative nature. Most employees understand that such meetings are for the purpose of disseminating information and can be prepared to inquire about matters about which they feel they need additional information.

The *regulative* function of communication is involved with the communication that is directed toward regulatory policies within the organisation or messages about maintenance of the organisation. For example, an employee might be informed by the manager that he or she has broken some rule or regulation and is not to break it again. Communication that involves the regulative function is often not pleasant, but it is essential to the smooth operation of the organisation.

The *integrative* function of communication is focused on coordination of tasks, work assignments, group coordination, or the fusing of work units toward a common goal. In other words, it is communication directed at getting people to work together and have tasks coordinated so that the "left hand knows what the right hand is doing." It is an attempt to get people to work together and make things run more smoothly. For example, consultants often will find employees duplicating each other's work, whereas if there were more integrative communication, one could do one task and another do a related task.

The *management* function of communication is directed toward the three goals mentioned earlier. It is communication focused on getting personnel to do what is needed, learning information about personnel to know them better, and establishing relationships with personnel. If one can meet the interpersonal relationship goal and the understanding goal, he or she might have a better chance at knowing "how to manage" the employees.

The *persuasive* function of communication is an outgrowth of the management function. Here the supervisor is attempting to influence the employee to do something in particular. Whereas simply issuing an order might accomplish the same function, this approach makes for much better relations between supervisors and subordinates.

Finally, we have the *socialisation* function. Although the other functions seem obvious and are rarely missed by either managers or employees, the socialisation function is often neglected. This is perhaps the most important function. The socialisation function of communication in the organisation is the one that can determine whether an individual survives well, or not at all, in an organisation.

Socialisation doesn't mean being "buddies" with everyone. It means being integrated into the communication networks in the organisation. It means being told whom one should talk to and what one should talk about. It also means being told whom not to talk to. It means being told what to say in certain situations and what not to say. It means being told how to address others (Ms./ Sir, Dr.). It means being told the informal norms of the organisation (what social gatherings to attend/ what to wear at luncheons, what things others find offensive). It means being told the idiosyncratic behaviours (and pet peeves) of others. It means knowing whom you should associate with and whom you should avoid (who are the "in" people and who are the "out" people). In a nutshell, it means survival! Today, many organisations realise the value of this function and will assign each new employee to an employee who has been with the organisation for some time so the experienced person can assist the newcomer in "settling into" the organisation the first two or three weeks. These guides help new employees "learn the ropes" without upsetting the system or saying things that could hurt them with the older, more established employees.

In summary, all of the functions are important. However, the function most important and probably most neglected by organisations is the socialisation function. Hence, if organisations neglect socialising us, then we have to do it ourselves.

The literature on communication generally acknowledges that the basic function of communication is to affect receiver knowledge or behaviour by informing, directing, regulating, socialising, and persuading. Neher identifies the primary functions of organisational communication as:

— Compliance-gaining
— Leading, motivating, and influencing
— Sense-making
— Problem-solving and decision-making
— Conflict management, negotiating, and bargaining.

Neher and Rogers and Rogers emphasise the social and organisational functions of organisational communication as a whole rather than focusing on the functions of specific communication exchanges. Thus they combine the functions of informing, directing, and regulating into the broader category of behavioural compliance. They also give greater emphasis to the role of communication in managing threats to organisational order and control, identifying problem solving and conflict management, negotiation, and bargaining as key functions of organisational communication.

Myers and Myers combine similar functions into a higher level common function and provide a particularly succinct and clear version of the functions of organisational communication. They see communication as having three primary functions:

— *Coordination and regulation of production activities*: This function of communication has changed the most over time. In traditional bureaucratic views of the organisation, prescription—clearly communicating behavioural expectations and the behavioural consequences associated with complying or not complying with these expectations—and monitoring are considered to be the basis of organisational order and control. This function of organisational communication was seen as involving fairly proceduralised, rule-oriented, one-way, top-down communication. Tasks in many organisations have become more complex, less routine and repetitive, tightly coupled, and interactive and, as such, the traditional bureaucratic view of organisational communication is no longer sufficient. Production activities of this nature require dynamic, reciprocal, lateral communications between production workers and non-routinised, two-way, vertical communications between production workers and managers. Communication as a means of coordination and regulation becomes more important, complex, and difficult.

— *Socialisation*: The socialisation function of communication is stressed in the human relations perspective of organisations which asserts that capturing the hearts and minds of organisational members is necessary to effectively coordinate organisational action in the pursuit of collective organisational goals. Communication directed at socialising organisational members focuses on articulating and reinforcing organisational values and aligning individual goals with organisational goals. It is directed at establishing an appropriate organisational culture and climate. This form of communication cannot be one-way or top-down. It must occur reciprocally between organisational leaders and organisational members.

— *Innovation*: The organisational communication literature is increasingly addressing the importance of communication in promoting innovation as well as control and coordination. Communication to promote innovation is associated with strong communication within and beyond the organisation.

This approach focuses on the functional goals of organisational communication, rather than on the near-term outcomes of particular acts of communication, such as to make a decision, to persuade, or to resolve a conflict. The more specific functions of specific acts of communication or sets of communication exchange (decision-making, informing, persuading, negotiating, problem-solving) are subsumed into each of the three higher-level functional objectives.

Organisational Communication Networks

There are two primary communication networks that exist in any organisational environment. These are the formal communication network and the informal communication network. The *formal* network is communication that follows the hierarchical structure of the organisation, or the "chain of command." It follows the formal, established, official lines of contact. In other words/ it follows the prescribed path of the hierarchical chart and tends to be explicit in terms of "who should be talking to whom and about what." The formal chart for this network often is provided to new employees the first day they walk in the door. It explains whom they report to and for what. There usually is little confusion about the formal communication network.

The *informal* network involves communication that follows the "grapevine." It carries the "scuttlebutt," the rumours. It is the unofficial network. This is the type of communication that does not follow the hierarchical path or chain of command. It tells you "who is *really* talking to whom and about what." We are not talking about "gossip" here. Gossip can exist in either network. We are referring to informal communication links that have grown out of relationships among employees and management and that have little or no correlation with the formal organisational chart. The informal network is very strong in most organisations. It usually works much faster than the formal network, and often it works with more accuracy. Until you have access to this informal network, you have not really become a part of the system.

An employee needs to be aware of both networks. Management has more control over the formal network than the informal, but employees have more control over the informal network than management does. It usually is relatively easy to learn the formal network, but specific information regarding the informal network may be more elusive. Being properly socialised assists an employee in gaining understanding about the informal system in the particular organisation.

It is critical that employees and management remember that the formal network is not the only network functioning in the organisation. One needs to remember that the informal network is a very powerful communication avenue and carries information that the formal network doesn't. The informal network tells you "who is playing golf with whom," "who is sleeping with whom," "who has an occasional lunch with whom," "who is distantly related to whom," "who protects or defends whom," "who promoted whom, and why." These all are things the formal network almost never tells an individual, but the informal network usually will when one is properly socialised.

In conclusion, you must learn the formal network, but don't forget to take the time to learn the informal network also. It, too, can make the difference between surviving and not surviving in the organisation.

References

Argyris, Chris. (1986). Skilled Incompetence. *Harvard Business Review* 64(5):74-80.

Blumer, Herbert. (1972). *Symbolic Interactionism*. Englewood Cliffs, N.J.: Prentice-Hall.

Conrad, C. (1994). *Strategic Organisational Communication—Toward the Twenty-First Century*. Fort Worth, TX: Harcourt Brace College Publishers.

D'Aprix, R. 1996. *Communicating for Change—Connecting the Workplace with the Marketplace*. San Francisco: Jossey-Bass Publishers.

McCroskey, J. C., & Richmond, V. P. (1996). Human communication theory and research: Traditions and models. In M. B. Salwen & D. W. Stacks (Eds.). *An integrated approach to communication theory and research.* Mahwah, NJ: Lawrence Eribaum Publishers, 233-242.

Richmond, V. P., & McCroskey, J. C. (1998). *Communication: Apprehension, avoidance, and effectiveness.* (5th ed.). Needham Heights, MA: Allyn and Bacon.

Sapienza, A.M. 1995. *Managing Scientists—Leadership Strategies in Research and Development.* New York: Wiley-Liss.

Tucker, Mary L., G. Dale Meyer, and James W. Westerman. 1996. Organisational Communication: Development of Internal Strategic Competitive Advantage. *The Journal of Business Communication* 33(1):51-69.

White, K.W., and E.N. Chapman. 1996. *Organisational Communication—An Introduction to Communication and Human Relations Strategies.* Needham Heights, MA: Simon and Schuster Custom Publishing.

3

Levels of Business Communication

Communication is the element that maintains and sustains relationships in a business firm. What person A says to person B not only can have an impact on those two people but, since organisations are systems, it also can have a meaningful impact on the total system. Your communication with your coworkers and supervisors in the organisation will be a major determinant of how satisfied you are with your work, and how satisfied *others* are with your work. For example, in one firm where we worked, there was a very gossipy, control-oriented person who would subtly let others know what he/she thought of his/her coworkers. Eventually, this type of communication made it impossible for others to work with this individual. When asked to work with this person, others would find excuses not to or would become "ill" when the time to do the work rolled around. This, of course, had a negative impact on the work of the total unit.

Communication in Conventional Business Firms

Communication within an organisation has some important functions which can be gathered in the following four groups: providing information, convincing and influencing, training, and unification.

Providing Information

Information exchange is considered to be the most basic function of communication. Information is necessary for the individual to have a harmonious relationship with their environment. On the other hand, employees need information as to what needs to be done, how, and why, in order to achieve the goals of the organisation. Organisational activities cannot be performed unless senior management informs the employees of the policy and goals of the organisation, the goods or services produced the methods of production, and innovations. Communication has a significant function in decision-making. Without the necessary information, problems cannot be solved, nor can a decision be reached on any issue.

Convincing and Influencing

Convincing is the process of affecting and changing the behaviours, opinions, and attitudes of the person(s) an individual is in interaction with. Influencing, on the other hand, can be defined as an attempt to change people's attitudes and behaviours, without contradicting their will or aims, over a longer period.

A significant part of the communication taking place in organisations in various ways aims to change people's opinions, attitudes, and behaviours. The requisite of the members of an organisation working efficiently is largely dependent on their internalising the goals of the organisation and their identifying with the organisation. This internalising and identifying will largely depend on the function of communication as to convincing and influencing.

Communication for Training

Managers communicate with their subordinates not only to inform them but also to shape their behaviours. Subordinates need training in order to perform in line with the goals of the organisation. In order for the training to be successful, positive communication between the trainers and trainees is indispensable.

Unification

People's interrelationships and interdependence in social life are made possible by communication. As well as gathering individuals around organisational goals, communication has a significant function in preserving these individuals' psychological integrity and balance.

Scott and Mittchel point to four main functions of communication in organisations: control, motivation, expressing emotions, and transmitting information.

— *The Function of Control*: Communication makes control possible by clearing up duties and responsibilities. In face of ambiguous problems, it is then possible to get down to the source of the problem and take action.

— *The Function of Motivation*: Communication improves loyalty to organisational goals and, therefore, raises motivation.

— *The Function of Expressing Emotions*: Communication enables emotions to be expressed and social needs to be satisfied.

— *The Function of Transmitting Information*: Communication is also used in transmitting the information necessary for decision-making. The making of effective decisions requires different options and information.

Organisational communication is an exchange of information and thoughts in the internal and external environments of the organisation aiming to keep its day-today activities running and its targets met. Modern organisations of our day continue their work in a changing and dynamic environment.

A dynamic environment pushes organisations to become open systems. Organising as an open system makes communication vital for the establishment of a relationship between the organisation and its environment. This importance arises from the need to constantly watch the environment, analyse the changes, and develop policies and strategies for the future.

Needs of Effective Business Communication

An organisation is a unit set up to achieve certain goals. In other words, an organisation is the structuring of organisational elements in a productive relationship. An organisation is a structural process in which individuals engage in mutual behaviours in order to achieve their goals. This process is run by the manager. The things that happen in an organisation are interdependent.

The word 'organisation' can be defined narrowly or broadly. In its narrow sense, an organisation is the specification of the work to be done to achieve a certain goal and the groups to carry out this work. In its broader sense, it is a structure where people bring together their physical tools and capabilities in order to reach a certain objective.

Organisations cannot possibly carry out their activities without communication. The coordination of employees is allowed by communication. Cooperation is not possible when employees are unaware of one another's needs and emotions. Communication helps implement the basic functions of management such as planning, organising, and control; and thus organisations can fulfil their duties. With efficient communication taking place, individuals feel more attached to their work.

Organisational communication is an exchange of messages in the internal and external environments of the organisation. Put another way, organisational communication is the structural communication of all the employees of the organisation with their internal and external environments.

Organisational communication is an administrative function crucial especially for executives in the implementation of organisational and administrative functions. Executives spend a significant part of their time on communicative activities. Doing his or her daily routine, arranging meeting schedules, speaking on the telephone, reading or replying to business correspondence, or fulfilling the control functions within the organisation, an executive typically engages in communication processes.

Effective communication is essential for the implementation of organisational functions. Efficient management requires thorough communication. Mell Grosz argues that the basic function of management is information processing during planning and control, and that this process continues through communication.

The need for the right information for the running of administrative activities and decision-making is met by communication, which is indispensable for increasing work efficiency and mobilising organisational resources. The implementation of administrative and organisational activities is helped by organisational communication. The existence of various departments and titles gives rise to organisational hierarchy, which underlines the need for formal and informal communication channels among those various departments.

Executives liaise with the relevant people through communication. In an organisational activity, communication is necessary, but not sufficient, for an executive. In order to get the message across, communication also needs to be perceived, that is, it needs to mobilise the employee. Efficient organisational communication depends on employees' communicative abilities.

Efficient communication in organisations is considered important for two reasons. Firstly, communication makes the planning, organising, guidance, and control functions of management possible. Secondly, it is an important part of the administrative process on which executives spend a significant amount of their time for coordination purposes.

Efficient communication in organisations requires an efficient use of management techniques. Communication provides various departments with information to enable them to guide, plan, organise, motivate, and control. Efficient communication is essential for the successful running of administrative and organisational activities.

Efficient communication is the principal device for the adequate implementation of administrative and organisational activities. For this purpose, management needs to specify the kind of communication system to be set up and the kind of communication devices to be used. Communication is vital for any organisation.

All organisations need information. The information needed closely concerns not only senior executives but also junior executives and all employees, even though they may not take part in the decision-making process. This information is provided through communication.

Goals

Communication takes place in view of an objective, and organisational communication aims to reach certain goals. These goals can be listed as follows:

— giving information on the organisation's policies and decisions, working order, long and short term objectives, remuneration system, reward and punishment system, promotion opportunities, and benefits,

- communicating the organisation's annual budget, revenue, activities, and projects to the employees and other interested parties,
- briefing the employees and the unions on the new technologies and management approaches adopted,
- introducing the various departments and executives of the organisation through internal publications, and raising organisational awareness,
- promoting the organisation in its external environment,
- informing the members of the organisation of the legal framework regulating their field of activity in order to prevent potential mistakes.

Organisational communication ensures the interaction of all the elements in the organisation and thus helps towards organisational integrity.

Efficient communication in organisations depends on communication being interactive. Interactive communication arises from various needs. The most important goals of interactive communication in organisations can be listed as follows:

- *Coordination of Work*: contributes to efficient coordination of organisational and administrative work.
- *Problem-Solving*: overcomes problems arising in various departments
- *Information-Sharing*: ensures the sharing of new information with all members of the organisation.

Conflicts between individuals, groups, or departments can only be resolved through efficient communication.

The four principal goals of communication in organisations are information, motivation, control, and organisational excitement. Organisational communication fulfils these functions. Organisational communication serves several important purposes for the organisation and its management. These are information-sharing, feedback opportunities, convincing, excitement, and innovation. The communicative process thus allows the sharing of information both inside and outside the organisation.

An organisation's competitiveness in both domestic and foreign markets depends on its keeping pace with the innovations in the production of goods and services. Communication mobilised the decision-making mechanisms within the organisation and provides information from the external environment. Adapting to the changes in the outer environment is possible through communication as a whole.

There are various modes of communication within organisations. Some are among individuals, others are about internal incidents, and yet others are between the organisation and its environment. Organisational communication is needed for the strategies designed to increase employees' participation. In this context, the function of communication is to raise mutual understanding and to create a spirit of solidarity among the members of the organisation. Ensuring loyalty and mutual decision-making, communication guarantees participation through free information flow.

Organisational communication is one of the basic functions of organisational management. The function of communication is also compulsory for organisational change. It provides the right information in line with the members' emotional expectations.

Organisational information brings two main goals to light:

— *Raising mutual understanding within the organisation*: Making everyone understand what is expected of them during work hours and raising awareness of the duties and responsibilities in work groups are important functions of communication.

— *Ensuring upward information flow*: Ensuring that each manager is aware of the behaviours and wishes of the employees under his or her command.

Improving management begins with communication. Managers use communication in many administrative and organisational activities such as decision-making, problem solving, explaining organisational decisions, using discretion, giving authority, motivating, organisation development, making suggestions, reconciling, managing conflicts, training, informing, planning, and setting goals and objectives.

Planned communication by management contributes to the improvement of the linear, vertical, and interdepartmental relations among employees, causing positive change in their expectations, morale, and behaviours. This change in behaviour increases staff productivity and energy in their functions.

Communication in Conventional Offices

With a systemic approach, communication in conventional offices can be looked at inside and outside the organisation. Inside the organisation, upward, downward, and linear types of communication can be distinguished depending on the structure being formal or informal. Outside the organisation, public relations, sales, advertising, etc. can be seen.

Communication inside the organisation contributes to coordination among office staff. Organisational communication is an important device that lets employees know what is going on and work with confidence. Its function is to meet the employees' needs for information. For this reason, communication needs to function healthily inside an organisation in order to raise productivity and efficiency.

In conventional offices, communication takes place within the hierarchical pyramid called the organisational structure, and is known as formal or informal communication. Formal communication is the type that works in specified structures within the organisational rules and towards the organisational goals. Informal communication, on the other hand, is the unofficial type taking place among staff as face-to-face or telephone interaction.

A two-way information exchange is noted in formal communication in conventional offices. It is an inter-status communication type following the organisational rules and abstracted from the members' identities.

Informal communication emerges from the natural relations among office employees without adhering to a certain structure. It is a communication type witnessed in the informal groups created by office employees.

Formal Communication Methods

Relations among various departments or individuals in an organisation are established through either pre-specified formal channels or unpredictable natural channels. Formal channels are those set up by the organisation to ensure communication inside and outside the organisation. The natural communication network, on the other hand, develops spontaneously and ties social groups together. Organisations employ various methods in communicating with their inner and outer environments. These methods can be examined under two headings in terms of the structure of communication and the direction of the message flow:

1. Communication in terms of structural functioning
   a) Formal communication
   a) Natural communication
2. Communication in terms of the direction of the message flow
   a) Vertical communication
      i) Downward communication
      ii) Upward communication
   b) Linear communication
   c) Diagonal communication

Even though most communication in conventional offices tends to be formal, a fast information exchange is sometimes entered into in order to speed things up. Formal channels are usually clearly specified in the organisational plans. Each employee knows who they report to, who they are controlled by, what their authority is, and whom to consult when problems arise. These relations happen in vertical and linear communication channels. After these channels are set up, the decision-making process works efficiently and significantly affects irregular practices.

In both their inner and outer structures, organisations are systems in constant mutual relationships. Internal and external relationships need to be regular in order for the organisational activities to be efficient and appropriate for the goals. Defined as an organisational function, communication regulates, controls, and ensures relationships among departments and individuals both inside and out.

Communication has a three-way flow within the organisation structure: vertical, linear, and diagonal. Vertical communication is the downward or upward communication type set up by the employees within the organisational structure and policies.

In normal circumstances, communication runs downwards and takes place in writing. Linear communication takes place between equals and arises from functional relations. Diagonal communication happens between different ranks within the organisational command network.

Communication in Virtual Offices

Virtual offices are equipped with powerful communication infrastructures backed with information technologies in order to keep virtual activities running. They increase organisational efficiency by largely improving the coordination and communication functions with the help of information technologies. Organisational change in today's context is brought about with the development of communication technologies.

In virtual offices, communication takes place through shared database, e-mail, intranet, computer-based meetings, softwares, groupwares, computer-supported cooperative work systems (CSCW), video-based communication systems (video conferencing), etc. The greatest use of these technologies in terms of communication and coordination is instant access to information through shared database. Communication technologies back up common functional work and improve coordination among offices.

In order to make good use of information and communication technologies in virtual offices, they need to be coordinated towards the following objectives:

— All information necessary for the office must be processed electronically,

— This information must be accessible at different times and different places,

— The electronic communication infrastructure must overcome communication and coordination problems.

The principal factor raising the importance of communication and coordination in virtual offices is that the tasks are carried out virtually. These are offices running on computers, printers, and integrated copying machines. Virtual offices cause significant change in coordination and communication approaches.

Today's offices make great use of computers in communication. Multimedia practices allow texts, graphics, photographs, film and sound data to be numeritised and used digitally in smaller formats.

Communication in virtual offices is important for two reasons: firstly, the need to equip employees with the information necessary to do their work and share this information, and secondly the need to create values towards coordination, performance, and job satisfaction.

In virtual work order, people choose their work places themselves. Choosing the work place can be as colourful as choosing a holiday destination. A laptop computer with a modem card and a mobile telephone connected to it are enough to get the work done anywhere.

The place chosen could be a holiday resort, a cottage, etc. Those who feel uncomfortable in formal work environments can get a work place of their own where they can work freely through telework.

Intrapersonal Communication in Business

Intrapersonal communication takes place within a single person, often for the purpose of clarifying ideas or analysing a situation. Other times, intrapersonal communication is undertaken in order to reflect upon or appreciate something. Three aspects of intrapersonal communication are self-concept, perception and expectation.

— *Self-concept* is the basis for intrapersonal communication, because it determines how a persona sees him/herself and is oriented toward others. Self-concept (also called *self-awareness*) involves three factors: beliefs, values and attitudes. *Beliefs* are basic personal orientation toward what is true or false, good or bad; beliefs can be descriptive or prescriptive. *Values* are deep-seated orientations and ideals, generally based on and consistent with beliefs, about right and wrong ideas and actions. *Attitudes* are learned predisposition toward or against a topic, ideals that stem from and generally are consistent with values. Attitudes often are global, typically emotional. Beliefs, values and attitudes all influence *behaviour*, which can be either spoken opinion or physical action. Some psychologists include body image as an aspect of intrapersonal communication, in that *body image* is a way of perceiving ourselves, positively or negatively, according to the social standards of our culture. Other things that can affect self-concept are personal attributes, talents, social role, even birth order.

— Whereas self-concept focuses internally, *perception* looks outward. Perception of the outside world also is rooted in beliefs, values and attitudes. It is so closely intertwined with self-concept that one feeds off the other, creating a harmonious understanding of both oneself and one's world.

— Meanwhile, *expectations* are future-oriented messages dealing with long-term roles, sometimes called *life scripts*. These sometimes are projections of learned relationships within the family or society.

Intrapersonal communication may involve different levels of communication activity: internal discourse, solo vocal communication, and solo written communication.

— *Internal discourse*: involves thinking, concentration and analysis. Psychologists include both daydreaming and nocturnal dreaming in this category. Prayer, contemplation and meditation also are part of this category, though from a theological point of view the argument may be made that this is not solely internal to one person. In Sufi tradition, this is similar to the concept of nafs, negotiating with the inner self. Example: Consciously appreciating the beauty of a sunset.

— *Solo vocal communication*: includes speaking aloud to oneself. This may be done to clarify thinking, to rehearse a message intended for others, or simply to let off steam. Example: Talking to yourself as you complain about your boss.

— *Solo written communication*: deals with writing not intended for others. Example: An entry in a diary or personal journal.

Direct Interpersonal Communication

Direct interpersonal communication involves a direct face-to-face relationship between the sender and receiver of a message, who are in an interdependent relationship. Because of interpersonal communication's immediacy (it is taking place now) and primacy (it is taking place here), it is characterised by a strong feedback component. Communication is enhanced when the relationship exists over a long period of time. Interpersonal communication involves not only the words used but also the various elements of nonverbal communication. The purposes of interpersonal communication are to influence, help and discover, as well as to share and play together.

Interpersonal communication can be categorised by the number of participants.

— *Dyadic communication*: involves two people. Example: Two friends talking.

— *Group communication*: involves three or more persons, though communication scholars are inconsistent as to the top end of the number scale. The smaller the number in the group, the more closely this mode resembles interpersonal communication. Often group communication is done for the purpose of problem solving or decision making. Example: University study group.

— *Public communication*: involves a large group with a primarily one-way monologue style generating only minimal feedback. Information sharing, entertainment and persuasion are common purposes of public communication. Example: Lecture in university class.

Another way of categorising interpersonal communication is on the function or setting of the communication.

— Organisational communication deals with communication within large organisations such as businesses. This is sometimes considered part of group communication, but communication scholars have built up a body of knowledge focused primarily on organisations. Example: Work-focused discussion between employer and employee

— Family communication focuses on communication patterns within nuclear, extended and blended families. Like organisational communication, this too is sometimes seen as part of the general category of group communication, but much research has been focused specifically on communication within a family relationship. Family communication can be enhanced by the long-standing and close relationships among participants as well as the likelihood that families have shared heritage, similar values, and social rituals. Patterns differ in communication between spouses, between parent and child, among siblings, and within the wider family context. Example: Conversation during a holiday meal.

Additionally, some scholars identify a category of impersonal communication. This is a distinction between impersonal and interpersonal communication on the basis of the quality of the interaction. Impersonal communication is that which involves functional short-term exchanges such as might occur between a shopper and a salesman; the label of interpersonal is reserved for communication that functions in deeper and more meaningful relationships

The process of interpersonal communication includes several stages over an extended life cycle. Communication scholar Mark Knapp has outlined one useful framework for understanding the coming-together process. Note that these stages can be applied to personal friendships, romantic relationships, business encounters, and many other types of interaction.

— The *initial encounter*: offers a first impression that can be full of communication data. Likes or dislikes can be instantaneous, though many people have learned that first impressions may be misleading.

— *Experimenting*: is the second step in interpersonal communication. In this step, information is exchanged on a variety of topics—general and "safe" at first, gradually becoming more personal and more self-revealing.

— *Intensifying*: follows when the experimentation leads to positive mutual conclusions that the relationship is worth pursuing.

— The fourth step in interpersonal communication is *integration*, in which mutual decisions are made that the relationship is fulfilling. This is the stage of intense friendships, close business partnerships, romantic commitments, and so on.

— *Bonding*: is the final stage, in which the relationship is sealed (often formally with contracts or written agreements) and generally is publicised (such as through announcements).

Knapp also outlined a similar reverse pattern for the unravelling of interpersonal relationships:

— *Differentiating*: mirrors the initiating phase but focuses instead on the differences that people notice about each other.

— Communication likewise plays a central role in the *circumscribing* stage, during which time participants in the relationship begin to minimise their communication and confine it to mainly functional topics.

— *Stagnating*: is the next stage, in which the relationship becomes flat and personally unfulfilling and is continued mainly for reasons beyond the relationship, such as religious or family obligation, contractual obligation, or social expectation.

— Overt unpleasantness is evident in the *avoidance* stage, in which the participants in interpersonal communication both avoid each other and express mutual annoyance when they encounter each other.

— *Termination*: if the final stage of breakdown, at which time legal, religious or other formal contracts are abrogated and the demise of the relationship is announced to others.

Mediated Interpersonal Communication

Mediated interpersonal communication involves technology that assists or links the sender and receiver of messages. This may involve immediacy (live, or so-called real time). It does not involve a primary context but instead uses technology to link the various parties in communication.

— *Dyadic communication*: includes two people, with some of the elements of interpersonal, but the context is not face-to-face. Example: Two business colleagues using the telephone or e-mail.

— *Group communication*: includes a small group of people. Example: Teleconference in a distance-learning class.

Mediated communication offers the advantage that it allows people to communicate over a distance or throughout a time span that would not be possible in direct communication. E-mail offers instantaneous global communication, and cell phones are highly mobile. Computer technology makes it possible for people to do their job without being physically present, allowing them to work from their home or from across the world.

Like direct communication, mediated communication may be formal or informal, personal or public. Feedback may be immediate or delayed. Machines even can assist in communication across language barriers (more on that in Unit 5 on intercultural communication).

Mediated communication has several inherent limitations, including the ability of telephone or Internet users to mask or disguise the source of the message, or the susceptibility of machines to various mechanical or technological noise sources.

Group Communication

Much communication takes place in the context of small groups, which are defined as those of three or more participants. The various and overlapping types of small groups lead to various types of communication patterns.

— Social groups are units such as families, friends living as roommates, and voluntary recreational groups such as soccer teams.

— Families also form primary groups, which are defined as those in which people share living and financial arrangements.

— Families also are an example of reference groups, through which participants gain a sense of identity and an awareness of expected behaviour

— Work groups are another pattern of relationships. These are built by people who are drawn together by a common task, such as students working together on a project or company employees assigned to a common job activity.

— Decision-making groups are brought together for the purpose of dealing with a question or policy.

— Similarly though distinctly, problem-solving groups focus on resolving a problem.

The working of groups has been the subject of much study, particularly from the framework of organisational communication. Leadership styles of small groups have been identified—generally in a three-part continuum ranging from high control (authoritarian leaders) through moderate control (democratic leaders) to low control (laissez-faire leaders). A fourth type, called abdacratic, involves the total collapse of leadership over uncontrolled group dynamics.

Psychologists and communication scholars have observed a pattern of group development, usually presented in a fourfold model

— The process begins with an orientation phase in which participants get to know each other and learn what is expected of them as a group.

— In the conflict phase, they deal with sources of conflict, usually in an effort to avoid conflict within the group. Too much conflict can prevent the group from functioning. However, some conflict is useful to avoid the pressure toward conformity known as groupthink.

— This norm emergence phase centres on compromise, the convergence of ideas, generation of alternative solutions, and eventually consensus. A technique often used to enhance the early part of this phase is brainstorming, in which unrestrained possible solutions and options are generated with no self-censorship or initial group evaluation. The purpose of brainstorming is to generate as many ideas as possible. Only after the ideas have been generated will they be evaluated, keeping the two steps separate and thus allowing the group to consider all possible options.

— The closure phase completes the process by concluding the group's work.

Conflict and Communication

Because much of the motivation for communication deals with the solving of problems, significant scholarly attention has been given to concepts such as problems, conflict, and consensus.

Conflict can be considered in various contexts, but much of the formal study of conflict has been at the interpersonal level. Principles and lessons from that level can be extended to the public and intercultural levels of communication, and the manner in which conflict is approached varies greatly from one culture to another. Even the resolution of conflict varies, from the seeking of clear winners or losers, saving of face (or inflicting shame), short-term gain versus the setting of precedence and long-term implications, and so on. Here are some issues associated with conflict.

Here are some principles associated with the study of conflict and the role conflict plays in interpersonal and other levels of communication.

— Consensus building is the creation of a mutually acceptable agreement, achieved through negotiation, built on dialogue, and resulting in the outcome of a commonly agreed-upon conclusion that at least partially accommodates the needs and interests of all parties.

— Conflict management is the process within an organisation or social unit that anticipates, researches, identifies potential solutions, and acts to address the problem. Conflict management focuses primarily on changing conditions within the organisation without addressing the internal or external cause of the conflict

— Conflict styles are the types of strategies and tactics for conflict management that are employed by persons or groups in communicating in a conflict situation. Five styles of been identified. Two focus on solving the conflict: an integrating style of conflict management involves a high level of concern for both oneself and others; a compromising style involves a moderate level of concern for both. One management styles is less focused on problem solving and more on control; a dominating style reflects a high concern for oneself and a low concern for the other. Two styles seek to steer clear of confrontation: the obliging style stems from a low concern for oneself and a high concern for the other; the avoiding style involves a low concern for both oneself and the other.

— Conflict resolution is permanent resolution of a problem or dispute achieved through dialogue and without physical or verbal violence. Conflict is inevitable. It is negative when it leads to violence, disrupts the communication relationship between the parties involved in the conflict, motivates people to become uncooperative, or prevents the parties from addressing real issues or problems. However, conflict can be a positive creative force when it increases communication, releases stored feelings, leads to the solution of problems, results in the growth of the relationship between the parties in conflict, or improves performance. Conflict is sometimes categorised either as expressive conflict rooted in a desire to release tension or as instrumental conflict that stems from a difference in goals or practices.

— Win-win strategies are positive approaches to resolving conflict in which each side gains something, though perhaps not everything sought.

— Win-lose strategies are negative approaches to conflict in which one side emerges as a clear winner and the other as a clear loser. These negative tactics usually are highly manipulative and are unlikely to lead to a long-term successful resolution of the conflict. Specific negative tactics associated with conflict and communication include steamrolling (hammering away at one's point of view until the other party gives in), force (physical or emotional coercion), blame (focusing on the cause of the problem instead of its resolution), silencing (prevention of the other side from engaging in communication), rejection (withholding love or affection, even acknowledgment of the other's existence), and escalation (taking the conflict to a higher level by causing even more serious actual or potential harm).

Sociologists and other scholars have researched how people of various racial and ethnic background handle conflict. Their findings suggest that, like many other aspects of intercultural communication, conflict management show some cultural patterns.

Many of the studies conducted in the United States have involved American co-cultures or microcultures (terms replacing the older concept of subculture). For example, European Americans show a preference for solution-oriented styles that, in Arab and Muslim countries, sometimes is interpreted as indifferent or lacking emotion. African Americans lean toward a controlling style. Arab Americans, Latino Americans and Asian Americans often make cooperative choices in handling conflict. The style of conflict management also relates to communication styles. For example, people often use emotional language and heated arguments as part of a dominating style of conflict management, whereas an unemotional discussion mode of communicating often is part of a conflict management style that focuses on problem solving.

REFERENCES

Arnold H. Schneider et.al., (1975). *Organisational Communication,* International Student Edition, McGraw-Hill Kogakusha, Ltd.

Brown, R., & Gaertner, S. (eds.). 2001). *Intergroup processes.* Oxford, UK: Blackwell.

Knapp, M.L. (1984). *Interpersonal communication and human relationships.* Boston: Allyn & Bacon.

Neher, W.W. (1997). *Organisational Communication—Challenges of Change, Diversity, and Continuity.* Boston: Allyn and Bacon.

Operrario, D., & Fiske, S. (2001). *Stereotypes: Content, structures, processes, and context.* In R. Brown & S. Gaertner (eds). *Intergroup processes.* Oxford, UK: Blackwell.

Pearce, Barnett. (1994). *Interpersonal Communication: Making Social Worlds.* New York: HarperCollins.

Trenhold, S., & Jensen, A. (2000). *Interpersonal communication* (4th ed.). Belmont CA: Wadsworth.

Tubbs, S. (1992). *A systems approach to small group interaction.* New York: McGraw-Hill.

4

Effective Team Communication

Teamwork is the ability of a group of people to understand the situation they are faced with, pinpoint their individual strengths, and then use these abilities to achieve an end result that is favourable. In a workplace, without proper teamwork it is often possible to have mixed results, miscommunication, and a situation where people do not achieve their full potential. As human beings we are first introduced to the concept of teamwork when we indulge in some form of team sport. A team sport allows you to understand the importance of allowing other members in the team to do their bit. It also teaches you key things like proper communication and the importance of sharing responsibility.

Working in a team does not in any way reflect on an single employee's inability to perform the task with effectiveness. The importance of teamwork in the workplace is highlighted in situations where in many people with diverse skill-sets need to come together in order to complete a task that needs different perspectives. Working in a team ensures that the completion of work is thorough. Effective teamwork can be imperative for proper completion of result oriented tasks. Another factor that needs to be taken into account while talking about the importance of teamwork in the workplace is the fact that it merely reduces the time taken to perform the task.

There are a number of reasons that can highlight the importance of teamwork in the workplace. First and foremost, with proper teamwoık it is possible to reduce the amount of work that generally becomes one person's headache. Sharing work means more focused attention on fewer things and also, a possibility of getting your work done much before you expected. It also helps to a great extent in reduction of stress levels of the employee.

With every employee it is important, that they feel like they are a part of a group. Team building and creating a bond between team members goes a long way in increasing the productivity of a business place. It is important for every employee to possess teamwork skills in the workplace and work with each other. Continuous interaction with other employees can also often increase the loyalty to the company. Another great thing about teamwork is that it helps create an atmosphere that has healthy competition. This goes a long way in improving the productivity of a company. Working towards a common goal and at the same time competing with each other to do better can help foster ties at the workplace.

Teamwork in the workplace and working with different individuals also enables quicker learning processes. You grasp concepts regarding the work better and with ease. Seniors in the team can always guide newer members regarding possible pitfalls, and help them learn pathways better. In some situations it has also been noticed that teamwork tends to increase creative output. A suggestion can lead to another, which like a pack of dominoes, can bring in some interesting results. All this can be credited to the importance of teamwork in business.

One of the most important reasons to encourage teamwork and collaboration in the workplace is to increase the rate of productivity and the time taken. Importance of teamwork in the workplace has also shown that it can in certain cases foster job satisfaction that bears a direct correlation with employee performance. These are just some benefits that highlight the importance of teamwork in the workplace. There are many other benefits that can be very specific to the team that you are working with. While for many people adjusting to an environment consisting of groups of people can be a stumbling block, their adaptability to the situation will improve, making them more receptive to teamwork.

Importance of Teamwork in Business

Businesses of today are largely concerned about their profits. They are taking every possible step to increase their turnover. The most important aspect that has a very substantial and positive impact on any business is teamwork. Effective teamwork is very significant for a company to use employee potential to the fullest. Teamwork is not only used in the corporate world to achieve targets on time, but also in the world of sports. If a team works towards a goal collectively, no one can stop it from reaching its goal. Due to the importance of teamwork in business, employers prefer to hire employees who are good team players.

For becoming a good and effective team player in your company, you are required to have a particular set of skills and capabilities. You most importantly should have a good listening skill. This surely proves to be useful in listening to ideas, views, suggestions and conceptions of other employees or subordinates. You should be able to discuss the ideas and strategies suggested by your colleagues.

You should encourage the participation of every member in the team for a collective effort to achieve a goal. You also need to be able to share knowledge and understanding among the team members. A not to be missed skill is to give respect to others. If you want to be a good team player, you should learn to respect people and their ideas. These are just a few essentials that are required for becoming a good team member. Now let us understand why is teamwork important.

Achieving Goals

It is a widely understood concept, that united we stand and divided we fall. Same is in the case of a team in a business. Collective team activities are very important if the company or a process wants to reach its goal. There are some tasks that cannot be done individually, but can be easily accomplished by working in a team.

Increasing Individual Learning

In simple terms, a team is a group of people who have come together for achieving a common objective. Therefore, in a group of people, there are many intelligent minds and brains working. When team members work together as a team, they can learn the skills and capabilities of each other and advance their knowledge. This certainly can be beneficial in your professional as well as personal life.

Resolving Conflicts

There are many types of conflicts that may arise in the company, which may in turn have an adverse effect on the collective output. In order to resolve business conflicts; the knowledge, understanding and expertise can be used efficiently for determining solutions to the problems. This significantly helps the business to grow.

Good Communication

Communication is an inevitably important factor in teamwork. When employees work in a team, they are able to pass on their ideas clearly. This rules out the possibilities of miscommunication due to complex hierarchy in the company. And due to ideas and concepts passed clearly, there is no scope for misunderstanding.

Generating New Business Improvement Ideas

If a manager encourages team members to participate in collective decision making, he will be able to reach a good strategy by considering views and suggestions from all members. The business can also think of incorporating ideas suggested by the team members. Employee participation in the management is a very effective tool in meliorating business strategies.

Effective Team Communication Skills

Effective team communication is very important in the world today. It ensures that decisions are taken well and with the consent of everyone involved. The various communication styles don't only improve the working environment but it is observed that employees are more productive when the communication is good. A team cannot perform its best if the output is on different levels of performance. Optimum output is expected from each team and this is possible only with effective communication in the workplace or a college/school even. Effective team communication will also make sure that decisions are taken considering all view points and are thus complete in their own being. A team which does not communicate effectively will experience low levels of employee motivation.

Learn to Convey

For effective team communication, a lot depends on how you eradicate the communication barriers and convey what you have to say. Conveying what you want and conveying it rightly, holds the most important key to effective team communication. People, colleagues in your team need to understand what exactly you want to say and they also 'have to' know why you are saying such a thing.

Don't Talk, Speak!

Another one of the effective team communication skill activities would be learning how to speak. Someone who just keeps on talking and doesn't make any sense is ignored and people seldom feel like communicating with him/her. Learn to be articulate and learn to make sense to people when you speak. Speak with a motive. Hold discussions and not speeches. Two sided conversations are very essential for effective team communication.

Be Open to Change

Another important skill required for effective team communication is being open to change. If you come across as someone who doesn't bother about other peoples' opinions and judgments, no one is going to bother giving them to you. Listening to what other people have to say and being open to change if needed. It is very important to consider and value every persons opinion in the team.

Be a Good Listener

Being a good listener is one of the best effective communication techniques. It is very important to listen to what people have to say and they'll say things to you only if they know you are willing to listen and not just listen because you have to. Importance of communication is sometimes understood just by the fact that people have the freedom to say things to each other in the team without thinking twice or feeling awkward.

Be Patient and Reasonable

Learn to be patient when you are dealing with anything in a team. Let it be deadlines or targets even. People sometimes have their own issues and you need to make them feel comfortable while discussing them. Freedom of expressing problems is one of the most important techniques of effective team communication. Also, you need to be reasonable. You have to understand the fact that you are dealing with different people and there are going to be more sides to everything that happens.

Polls for People

One of the best things to do if you want effective team communication in the office or anywhere else, is to hold polls for everything you can. Polls make the people feel that their opinions are taken into consideration and what they have to say matters. After these polls, it is also important to take decisions according to those polls. Proper action need to be taken regarding the conclusions that have been drawn out of the polls.

Group Meetings & Discussions

If you want to see some effective team communication activities, organise some group meetings and discussions where this can be developed. Meetings, discussions and similar platforms work best when you want to see some communication happening. In these meetings, get to know the team members as a first step and then start discussing the points you'll need to. Breaking the ice initially is very important.

Suggestions Box

Having a small suggestions box in the office is one the best effective communication strategies that you can develop. Allow people to anonymously put in their suggestions. Keeping it anonymous will help people to be frank about what they feel needs to be done. Secrecy is sometimes required to keep your dignity and this option will certainly help the cause. This strategy will surely help you achieve the goal of effective team communication.

Transparency & Combined Decisions

Transparency is of utmost importance in any team for any purpose. Everyone in the team should have equal rights and duties and these should be known to one and all. The basic idea of a team is where a group of people work towards a common goal and this makes it important for everyone to know what is happening. Similarly, a combined decision will make sure that everyone is equally a part of what is decided.

Communicating in a Work Team

Some of the most important communication in any business organisation occurs within work teams, but workers name workplace meetings as the *least* productive communication events of a typical week. Worker satisfaction is directly related to the perceived productivity of the teams in which they work, and team productivity is directly dependent on the communication that occurs within them. Productive communication within work teams is thus an important part of a person's overall effectiveness as a communicator, but most workers find it to be one of the most difficult set of skills to master.

Some of the complexity of team communication comes from the close interpersonal relationships that are part of the team experience. Another major source of difficulty, however, is that productive team communication is simply a more complicated communication task. Rather than *one* sender predicting the needs of *one* receiver and creating an effective message to meet them—an already difficult task in many situations— team work requires *several* communicators to maintain continuing shared perceptions over the course of a project, engaging in *common* communication without outside audiences, who might themselves be dynamically changing over time. Team communication simply never "sits still" long enough to make it seem manageable.

As you join any organisation, you will enter team situations that are already underway, but an easy way to understand much of a team's communication is to think in terms of its development process. Productive team communication is built in a series of stages, each of which includes several important communication components.

Getting Acquainted

A sense of team identity and cohesiveness among team members is a key factor in group satisfaction and productivity. Any team will be more productive when it spends at least a short period of time getting acquainted before jumping into its task. In a large, formal team situation, a well-run kick off meeting is an excellent forum to meet each other and begin to develop a sense of common goals and team identity. Even if your team is a short-term, informal group, though, spend some time communicating with each other in a "social" way to get acquainted with each others' goals, talents, and personalities.

Team Roster

Clearly defined membership is crucial to a successful, cohesive team, although team creation is sometimes a difficult exercise. Tasks are sometimes assigned before the group is even formed, perhaps because individuals must be hired to do specific parts of the project, or because workers must be released from other assignments. Sometimes the politics of team membership get ugly.

A group of individuals cannot become an effective team until everyone in the group knows who is "really" a member. If a team is formed at a face-to-face kickoff meeting, the roster is formed intuitively. People look around the room and make a visual identification of the team membership. Because they already work together, it is easy to find each other's phone numbers or office locations, but most business teams will still create a written team roster as the official act of recognising each other as members of the team. The roster is often circulated to the rest of the organisation, often with a copy of the team charge, so that everyone knows who is responsible for the project and how those individuals can be contacted. Obviously, the more distant or vague the team boundaries are, the more important it is to create a team roster before beginning any team communication.

— A boss wants to assign her favourite worker to a team, but Human Resources insists that others be given a chance at the responsibility.

— Upper management assumes the heads of each function will form the group, but two of these people work out of town most of the time, one is getting ready to retire and doesn't care about the project, and several people who are affected by the project want to attend the meetings, even though they aren't department heads.

— An individual sends an email to several people asking them to handle a situation. They can all see each other's names on the email, but some of them have never met, and none of them knows whether everyone else got the email yet.

If the team will be involved in a long-term or complicated project, two common documents are used to help team members get acquainted with each other as "real people" and create a sense of identity and common purpose.

Team Personalities

As with any interpersonal relationship, getting off "on the right foot" makes all the difference between success and failure. Many people will judge the quality of a group on the basis of its cohesiveness, camaraderie and group identity, calling a "good group" one in which people get along, even though getting along has no direct effect on team productivity.

You will be willing to spend more time interacting if the atmosphere is pleasant and sociable, which will lead to more participation in team activities and a better outcome. The team members will interpret those pleasant feelings as cohesiveness, a rather vaguely defined sense of attraction and togetherness, which leads to the real heart of team productivity, an honest desire on the part of team members to cooperate and work hard to do whatever the rest of the group wants to accomplish.

Of course, just liking each other does not guarantee productivity. Nor do the individual group members have to like each other for the group as a whole to become cohesive. Getting acquainted does involve a few key elements, though, when the point is to create good working relationships:

— *Get acquainted in a completely social atmosphere*: Even though this is a business situation, and everyone wants to get to work as soon as possible, groups do not become productive until *after* the members have gotten past the basic human tension of interacting with strangers. You'll get acquainted more quickly and eliminate much of the "storming" seen in new groups if you put yourselves in a context where your natural social inclination to make friends can take over. Groups become cohesive when they communicate in the expressive, emotional ways that friends do, and that doesn't happen as easily in the hierarchical atmosphere of most workplaces.

— *Be sure that all group members are present*: A key component of cohesiveness is a clear sense of who is in the group—and who is not. Attendance at a first team meeting will allow the members to identify each other as "us" and everyone else in the universe as "them." Everyone who is on the team must show up, and be sure as well that you are meeting *away from* other workers who are *not* on your team. It is crucial that the team membership is clearly marked so that you can take advantage of the social instincts that cause you to bond with your "own" community.

— *Discuss your personal goals*: Cohesive groups influence their members to do whatever the group wants, but if the group wants to socialise or loaf, it will be a very *un*productive group!. If you do want to be a productive work team, you will need to discover reasons all of you are interested in moving in the direction of the work task. While you are still "individuals" you control the way the team develops by finding things you have in common. If you chat about how much you hate your jobs and wish you could be doing other things, you'll find that the team becomes cohesive in supporting each other's attempts to avoid work! Instead, your getting-acquainted conversation should focus on how each of you is going to get something out of completing the project.

— *Talk about your work related skills and preferences*: Even a cohesive group can lack the skills or resources to do a particular task, so it's a good idea to start early to make sure that you do have everything it takes to get the job done. The most productive "knowledge work" teams have a diversity of knowledge, perspectives, and skills, and they are willing to disagree with each other, come up with new ideas, and be critical of each others contributions. Furthermore, cohesive groups are characterised by a sense that each person has a meaningful role within the group. None of this develops unless you become acquainted with each others skills, work preferences, thought processes and backgrounds.

Team Charge

The team charge is the official instruction to do a task as a team. This might be a memo from the boss, a letter from a client, or perhaps a statement of purpose that a team creates for itself. The team charge will sometimes be called a vision or a mission statement. The charge is not a complete description of the project or task, which comes later. This is an articulation of how the team's task fits into the organisation's broader goals. It provides "boundaries—in terms of constraints on the team as well as areas of autonomy". A clear mission should clarify any constraints such as budget limitations, delivery schedules, quality standards, legal restrictions, or technical requirements and clarifies areas in which the team has autonomy. Teams with a clear mission have higher performance than those without, as they are able to decide more effectively how to spend their efforts, and less likely to experience negative conflict within the team.

Defining the Task

Once your group of individuals has become a cohesive team, you will be more *motivated* to get the job done, but success requires another key step: you need to "understand together" exactly what the task is. A lack of goal setting and task definition is one of the key reasons groups fail.

Just understanding a task by yourself can be difficult. Some students, for example, think of themselves as very "task oriented" because they really, really want "good" grades and are willing to work "really, really hard" for them. That kind of high motivation is a good thing, but it doesn't really help you see what it is you need to *do* really, really hard to get those good grades.

The student who actually *gets* good grades translates the vague general goal of "good grades" into specific, operational plans:

> "I want to get a B or better in Cost Accounting by doing all the homework and identifying areas to ask questions about during the study session before each test."

This makes it easier to set up a schedule to actually get the work done, provides a benchmark for success, and helps the student pinpoint the places where you will need to access outside resources (i.e. the professor's study session).

Your group situation is similar, but multiplied by five or six minds. You not only need to make sure that your goal is operationalised into specific task steps, but now you must make sure that all of you understand both the goal and the steps in the *same* way. Not only that, you probably have a client or boss whose understanding of the task is more important than anything the team thinks!

The step of clearly defining your goals is thus not simply a motivational conversation to get your team pumped up. This is a conversation about translating general desires into specific, concrete *tasks*, deciding what your team's *deliverables* will be, and determining the *success criteria* that you will use to measure your team's productivity.

Create a Task List

Every job that requires several people is complicated enough to require several steps. These might be sequential steps, like the to-do list you'd follow in planning a party, or they might be components that need to be put together, like a blueprint for assembling a bicycle. Often, as with both parties and bicycles, some of the steps could be done in any order, but others must be done in a certain sequence in order for key decisions to be made on time or for parts to fit together properly. You probably will not create a complete task list for the entire project in your first meeting, but ultimately, every aspect of the team's job must be broken down into tasks: concrete, observable duties, activities or behaviours that a single person can do in a single sitting.

Determine Project Deliverables

The term "deliverables" is a good one if it reminds you that your team goal must be translated into something "real" that you could carry or mail to someone else. Business teams are never created to sit around and chat and come up with great ideas. They are created to produce something for someone. Whether the product is a car or a marketing plan or a customer response decision, your team must deliver something...the car, a report, a memo...to someone. Certainly the marketing ideas inside that report are the most important part of it, but your team will be more productive if you decide early in the process exactly how those ideas are going to be packaged for delivery. You'll be able to see more clearly what steps need to be taken, and you'll be able to talk more productively about what needs to be included.

Define Success Criteria

Group success can be defined in many ways, and without a specific conversation about what your team wants to accomplish, you are likely to find yourselves thinking you've done a great job just because you came up with some great ideas, or enjoyed your meetings, or didn't create any enemies in the sales department. In business teams, in particular, it's important to realise that how you *feel* about your group is not as important as whether or not you meet the expectations of your client or boss. As with everything else about task definition, this will mean defining your expected outcome in terms of some concrete, measurable standards. The specifics can vary from project to project, but the basic parameters will include

— *A time frame*: How soon does this project need to be completed? If something comes up, is timeliness more important than cost or quality?

— *The cost*: How much is the client willing to pay for this product, in terms of money, time and other resources? If some part or step looks like it's going to cost more than the budget allows, should the money (or time) be spent anyway, or should a solution be found that might take more time or reduce quality?

— *The quantity required*: How big, how much or how many are expected? Will this be a one-page report of a few ideas, or a fifty-page analysis of every suggestion made over the past year? Is the emphasis on generating the most possible alternatives and choosing one, or is the team expected to find the quickest "satisficing" solution?

— *The quality desired*: Does the boss want the team to produce a great widget, a mediocre widget, or a "down and dirty" widget? Perhaps more important, does everyone agree on what a great widget looks like? Has anyone seen one? If it turns out that it costs a lot to make a great widget, will an okay widget do?

Talking about Resources

Before you ever begin the project, you must identify and locate the resources you will need. Will you need information from another department or from the library? Will you need to use a programme or a programmer to complete some parts of the analysis? Will you need to allocate a large amount of some group member's time to write up the results?

A comprehensive conversation about resources will be crucial to your overall success. Sometimes, it is difficult for team members to talk about the resources because the group is unsure of how to do the task in the first place, but you can come up with a general list of job requirements by brainstorming about the possible things that could come up. Use this checklist to guide your team's communication about resources. If an answer is "we don't know," don't assume you don't need the resource! This just means your group's first responsibility is to find out more about how to do its task.

Task Resources Has someone in the group done this kind of task before, or do you have access to a guideline for doing it? Do you have the skills among you that are required to do the task? Will you need to hire, borrow or trade for expertise in some area? If you are expected to learn some concepts or skills in order to do this job, do you know where to get that training or experience? When will it be available? Do you have team members who enjoy and are good at the various elements of the job to be done?

Information Resources: Will you need factual information to do this job? Is there research on some aspect of the subject that needs to be performed? Will you need access to files, the Internet, a library or specific people who have relevant knowledge? Is any of the information restricted? Available on a limited time schedule? Will the information need to be reformatted, analysed or censored before it can be used? Do you have group members who know how to access all the information required? or, will you need training or help to get everything you need?

Administrative Resources: What office equipment, space or supplies will you need to get the job done? Do you need secretarial, programming, or accounting support? Do you have access to necessary computers, software and sufficient time to do the work? Is calendar or project management software available to help you track the job? If not, do you have someone in the group with sufficient project administration skills to keep track of the task you will be doing?

Relationship Resources: Working together will require a variety of relationship maintenance, conflict resolution, and general "people" skills. Has everyone in the group developed these skills, or is there a mentor available to help you learn them? An important group resource is shared norms: do you all agree on what "quality work" or "fair share of effort" means? Do you all understand "how meetings are done around here"? Do you have common, complimentary or contradictory goals? If you don't already have shared norms, will you have the time and guidance needed to create some?

Communication Resources: Do you have access to phones, email or other communication devices needed for effective project administration? Do you have a space for meetings with tables, white board or flipcharts and note-taking equipment? Is there someone who can take minutes? Do you have the equipment, skills, and time to create the documentation, presentations or status reports required by the project?

Planning Project Communication

Once the team is formed, productivity depends on the management of resources to accomplish its task, which by the very definition of "team" work requires productive communication within the group. Just as you aim for clear, concise, efficient communication to be a more productive individual worker, your team needs to use clear, concise and efficient communication to insure its productivity. The first task of any group is to define its own task. This is itself a communication process. The specific goals and standards envisioned by each group member must be shared and confirmed in a feedback process so that the group can productively work collaboratively. Then, the group's understanding of the task must be shared and verified with its supervisor or client. Productive groups communicate the task definition process with several key documents:

Team Charter or Mission

A team's first document should be its own statement of goals and objectives. Ideally, a team sets its own specific goals in cooperation with management. Often a team will be given a specific task when it is formed, but even then, the group should spend some time creating a restatement of those goals in their own words, paying special attention to,

The team charter should include:

- the team's mission or overall purpose in terms of how the team's task fits into organisational goals or the business's strategic mission,
- immediate goals in terms of what the team is supposed to accomplish, including time commitments and major deadlines.
- How the goals will be met in terms of delivering specific, measurable, accomplishments or products.
- How success or completion of the task will be measured

The process of creating the team charter can be lengthy. Often the team will need to meet together several times, gathering information about the task from a variety of sources before it can come to a clear agreement about what is involved. Usually, a representative will meet with a supervisor or client, as well, verifying that the emerging team goals are compatible with the organisational or client goals.

As a finished document, a team's charter can take many forms. Sometimes a team simply keeps the informal meeting notes as part of the project records, using them as the basis for the more formal external documents that will follow. Other teams have their missions engraved on plaques, pens or mouse pads and distributed to all members as a method of increasing both team identity and member motivation. Often a team charge will appear as the first page for the final project documentation.

Memo of Understanding

As soon as the team has defined its task, a document is usually sent to the client, supervisor, or major stakeholders to verify that everyone understands the task in the same way. The document could be a pro forma memo kept on file, a binding contract, or a series of substantive emails that clarify key details.

Whatever the circumstances, this document sets up a feedback loop, which should be designed so that several key topics are summarised and verified:

— Team identity Your group membership should be defined, identifying the person within the team who will be the client's contact. Often contact information for everyone on the team is given and sometimes additional information regarding each member's affiliation, supervisor or team responsibilities.

— Task parameters A brief but complete description of the project is the main body of the document.

 — *Client*: Generally the memo is addressed to the client (whether an external client, internal client or a direct supervisor) but sometimes you need to clarify multiple clients or cross-functional lines of authority.

 — *Organisational goal and context*: The memo should specify both long term organisational goals and the specific tasks that the team has undertaken to help meet them. If the project is part of an ongoing effort, the memo should clarify its current status with respect to completed phases or interrelationship with other teams involved in the project. This would also be the document to review previously determined constraints, concerns, or warnings regarding the successful implementation of the project. Be careful to spell out any assumptions that you are making regarding success criteria, resource availability, anticipated environmental changes, or strategic choices yet to be made.

 — *Contingent choices*: If there are any significant contingencies built into the project, they should be specified here, along with the dates that decisions will need to be made and the person or persons who will be responsible for making them. Be sure to indicate whether any resources or timeframes are dependent on these decisions and, if possible, the alternate deliverables that will result.

— *Deliverables*: This is a concrete description of what you will accomplish, create, or decide, and a commitment as to when, where and in what format it will be delivered to the client. Include information about interim or additional work that will be delivered at other times or to other people.

— *Standards*: What standards of quality, quantity, timeliness and cost are to be met in this project? It is also a good idea to spell out the priorities that the team and client have agreed upon in case conditions require that changes be made to the project scope or processes.

Resources: Specify any resources you expect to be able to use over the course of the project, including people, equipment or funds. You should be clear whether you have already secured the cooperation of resources, are expecting your supervisor or client to provide them, or will be locating necessary resources as part of your project responsibility.

Documentation: Specify the communication that will occur within the team, between the team and client. Any dates and format for interim and final reports should be included, along with information about where they are to be sent or stored.

Work Plan

Project management, by definition, requires the use of management tools, and documentation will be your most important tool. A complete project work plan, includes all elements of the team's scope and objectives, as well as the specific phases or steps involved in completing the work. This document will allow everyone in the team to know where it is going, and how much it has accomplished at any given moment, and what remains to be done.

The key information in an effective work plan includes:

— *Project Steps*: Every element or step of the project must be listed. Generally, a team will attempt to put the steps into chronological order, although most projects involve interrelated steps and information flow that allows or requires that some steps be completed simultaneously. When these interrelationships become very complex, a Gantt chart is often the best way to visualise the flow of the project.

— *Sub-steps and Tasks*: Each major element of a project is broken down to the level of a task: the work that an individual can accomplish in a single work session (generally figured at two to four hours).

— *Task Sequence*: Each task should be reviewed for elements that must be completed in advance. It is at this stage that a team will discover that the original chronology is incorrect or incomplete. If project management software is being used, the final result will accommodate these interrelationships, but if a team is using a simple table or spreadsheet, the prerequisites are listed for use when the calendar is created.

— *Time Estimates*: The estimate of the time a task will take should never exceed the amount of work one person can do in one sitting. Project elements that exceed about four hours should be further subdivided so that each discrete step can be adequately planned. Indicate multiple time estimates if a task requires the time of two individuals.

— *Task Assignments*: Productive team work requires that tasks be assigned on the basis of skills, access to resources, and work preferences. In many cases, work assignments are made to minimise the need for extra communication. A person who completes a sub-task, for instance, might be involved in a later step, allowing him or her to use the information learned at the earlier stage of the project. Review the assignments carefully to insure that each individual has access to the equipment, time and skill resources needed to complete his or her tasks.

Project Calendar

Once the work plan is completed, the team will create due dates for the various steps of the project. These are generally created "backward" from the final project completion date, picking up the time required for prerequisite subtasks and accounting for resource availability, communication requirements, contingent decisions, and any other elements that will require time for completion. The conversion from work plan to calendar can become complicated by elements that have yet to be decided, but *all* project elements should be accounted for, even if the exact parameters of the element are not yet known.

Adjustments might be required to balance a team's workload. Individual tasks and times are added to complete team calendar.

A project calendar is created in the same way a personal calendar is created, although accuracy and completeness are more important when several people must coordinate their work. In a complex, multi-phase project, a Gantt chart is often used, creating a visually intricate calendar that helps the team plan its work. Punch lists, spreadsheets and flow charts all offer advantages for various kinds of projects or processes, and some industries have specialised methods or software packages to facilitate their unique projects. Some teams work with sophisticated project management software that combines the work plan and project calendar, often with additional communication features. Others keep the project planning documents in a simple three-ring binder. You might also use a web-based intranet or a document management system that connects everyone on a "virtual" team electronically.

Whatever the communication technology used, the typical business team will organise its work chronologically, and the project process will be controlled on a *team calendar* of some kind. Once the team's overall work plan is completed, each team member will be able to locate to his or her own well-defined tasks, deadlines, and deliverables.

As you plan the task steps, locate the points at which you will need to communicate with each other, with your client or supervisor, and with anyone who will be providing resources to the team. Productive teams communicate about key topics: scheduling and coordinating of task elements, review of team and individual performance, and review of environment. Furthermore, they plan communication events to accomplish the discussion.

Regular routine communication is a factor in team success, since the regularity insures that lapses and contingencies are handled, and sufficient interpersonal contact is available to get acquainted, develop norms, and work out differences. On the other hand, one of the biggest mistakes teams make is to arbitrarily schedule regular meetings without considering the optimal length or frequency, simply assuming that the project will be most effectively accomplished with face-to-face communication of the whole team at frequent intervals. Not only are such meetings extremely expensive in terms of member time, but they are generally a far less efficient channel of communication than the phone or email. Don't plan to do all your communication at meetings, and don't schedule meetings without a rationale.

Often, teams will use an electronic calendar system to plan a project, which can then be accessed and adjusted by all team members on a continuous basis. Most large organisations will use a software package that integrates team communication, the project calendar, and all documentation for multiple interrelated business activities.

Managing Team Communication

Productive management of team communication involves monitoring, evaluating and correcting processes over the course of the project. Furthermore, productive team communication involves every member of the team. In collaborative work, every member of the team must be in a position to know what needs to be done, what the next step is supposed to be, and whether any problems are looming on the horizon.

To meet this challenge, productive teams manage their communication with effective project documentation. Documentation can take various forms. The team might use a three ring binder that travels to each meeting. It might create an intranet that each member can access from his or her own workstation. A team might have an administrative support staffer who distributes copies of team documents for each member to store electronically. Whatever the format, a few key communications need to be recorded and made accessible to everyone involved in the project.

Creating a Communication Plan

Create a communication calendar: Once a team has created the overall work plan, it can determine the times it will need to engage in communication to complete its tasks.

— Determine the dates on the calendar at which:
  — information must be transferred,
  — decisions must be made,
  — resources must be secured, or
  — external stakeholders require communication or interim deliverables.
— Determine the optimal kind of communication format for each date. Generally, information transfer is best handled electronically, decisions are made face-to-face, and client/supervisor contact is done in writing.
— Create another calendar for the team's emails, meetings and status reports. Many teams will combine their task and communication calendars so that all team activities can be monitored at once, but budgets and status reports generally require that task work (i.e. "billable hours") and communication work (i.e. "administrative hours") be calculated separately.

Create communication processes: In addition to planned task communication, every project requires a great deal of communication about unplanned events. A productive team will determine how communication should take place when:

— the client, supervisor or resource availability necessitates a change in plans,
— unexpected decisions are required,
— follow-up or discipline of team members is required
— Determine the procedure that one member of the group should use to make a decision "on the fly" and the level or type of responsibility that each person has for making such decisions without whole group approval. Most groups will decide on a dollar amount, for instance, that a team member can spend over a budgeted expense, or determine a range of product specifications that will be acceptable, allowing the person assigned to the actually purchasing trip to make the final choice in the vendor's showroom.
— Determine the procedure for annotating the team's work plan, calendar, and documentation. Most disasters do not come from an

unexpected change in the teams work; they arise because a client was not informed of a change or a subsequent task on the calendar was not adjusted to reflect the changed circumstances. If there is one "most" important communication in a team situation, it is the communication that informs others of changes that have taken place over the course of the team's work.

Optimise communication channels: Although meetings, emails or phone calls are already scheduled to accomplish the team's task, a second level of communication is required to handle the contingency events, interpersonal issues, and misunderstandings that are a normal part of team work. This requires that all team members are aware of the optimal methods for communicating with each other under various circumstances.

— How is each group member best reached? (email? pager? voicemail?)

— What is the timeframe that responses can be expected? (within an hour? overnight?)

— What are the cost issues to consider? (phone vs. computer? meeting vs. phone?)

Specify communication responsibilities: Obviously every team member is responsible for maintaining the communication plan, but several key duties will probably be assigned to specific individuals:

— Organising and facilitating planned group meetings

— Maintaining and updating the team work plan and communication calendars

— Client and/or supervisor contact

— Creating and maintaining team work and communication documentation.

Managing the Communication Process

You might imagine that you are now ready to get to work, which would be true if you were working alone. In a team situation, though, one more crucial step is needed for success. You must decide how you are going to share information, make decisions and deal with changes as they occur over the course of the project. When a job that is complicated enough that it needs several minds, success depends on having a workable system for sharing knowledge among those minds.

This coordination of knowledge is not a process that happens automatically or magically. In fact, in a complicated, long-term business project, team communication might be a full time job for one of the team members. Regardless of the project's complexity, success requires that a team agree on *what* needs to be communicated at every stage of the project, *how* that communication should happen, and *who* will be responsible for participating in the various communication events.

Anticipate Communication Topics

Any job that a team undertakes will necessarily involve the coordination of resources, information, and changes. Before you ever begin the project, you must identify and locate the resources you will need, and then your various resources must deliver their information, materials or products at the right time, to the right person, over the course of the project. How will each resource know it is needed? Will someone need to call and notify the client that information is needed? Does the office administrator need a calendar of when the conference room should be scheduled? Will there need to be negotiations with a team member's supervisor regarding attendance at an off-site retreat? Go through your resource list carefully, noting these communication tasks, and put them on your project calendar.

Similarly, teamwork always requires a systematic distribution of information among team members. From your task list, you can predict some of the major information transfers that must occur. Schedule these on your project calendar. You should also identify major categories of information that team members have, which others will need. Your programmer might have the specs for the software design, while the marketing rep knows whom to call at the client's office for some user input. The team leader will obtain the audit schedule from the client, but needs to know from the human resources department when each intern should be paired with a team member. While this kind of information is not always scheduled, your project records should include the key contact people for various types of information.

Finally, your team will be communicating change. The client might change his or her mind about how the project is to proceed. The market situation might change the parameters of what your team can accomplish this quarter. You might suddenly discover mid-project that a key supplier will not be able to provide parts on time. You won't know what change will occur, but you can be sure that somewhere along the line, an emergency will come up, a plan will be changed, or someone will discover a problem the team hadn't anticipated. As you plan your communication, you should include "changes" and "problems" as a topic, and decide how they will be handled.

Plan Communication Procedures

Select Communication Channels: Once you know the topics of conversation, you'll need to chose the best channels for each communication that must occur, and when possible, the best times. Many teams have a communication "plan" that consists of a single question, "when shall we have our meetings," but meetings are without a doubt the most expensive channel of communication your team could select, and the least efficient for routine information transfer.

A much better method of planning communication is to go back to your project schedule and locate all the points at which information must be transferred, decisions made, or knowledge shared. Then select the best method to accomplish each of those tasks, and add the communication events to the schedule.

A crucial part of planning the communication is making sure that each team member knows what to expect. It isn't enough to plan good information flow; team members must be able to recognise and resolve information deficiencies. Make sure that everyone understands what should happen if expected information doesn't arrive, or isn't clear.

Plan Special Communication: Your team's task might also require some specialised communication, which must be included in your planning. If your team will be functioning as a decision-making group, you'll need to know methods you'll be using to make the decision. Teams can use anything from voting, to drawing straws, or finding consensus, but will be productive only if everyone agrees on the method and is skilled in the procedures. Decision-making groups should also pay particular attention to their social communication. People who "feel good" about the people in the group will be more satisfied with any decisions reached, which is especially important when the group is also responsible for implementation of its decision

If your team will be engaged in supportive activities, perhaps because you anticipate a great deal of difficulty or stress in the project, your communication plan might also include opportunities for more intimate conversations that involve caring and concern, empathic listening, and emotional expression, in a supportive, noncompetitive context. You might schedule an off-site get together now and then, where the topic is not work per se, but the human side of coping with the work. Humorous, playful activities can generate warm feelings in the midst of a stressful project, as can a pizza or do not delivery, and these events will create an environment in which supportive communication can occur.

Discover Communication Norms: Finally, your communication plan must include some attention to defining the group's communication norms, those expectations of polite, smart, decent communication that define any community. If there is a single cause of "storming" in groups, it is a failure to discuss those deep-seated expectations of how people "ought to behave" within the context of the team's work together. If the arguments, misunderstandings and conflict get completely out of hand, a group will eventually create some kind of group norms, but usually the group just goes along with whoever grabs power. Someone finally gets tired of the hassles and takes control, while others give up or decide they don't care much any more what happens to the group (or its task).

What will count as polite social behavior? Does getting to an appointment on time matter? Returning phone calls? Whose emails need to be answered immediately, and whose can be ignored until their information is needed? In many groups, people with higher status in the company to work harder and follow procedures, or members with very important skills are allowed to violate the rules more often than others. To a certain extent, it doesn't matter how your group defines polite relationships, as long as you are all comfortable with the rules, but some rules do make a group more productive: you should not give a person special privileges within the group just because he or she has a higher status in the organisation, and you should not let your desire for social relationships get in the way of critically evaluating ideas, information or opinions about the task at hand.

What counts as valid information? Since information must be shared within the group, everyone must have a sense of confidence in the facts, evidence and analysis provided by others. Can information from a website be used without a background paragraph about the website's sponsors, history and current customers? When focus groups are conducted, does the team need complete demographic information on the participants? Does everyone in the group understand the statistical methods that will be used in the project, and what types of data will be needed for a valid analysis? Is everyone on the sales team collecting the same information on potential client needs? Is that information in the same format the programmers can use? Obviously each project will use different kinds of information, but finding out mid-project that team members don't mean the same thing by "good information" will be a disaster.

What is proper conversation? Finally, your group should talk a bit about how to talk. In general, groups do best when communication is perceived as "open" and "supportive", but those words can mean different things to different people. If "supportive" means to say nice things about a team member's idea, even when you think it's not a very good idea, your group will lack the confrontation it needs to make good decisions. If "openness" taken to mean that interpersonal conflict is acceptable, you'll find the group distracted from task at hand and unable to engage in optimal conflict resolution strategies. Take some time to talk about how discussions should be conducted, how criticism should be handled, and what counts as constructive discussion. You might discover that one of you comes from a family of "screamers" and another from a family that uses the "silent treatment" to convey disapproval. You can learn to communicate with each other, but it will be much easier if you find out about your different expectations *before* the project problems start.

Decide Who is Responsible

No amount of planning will actually get the job done. The plans must be followed, and with any group activity, that requires some communication to keep all the information flowing. Your team will avoid innumerable "communication breakdowns" later by installing some effective management procedures *before* you get started on the project.

Sometimes groups find it easiest to name one person a "project facilitator" or "communication specialist." This does not have to be a person with any other kind of power in or out of the group, but a group will be most productive if someone is in charge of the information flow, both inside the group and with its external resources and environment. Complex or risky tasks, in particular, are not done well when coordination and control functions are too widely shared. In most groups a "social leader" will also emerge. Regardless of the work done by a formal or informal administrative leader, someone will take on the informal responsibility of social communication, doing whatever is necessary to maintain "group unity and satisfaction".

Meeting Facilitation

Team meetings are a common type of regular communication and so important that special documents are used to plan, facilitate and record them: the meeting *agenda* and meeting *minutes*. Most people think of meetings as a single occurrence of oral communication, but business meetings involve a series communications, generally in writing, before, during and after the oral conversation that insure the group achieves the objectives. Taken together, the pre-meeting, meeting, and post-meeting communication are most productive when they follow the standard business structure of productive communication.

Starting the Meeting and following the Agenda

In general, individuals should be allowed to leave a meeting that lasts longer than scheduled. It is up to the meeting facilitator to schedule sufficient time to cover the planned topics, and to keep the conversation efficient about covering those topics. Participants should not be expected to suffer the consequences of a poorly managed meeting.

It is generally the responsibility of the person who prepares the agenda (who is usually the meeting facilitator as well) to pull together all these potential agenda items, estimate the amount of time to be allotted to each item, and insure that sufficient meeting time is available to accomplish the agenda. If there are too many items to be productively handled, some should be "tabled" for another meeting or an alternative mode of communication should be created to resolve the item.

Unless a general category is designated for "new business," meeting participants are expected to ask the meeting planner to place items on the agenda before it is distributed.

Then everybody should leave the meeting! If meetings consistently drag on because more agenda items are being thought up as you go along, or people are standing around afterward discussion important issues that were somehow never included in the agenda, the team should take a hard look at its agenda creation process.

Meeting Facilitation

Once everyone arrives, agenda in hand, effective team meetings are characterised by starting and finishing on time, staying on the agenda, full participation, and some time for socialising. This productive conversation is not accidental. One or more people will "facilitate" the meeting by paying attention to the communication that occurs and insuring that the agenda is followed.

The facilitator can be a supervisor of the group, a member of the group, or an outside specialist in group processes. Generally, one person is thus considered the meeting's formal facilitator, but it is important to remember that everyone in the group is equally responsible for communicating in a way that insures that the group achieves its planned objectives. The more members who understand the meeting process, the more effectively they can cooperatively facilitate productive conversation. Some groups—and student groups are a good example—do not have a designated facilitator. In these groups it becomes especially important that the group members understand and follow good communication practices.

Whether or not there is a designated meeting facilitator, everyone who attends a meeting plays a part in keeping the group's communication on track. As the new person in the company or on the team, don't feel that you have no control over how well things are going. In fact, sometimes the new person can be in a great position to clarify goals and expectations because you get to ask questions about just about anything!

— Make sure you see the agenda. If the facilitator "forgot" to prepare one, ask that the group make a quick list of the meeting's goals and topics.

— Take meeting notes right on the agenda. This will help you to keep track of what is going on, and you can offer to make the group notes or take the minutes if those jobs aren't being done.

— Keep an eye on the clock. If conversation is getting bogged down, or if conflict seems to be unresolvable, it is proper to suggest that the group "move on, in the interests of time." Unresolved issues should be rescheduled for a better time when information, resources and/or open-mindedness are more available.

After *each* agenda item, verify that the group is in agreement

— That the agenda item has been adequately covered

— On the decisions that have been made

— On any "new" issues that need to be added to a future research or communication agenda

If an agenda item is taking longer than anticipated, the group may agree to extend the conversation, but other agenda items should be eliminated so that a meeting's overall time is not affected.

Most good facilitators will create a written set of meeting notes, which acts as a visual trace of the conversation as it happens. Even though several individuals are usually taking notes (including someone who might be creating the meeting minutes), the whole group needs to be able to share a *common* perception of how the conversation is progressing. Everyone in the group needs to maintain constant awareness of what information the group is finding relevant, and the decisions that are being made. This allows people to verify the group's decisions as they go along and saves disagreement among individuals' notes.

The meeting facilitator is often the person to make the group notes, usually on a white board or flip chart. Flip charts are useful because they can be torn off and posted all over the walls so that everything remains in sight for the entire meeting. Electronic whiteboards are handy for creating a permanent and accurate copy of brainstorming results, diagrams that perfectly capture the group's creative ideas or the exact wording of decisions or results.

Whether or not the group keeps these meeting notes depends on the circumstances, but they are often brought back to later meetings to insure that key ideas or tasks have not been forgotten. Sometimes, items come up that the group will need to resolve or discuss at a later time, and the meeting notes should also create a "group memory" of anything that must be done by anyone after the meeting ends.

Discussion and Decision Records

The most important part of productive team communication is the continuing record of decisions that are made. Whether a decision is made in a meeting, or on the phone between two members, or in a chance meeting with the client, it must be communicated to everyone on the team who will need to act on that decision. Further, it must be recorded so that time need not be spent in another conversation, discussing and making the same decision all over again.

Project Data

Virtually any team is more productive when all team members have easy access to key information that is needed. Generally, a team will create some kind of central depository of information, which is sometimes kept separately from the rest of the project documents. The format will vary depending on the work, but blueprint files, bibliographies, spreadsheets, bound reports and trays of tissue samples are all examples of project information depositories. Internal team documents will also include copies of the key documents the team produces, which might be kept chronologically as a record of the team's work, or as separate archive documents.

Sometimes, project records are used to document that legal or auditing requirements have been met. They are used to bring a new member up to speed. On a long, complex project, a team can refer to project records to remember why certain decisions were made, or to locate information details. Sometimes the only thing between you and a lawsuit is a clear paragraph explaining how a particular client requirement has been met.

External Communication Records

In addition to your own internal communication, members of your team will also have regular communication with some combination of supervisors, resources, or clients. As part of its task definition step, the team should determine exactly what communication is expected by supervisors and clients, who generally expect to communicate at regular intervals throughout a long project. It is crucial that a team keeps a written record of this communication, which can often involve changes in the team's mission, its resources, or commitments from others in the organisation.

Communication Log

A log is an easy way to keep a complete record of communications as they occur, without having to categorise and file the information and decisions, and regardless of who on the team engaged in the communication. A sales team, for example, might keep a web-based prospect book, to which each team member posts every contact. Each time a team member is about to call a prospect, he or she can see the complete record of previous calls, including entries about the product requirements, special offers that have been made, and even personal information about the prospect's likes and dislikes.

Status Reports

A productive team will engage in informal status and formal reporting with a range of key resources, clients, supervisors or stakeholders. The nature of these reports can range from specific coordination of resources to ambiguous but politically important warnings that things aren't going as planned. Some are "accidental" in the sense that you do not plan them. For example, a team member might "run into" a client at a business mixer and casually mention that some promised information did not arrive as expected. Some are carefully planned, as when a production team sets up a regular conference call among its key vendor reps, but the exact content of the report is not pre-defined. Regardless of their format, records of these reports should be kept as a complete chronological record of the team's commitments.

A formal status report should include some key information:

— a recap of the work you have performed during the reporting period

— explanations of any deviations from the work plan or project budget, and

— projections for the next reporting periods, including especially any schedule, budget or resource changes that are being made from the current work plan.

Informal status reporting is often oral. Be careful not to neglect these important conversations, or fail to record their outcomes.

Evaluating Communication Procedures

As you are planning your team's communication procedures, create a system to monitor the occurrence of any planned communication. Just as you would create benchmarks or metrics to monitor the success of any critical path event, you should have some kind of calendar, schedule or feedback loop to insure that scheduled phone calls, meetings or reports have actually been produced. Everyone should be clear as to the proper mechanism for coordinating subtasks and resources. In addition to routine communication, you should have procedures in place for non-routine communication events. Decide what the mechanism will be to communicate changes in task, procedures, and resources.

With a complete plan in place, it is relatively easy to see whether communication has been done according to that plan. If your team has a designated administrator, that person might engage in a systematic process or reminders, follow-up and documentation. More often, teams self-monitor their communication processes. As individuals note any communication failures, they bring them to the attention of those who are involved and make ad hoc corrections.

Sometimes it becomes apparent that a communication system is not working as intended. For example, team members might decide to exchange key information in early morning emails, but one team member is unable to log on to email at her workstation until after a sizeable data download is accomplished. Rather than delay its work every day, the team decide to modify its procedure, refreshing the intranet links to team members' information overnight, allowing each team member to upload the data as needed.

In addition to insuring that communication takes place as planned, communication management involves insuring that the interaction accomplished its purposes. In general, this means the team will engage in some systematic feedback activities to insure that information exchange, knowledge sharing, and critical evaluation of data is actually happening as intended. People tend to think that everyone else at a meeting understood what was said in exactly the same way, while in reality this is seldom the case.

Team communication is greatly enhanced when efforts are made to insure that feedback loops are in place to catch misunderstandings before they become problems. For example, at the end of every meeting, *everyone* in the group might summarise his or her own perception of the key decisions and commitments that have been made. Or, a meeting facilitator can meet one-on-one with group members on a regular basis, insuring that everyone is hearing things the same way. Group members might review agenda items with their respective departments prior to each meeting, then compare notes on how different groups throughout the organisation are viewing the issue. When quality information is especially important or difficult to obtain, a team might even defer all decisions until verified outside the group environment.

Most students have worked in groups, but the projects in a school semester lack one crucial characteristic of work teams. In business, you will seldom start with a "zero history" group that has never worked together, and typically you will not disband after each project is completed. If something is not going well in a work team, you can't simply ignore it and wait for the semester to end. You *must* identify the problem and solve it. Not only is the immediate task more important that a school assignment was, but your team will be working on many more tasks in the future, and you want to be very sure the same problems don't come up over and over.

Your team should have some communication scheduled to make sure that procedures and processes are evaluated. These conversations usually occur at the boundaries between one project and another, or between one project stage and another, or when team membership changes and a new individual must be acculturated into the team's goals, norms, and procedures. You might schedule a special "task redefinition" session to talk about any changes in project direction or scope, or hold a "get acquainted session" to introduce a new team member. Or, you might include a short "how are we doing" session at every meeting of the entire group.

DOCUMENTING TEAM RESULTS

Whatever your team does accomplish, the outcome will probably need to be communicated to others. The effectiveness of that communication is at least as important to the team's final productivity.

User Documentation

Many teams are charged with the creation of a product, service or procedure that will be used by other employees or a client. A group is asked to decide on a new employee dress code, for instance, or a design team creates a new line of products. The deliverable, in these cases, is not merely the decision or design, but whatever instructions, explanations or procedures are required to allow someone to *follow* the new dress code or *use* the new product.

Quality documentation in this scenario requires more than simply recording of the team's decision in the project records. The format and content must take into account whatever accessibility, readability, and usability issues will affect the ability of the user to actually perform the desired behaviours or use the team's output. User documentation will often require extensive editing and reorganisation of material so that it provides a context for understanding the process, clear functional expectations, and clear instructions for behavior.

Transfer Documents

In addition to whatever documentation goes to the users of a team's outcome, there is often an additional transfer of the team's work responsibility. A quality team, for instance, might reach its reengineering goals and transfer the project responsibility to a production team. An emergency response team might wrap up the immediate disaster with a cover memo to some future team that must solve a similar problem. For security reasons, an audit team might disband and allow a different group of individuals to handle the client's next annual review.

Often the transfer document is written for an unknown audience; the team has completed its own responsibility, but does not know exactly who will be responsible for the next stage, or even exactly when that will happen. Sometimes the transfer is part of a proposal, which must include incentives to continue the project as well as instructions for how to do so.

The transfer document is therefore a relatively comprehensive document, summarising the team's aims and goals as well as specific results, anticipated future work steps, and available resources for continuation of the project. In a project with minimal written documentation, the transfer document might be formatted as a report, including resources and project records as appendices. If the team has created a large set of binders to house the project records, the transfer document might be a short memo inserted as a first page in the first binder. Teams that use an intranet or electronic communication technology might create a transfer document in html, which is then uploaded as a permanent home page for the project, with links to resources, records and appropriate background materials. In short, there is no rule about the required format for a transfer document. The team will use whatever resources are suitable to move project knowledge from one team to another.

Collaborative Work Communication

Writing Projects

Regardless of what other work a team will be charged with accomplishing, there will undoubtedly be group effort in creating its documentation. Even when individuals do not work within a team structure, they will often write collaboratively. One study found that 87% of business writing was accomplished in a team or group, and even the individual who writes a document "alone" can expect three to five levels of review before it is complete. In fact, even the writer whose work is so routine that it simply goes "out the door" without review will realise that his or her writing is constrained by corporate formats, organisational expectations, and an internal "ear" that has learned to write in a way that acknowledges and represents the views of everyone in the organisation. A letter from a company is never "just" from its writer; it also represents the company as a whole and all of its employees.

Time and resource management issues with respect to the writing process are just as large a part of the management job as any other resource management. Perhaps writing is even more important when the organisational impact of written communication is considered. Continuing issues should be resolved and not dismissed as just the "disadvantages" of collaborative writing. Certainly collective authorship is unlike individual authorship, but it is a communication practice that accomplishes important organisational purposes.

The basic steps of the productive writing process do not change with the addition of authors, reviewers or corporate expectations. Efficient collaborative writing does require, however, timely and productive communication at each stage of the *prewriting*, *drafting*, and *editing* process.

The Collaborative Writing Process

Group Cohesion

No team project, including a writing task should be started before the team is ready to take on collaborative work. The first job of the team is to get acquainted and communicate about its common goal or mission. For a writing task, in particular, the development of a clear and consistent "voice" often requires high levels of understanding and agreement among group members.

Task Definition

When multiple researchers, writers or editors are involved, an initial meeting should set up the project time-line, set intermediate tasks and due dates, allocate resources and responsibilities, and decide on a consistent format and style. A newly formed group that has not had experience with writing together should set multiple intermediate due dates, expecting to spend quite a bit of time talking through the various ways to express ideas.

An individual's writing is of higher quality when information requirements and audience expectations are considered before beginning to draft a document. With a group of researchers or writers, the process becomes even more crucial. A team will find it still has misunderstandings and disagreements after the drafting begins, but the most productive teams will at least come to an agreement on audience and goals, structure, research or data collection needs before attempting to write.

Schedule enough interaction among those who are making decision about the document's purpose, expected audience, and persuasive strategies. If a group has not worked closely together before, of if the organisational "voice" is unfamiliar to the writers, be sure that everyone agrees on definitions, expectations and goals.

Task Process

The actual typing at a keyboard is obviously an integral part of any writing project, but keyboards are designed for single writers and collaborative writing is necessarily accomplished by coordinating the keyboarding of several individuals. In reality, the drafting of any document is actually a series of decisions, drafts, revisions and edits, which can be distributed among a group in multiple ways.

— Different people can draft different sections of a document, which are then distributed to the entire group for editing and revision. Sections can then be redrafted by the same person or shuffled among members, especially on important projects that require careful attention and full knowledge distribution.

— One person might draft the entire document, which is then sent to others for review. The reviews can be conducted simultaneously, with the same or another person combining the comments in the next draft. Alternatively drafts can be created after each rereading in a hierarchical review process.

— Different individuals sometimes draft different sections of a document, which are then forwarded to a single individual who rewrites item to achieve organisational coherence as well as a consistent style and format.

Whichever drafting flow the group uses, it will find the process most effective when it allows sufficient time to reach agreement. Otherwise, an alternative editing process must be used to create a single coherent document. Many successful groups takes advantage of collaborative writing software, which can greatly speed the comparison and revision of documents.

Resource Allocation

Along with the information and production elements, collaborative writing requires attention to the creative, cognitive and language resources within the group. Writing ability is often perceived as an extension of ones own personality or "voice," and writers can be very possessive about their own personal choice of words. Collaborative writers must "be able and willing to overcome differences in writing styles, working styles, and personality traits", taking full advantage of each others' differences as additional writing strengths available to the group rather than interpersonal differences to be resolved or ignored.

Review and Revision

Communicating Change

During the course of a large project, it is common to find that the goals and purposes have changed, the audience has changed, or circumstances have changed sufficiently that a document must meet different goals from what was originally discussed at the prewriting stage. If document drafts are being prepared by individual writers, it is a good idea to schedule additional time for the group to review these issues and make sure that individual writers are responsive to the changes.

Editing

Usually, one person drafts a document or document section, which others edit, and typically one person does a 'full' or 'final' edit for perfect stylistic and formatting consistency. Whatever task process is selected, be sure that anyone editing a document is clear about the content, format and style decisions that were made during the prewriting, and about which editing step is to be done at the moment. The review and revision process is built on the assumption that two heads are better than one, but some heads are better editors than others. The best editor is not always the best writer, or English grammarian. The best editor is familiar with the writer's goals and with the audience and able to anticipate how an audience will respond to a document.

As a team, be even more careful to follow a systematic editing process, discussing content, format, style and language errors in that order. Conflict can arise when writers don't make careful distinctions between personal judgments about a businesslike "style" or "tone" and the rules of grammar or punctuation.

Editors should carefully distinguish between acceptable style differences and desirable format or style consistency. Conformity to a set of language and format rules is important, however, for a clear, consistent corporate image. A competent editor must also know the difference between style decisions and grammatical errors. Nearly any written format or style or construction is "correct" in some context, but it might not conform to the accepted norms of your group.

A good editor will explain his or her comments, suggestions, revisions and editing to others in a clear, constructive and reliable way. Telling someone 'it doesn't sound right' is useless in terms of making future decisions, and it conveys the message that you haven't thought carefully about the goals and strategies of the writing job at hand.

Generally, the more individuals who proofread the final document the better. Even the best editor will miss some errors or omissions. Nevertheless, the team must insure that its best editor has sufficient time to carefully read the documents. The final document should also be compiled as a single word processing document. This facilitates final editing changes and also allows electronic document control, now a standard practice in most large organisations.

Team Presentations

Virtually all oral presentations of team work, from proposals to status reports to final project reviews, are conducted as collaborative presentations. As with preparing a written document, the shift from individual to collective speech preparation requires some additional steps.

Collaborative Preparation

When working in a group, don't expect one person to "make the slides" and consider the presentation as a whole to be complete. A series of individual speeches is not a *team* presentation, and many supervisors will judge the team's overall effectiveness by watching the interpersonal dynamics that are all too apparent in a team presentation.

A public presentation is unique in that it displays the team's own interactions to others. An audience will be able to tell instantly whether the team members genuinely like and respect each other.

Instead, draft the presentation as a group, working out the conceptual flow of the whole, leaving spaces and holes to be filled – perhaps by individuals—as the presentation takes shape. One person should act as the "editor" to keep the voice consistent, but should never work in isolation. All members of the team should be present in the room, tossing out ideas, suggestions, clarifications, and potential questions to clarify (and shorten!) the presentation. Writing as a group means that everyone understands the purpose and meaning of every word of the presentation. In the end, each member of the team fully understands and can deliver the entire presentation, not merely his or her own area of expertise.

Choreographed Performance

Most groups will entrust the delivery to one or two lead presenters who might tap secondary speakers to contribute on specific points, although a really superlative group presentation is "a series of multiple star turns, with each member of the team contributing equally". The ideal team "rehearses and pitches together so often" that each member is "instinctively" aware of what is in everyone else's mind during the whole presentation.

A presenting team should be like a "seasoned basketball squad" says Fallon Worldwide's Chief Marketing Officer, Mark Goldstein, "One of our presenters could throw a behind-the-back pass that might take the crowd completely by surprise, but that the person on the receiving end fully expects."

As you plan and rehearse the presentation, consider the placement of all the "actors" in the "scene" and insure that their movement and "script" consistently support the presentation as a whole. Often, one person will handle technical and hardware issues, leaving the "speakers" to concentrate completely on interacting with the audience.

Be very careful that someone is *always* building rapport with the audience. It is extremely impolite for a team to ignore its audience while it is engaged in conversation, setup, or troubleshooting.

Developing Team Communication Skills

Developing effective communication skills within the team can be done easily by imbibing some basic manners, professional etiquettes and keeping an open mind.

Follow the tips given below and start practicing them within your team:

— Always respect all your fellow team members, irrespective of whether you are just a team member or a team leader.

— Ensure whether all the team members understand the project requirements thoroughly and know what the project targets are. Ask questions or have discussions to clarify the same.

— Organise regular team meetings to understand the doubts and queries of every team member and provide solutions accordingly.

— Keep every team member informed with the latest project updates or project issues.

— Define the role and responsibility of every team member clearly to avoid confusion or un-necessary re-work.

— When in a meeting or discussion, let every one have their turn to speak and suggest. It is of no use if you alone keep talking and ignore what others have to say.

— Listen to others' opinions and use their suggestions if found to be effective. Listening plays a significant role in effective communication. Repeat others' words to acknowledge their point of views.

— Ask for feedbacks and suggestions from your team members.

— Always speak in a clear and slow manner. Give sound and logical reasoning to your opinions.

— Always be polite in your way of speaking and behavior. Using rude tone or body language may bring upon negative feelings among the team members.

— Clear out personal differences and misunderstandings by speaking it out with the concerned person. Keeping it inside and harboring grudges against one another may affect the team spirit and have a direct impact on the quality of your work.

— Make appropriate use of emails, telephones, voice messages and instant messengers while communicating with the fellow team members. Follow the professional etiquettes while writing emails, greeting over telephones, leaving voicemails and sending instant messages. These modes of communication also have a lot of importance in today's work place.

— Avoid using unpleasant words, expressions, giving out sensitive and confidential information while using the above modes of communication.

— Display acknowledgement and appreciation through face to face interaction or electronic modes when a team member performs well. Just a pat on the back, a warm handshake or two lines of an appreciation mail can have a great impact to motivate a team member.

— When appreciated or praised, thank the person in a polite and sophisticated manner. Avoid continuous rejoicing about your personal success. This might create an uncomfortable situation for your other team members.

— Always have a friendly attitude towards each other. Help others in need and you will get back others' help when you require the same.

— Deal with tense situations with a calm mind. If words of any team member make you angry try to keep a cool head and put your point forward. Avoid using harsh words in return.

— Avoid blaming others continuously when any work is not done. Instead, try to find out the root cause and see to it that it is not repeated in future.

— Find out if any team member is facing any problem and have a discussion with him/her to address the issue. Speaking and constant interaction with each other always help in developing a healthy team spirit.

Activities for Team Communication

In any relationship, be it personal or professional, communication is what binds it together. Without communication, no relationship is going to be successful. The value of communication increases manifold when it comes to teamwork and team building, because of the larger number of people involved with all their individual viewpoints and varied perceptions. In order to carry out any activity or function, communication within a team is essential, which is why building healthy workplace communication becomes a necessity. Here are some effective team communication activities that will help colleagues forge a strong bond with each other, and help understand each other better.

Before we take a look at these team communication exercises and activities, it is important to first accept that there is no right or wrong in any of them. Each individual is entitled to her/his own opinion, and this opinion only enforces the team building process. Take a look at some great team building and communication activities.

Colors of the Day

This activity involves every member of a group associating a day with a particular color. Every individual is to close their eyes and imagine a color that they associate with the day of the week, and then write it down. Once everyone is done writing their choice, they are asked to speak about the color they associate with the week, and why they do that. It gives an idea about how human beings perceive different situations. For instance, some may speak of 'Monday blues', while others may associate the color red with the first day of the week as a fiery start. It is not necessary to see a color with a day, and some may not be able to make an association. Others may tend to associate other objects or feelings with a particular day. There is no right or wrong in this activity. Such team communication activities just enhance team bonding by helping members of a group understand each other and the differences in their viewpoints about complex situations.

Walk the Talk

An important method of team building and communication, this is also one of the many trust building activities that involves dividing people into groups of two. One person from the team is blindfolded, while the other is to guide her/him through a path full of obstacles. This helps the guide develop leadership qualities, and enables the follower to develop trust in the leader. The leader will also develop a style of communication that she/he perceives as best understood by the follower.

Filter

This is one of the many fun team games that shows how excessively filtered information gets affected and changes drastically from the actual information. Filter is the game you would call 'Chinese Whispers' in layman terms. The idea is to have a small number of people sit in a group, and have one person speak a sentence into the ear of the person sitting next to her/him. Ideally, the statement should be one full of gossip. The person will then repeat what she/he heard in the ear of the person sitting next to her/him and this will continue until a full circle is completed. The last person to hear the information will then speak out the statement. It is a humorous game where you will see how the statement was altered by the time it reached the final receiver, simply because of excessive filtering. It also helps forge a strong bond among team members by teaching them the value of effective team communication.

Perceptions

Similar to the aforementioned game, colors of the day, as the name suggests, this game is about how group members perceive different situations and enables them to put forth their viewpoint where group communication is essential. To conduct this activity, pass around a picture and ask everyone to write down what they derive from the picture. Have them talk about their perception about the picture after everyone has written down what they see. Every viewpoint is personal, and it helps provide a little insight about the individual that makes up a team. It also shows how each member will react and perform in group tasks, to come up with unique problem solving methods. This activity may also be performed by dividing everyone into groups of two and three, to figure how the group mindset functions.

I Will Survive

In this team building game for the workplace, people are divided into groups and are presented with a scenario. The scenario can go something like this, 'You are stranded on an island, and you are given the choice of ten objects for survival. Choose wisely.' This will require the group to put their heads together, to come up with the ten items that are necessary for survival on a stranded island. This activity provides an insight into group behavior. It will give rise to a certain amount of conflict, emotions, and will help them realise the importance and effectiveness of group decision making. There may be situations where one member of the group will change their decision just to maintain calm in the group. Note down all this and relate it to the group later, to be able to help them understand their positives and negatives as a group. Also provide some team building ideas to improve their function as a unit.

The development to team communication skills, and activities to enhance them have found their place particularly in large business organisations, that can function effectively only when the teams that comprise it are at their best. While a lot of elements go into healthy team building, communication is one of the most important of them. As such, the use of team communication activities to help colleagues familiarise themselves with each other will enhance this process, and eventually, the productivity of the organisation as a whole.

References

Bales, R. F. (1950). Interaction Process Analysis: A Method of Study for Small Groups: Addison-Wesley.

Chen, G., Donahue, L. M., & Klimoski, R. J. (2004). Training Undergraduates to Work in Organisational Teams. *Academy of Management Learning & Education*, 3(1), 27-40

Cohen, S. G., & Bailey, D. E. (1997). What makes teams work: Group effectiveness research from the shop floor to the executive suite. *Journal of Management*, *23*, 239-290.

Fisher, B. A. (1985). Leadership as Medium: Treating complexity in Group Communication Research. Small Group Behavior, 16, 167-196.

Gladstein, D. (1984). Groups in Context: A Model of Task Group Effectiveness. Administrative Science Quarterly, 29(4), 499-517

Hackman, J. R., Brousseau, K. R., & Weiss, J. A. (1976). The Interaction of Task Design and Group Performance Strategies in Determining Group Effectiveness. Organisational Behavior and Human Performance, 16, 350-365.

Jackson, S. E. (1992). Team Composition in Organisational Settings. In S. Worchel, W. Wood & J. A. Simpson (Eds.), *Group Process and Productivity* (pp. 138-173). Newbury Park, CA: Sage.

Levine, J. M., & Moreland, R. L. (1990). Progress in small group research. *Annual Review of Psychology*, *41*, 585-634.

Manz, C. C., &Sims, H.P. (1987). Leading workers to lead themselves: The external leadership of self-managing work teams. *Administrative Science Quarterly*, *32*, 106-128.

Tullar, W. L., & Kaiser, P. R. (2000). The Effect of Process Training on Process and Outcomes in Virtual Groups. *The Journal of Business Communication*, 37(4), 408-427.

Weingart, L. R. (1992). Impact of Group goals, Task Component Complexity, Effort, and Planning on Group Performance. *Journal of Applied Psychology*, 77, 682-693.

5

Business Writing

Communication is a part and parcel of everyday life. We cannot not communicate. It is one of the most essential and integral part of our existence, and the absence of communication can lead to many problems and misunderstandings. In order to have an effective dialog, it is necessary that effective communication skills be developed. Communication can be divided into verbal and non verbal. Verbal communication means any communication that involves spoken words or sounds. Non verbal communication includes any communication that does not use oratory media for communication. Written communication comes under non verbal communication. Having good written communication skills is a pre requisite for almost everyone today. Read ahead on how you too can enhance your skills and reap the benefits.

Importance of Written Communication

Written communication involves the use of written words to send a message from one point to another. Given below are some points highlighting the importance of written communication in day to day life.

- Written communication is important for any business entity to carry out the daily business activities.
- It helps in maintaining records of business transactions.
- Written communication like brochures and catalogs help companies to showcase their products effectively.

— Print advertisements help to market products.

— Contracts, inter departmental memos and notices, emails and other such intra organisational communication serve as a permanent record of the business communication that takes place.

— Written documents can serve as evidence in a court of law if and when required.

— Written words are believed more than spoken words. It's just human psychology to believe something that we see in writing (even if it may be false) than something someone says (which may very well be true!)

— Personal written communication like letters, emails, post cards, greeting cards, etc., have their own charm and special meaning to the ones sending and receiving them.

Business writing is one of the most important aspects of the business world. Writing is still one of the number one methods of communication in the world. With the introduction of email, writing became even more important in the work place. There are many different types of business writing. Each type is designed to work toward a different goal. Being aware of the different types of business writing and also being able to write in several different business styles will help a person become a great business communicator.

Business writing has been around as long as business and writing. Thousands of years ago business people kept track of transactions and inventory through writing. As more international business became usual, business letters became a huge aspect of the business world. After the invention of the phone business writing became less common, however, when email became popular for business use, business writing again became a very necessary part of the business world.

The purpose of business writing is to communicate to other business people through the means of writing. The different types of business writing will communicate information differently to the recipient. For example, emailing someone information is one of the least formal methods of business writing. If a letter is sent in the mail, then the information included is generally considered to have more formality and legality. A lot of companies do much of their advertising in business writing format.

There are several main categories of business writing. First there is email. This is the least formal communication method, and is generally used when people are not able to physically get up and talk to someone, or to communicate without the use of a phone. Research and technical writing is used in the business world to create presentations and document new ideas for companies. The business letter is a more formal way of communicating information to a colleague or superior. The business letter is often used when applying for a job. Memos are also often used to send important information to groups of people.

Business writing is very important because it is one of the number one ways that people are viewed professionally. If someone has a sloppy writing style, then he will be seen as a sloppy person. People who can communicate clearly through writing in the business world will have a higher chance of receiving promotions and job offers. It is also important that business writing be done in a clear and concise manner so that the recipients of the writing can actually understand the point of the writing.

Types and Styles of Business Writing

Style is a critical element of business communication, since you have to manage to obtain a fine balance between being personable and being polite. Here are a few types of business communication writing that you might come across in your work: advertisements, emails, letters sent by post, manual writing and writing about technology, recommendations and research proposals, papers, and summaries. People use business writing to ask for a job, to inquire about opportunities, or even resign from a current position.

Many companies use business communication to advertise their company's products, services, or goals. Business writing adds a level of seriousness to the advertisement, and makes the documentation seem official. Emails are often designed in a way that business communication writing is utilised to give easy access to information.

Business writing gives a formality to the writing, and can result in an increased profit—especially when coupled with less formal slogans and styles in a strategic format. Consider the fact that some businesses even count memo emails as official business documents: it is to your advantage to learn how to write in a formal, business style because it is an important part of most people's everyday life.

The main feature of business writing that ties all forms (memos, emails, letters, documents, etc.) together is the style. No matter what kinds of documents you are writing, you have to aim to be concise, to be clear, and to convey information in an effective way. Make sure that when you write, you can ensure that the writing style is simplified, streamlined, and organised.

If you are describing information for the benefit of another party, or if you want to showcase your skills, use effective, targeted language that will be very clear for a reader who skims your work. Even though there are different types of business communication writing, you can know that the simple style is effective in all sorts of written documents.

Business Letters

Business letters are the unique form of business communication with all the stake holders of the company. The stakeholders include all those who are interested in the running of an enterprise. The business letters are used to convince these stakeholders or persuading them to agree with the writer regarding the topic under discussion. These letters are written as a way of persuading the customers or clients to accept the contract or proposal or enter into an agreement. It is a modern way of communication between both the parties. This is a method winning a contract or bringing business to an organisation. A well-written and formatted letter represents the business identity as well as conveys the professionalism of a company.

There are many reasons which can make a marketer or an entrepreneur write a letter. One can send a Letter of Inquiry as a follow up for the sent business proposal to a client. You can use these letters as a follow up for the business proposals that you have been sending to your potential client. An entrepreneur can also send an order letter to place orders for the required product as raw materials. Marketers also send acknowledgment letter to the customers for informing them about the deliverability of the product to the right destination. Aspiring candidates can send a cover letter along with sending a resume to the Human Resource Management of an organisation. A cover letter introduces a candidate, elucidates on the work history and other points that highlight other capabilities of a candidate. A marketer of a particular organisation can also send a Complaint Letter to a legal firm for communicating the grievances while dealing with any other business firm. You can send such letter to the concerned firm for the purpose of requesting the firm to take a needful action.

A proper formatting and flawless grammar can make such letters a perfect means of presenting and communicating thoughts to the concerned party. These letters can also be considered as a modern way of communication of business thoughts. They are the means of abridging any kind of gap between the organisation and the stakeholders.

Business Letter Writing Etiquette

Following are the important parts of a business letter.

— *Heading*: How to write a business letter heading? You should write your name and address here. Nowadays, different types of letterheads (different colors, paper types, etc.) are used for business writing, as compared to plain boring ones used normally. Your name and address should be located on the top right-hand corner of the paper. No punctuation (commas, full stops) is required in the address.

— *Date:* The date is useful for filing and determining priorities. Date is important while taking any legal action. Date is written immediately under your own address. Writing a date in the form '10 March 2009' is the clear and concise form, which is least likely to lead to any kind of confusion.

— *Reference:* You can write down in short the reference if any, or the purpose of this letter in 5-6 words.

— *Opening*: The opening part of the business letter includes the name, title (doctor, professor, manager) if any, address of the recipient and the salutation or greeting.

— *Body:* Here you are expected to write the message you wish to convey, in a clear, concise, courteous tone and language. The reason behind letter writing decides the exact content of the letter. Not a single sentence should lead to any confusion or misunderstanding. Language should be simple and not ornamental. Use of unfamiliar words should be avoided. A good beginning, short description of the purpose in the middle part and a precise ending will ensure effective communication.

— *Closing*: You are expected to offer thanks to the person for any help given, through professional letter closing. You can sign off the letter by writing 'Yours faithfully' when you don't know the name of the recipient or 'Yours sincerely' when you know the name of the person, whom you are writing. Your signature can be on the right hand corner, if you have written your address in the right hand corner, at the top of the page. Your own address at the top and your signature at the bottom can be at the left hand corners respectively.

— *Enclosures*: If you have enclosed any documents like resume, along with your letter, then you have to mention it at the bottom of your letter. If there are more than one documents, then you should make a proper list of them at the bottom of the letter.

Business Letter Writing Format

While writing business letters, a block format has to be followed. Your letter can be left justified and single spaced. There can be a double space between the paragraphs. A little bit variation in this format, regarding writing the address or date is observed nowadays. The 'Times New Roman' font, with size 12, is the commonly used but there can be variations of font also.

In schools, letter writing is included as a part of the language study, with an emphasis on business letter writing. You can have a look at the business letter writing example below and know more about how to write a business letter.

Your name/Your designation
Name of your organisation
Address of your organisation
Your telephone number
Date
Employer name/Hr Department
Employer address

Ref: Letter of resignation

Dear Sir/Madam,

I (your name), working since (your date of joining), at the position of (your designation), in your esteemed organisation, hereby tender my desire to resign from my services. The reason behind my resignation is (what you wish to mention). My date of resignation will be (the desired date), which is one month away as per our contract.

Resigning from this job is really a tough decision for me. For me, it has been a very good experience working with this organisation. I am grateful to the management and my colleagues for the support and love they have bestowed upon me, during my tenure in this organisation.

I kindly request you to accept my resignation and relieve me on (desired date). I will readily abide to all the exit formalities.

Yours sincerely,

Your name and signature.

How to Write a Proposal for a Project

A proposal for a project, or rather a business proposal is usually written by one party to another in order to initiate a certain business activity or economic interest that would require contributions from both the parties and would also benefit both the parties. Thus, the proposal is basically a formal request and invitation that is send by one party to another, seeking help, resources and partnership contribution that would benefit both the parties. The project proposal is sent, quite commonly, to initiate business activities. Here the project proposal has been discussed.

The project proposal is principally, a summary of the proposed economic or business activity. It is usually, in the form a prolonged letter and in real life it stretches up to a few pages, and carries an appendices giving proofs or presenting facts. You may also read on how to write a project proposal.

Now, the query 'how to make a proposal for a project', is quite evident. There is no concrete project proposal format, that is followed, however there are certain conventions that are followed in business writing and the corporate world. An example of a proposal for a project, has been given in the following paragraph. However, here is a general format that you can implement while writing the proposal for a project.

- The header or the sentence on the proposal is the title or the head of project. This title principally provides the basic emblem for the title, as it conveys the purpose in a few words.
- The next section is the project overview. Again, this section is a short one and it usually extends for a single paragraph, giving an over view of the said businesses.
- In some cases, a brief summary of the background is also put into the proposal.
- The next part is an important one and states the actual, specific details of the proposed project. This extends for a couple of pages and also cites references from the appendices.
- Evaluation of the plan, or the result that is expected is elaborated next. Approximate figures and outputs with estimates and backup plans are elaborated upon in this paragraph.
- The last section is of course, the appendices of the plan, in which the proofs and citations are given. This includes the quotations, reports and observations, of the proposing party.

Throughout the proposal, connect with the reader and make sure to deliver the information that the reader needs to know. Hence, you need to frame the entire proposal bearing in mind what the reader would be interested in, and in what cases you need the reader's help.

Sample of a Proposal for a Project

The following is a brief project proposal sample. In this project proposal example, a fictitious summary of project proposal has been given, hence, note that the content of every section is significantly smaller. When you write your own proposal, the content would be significantly detailed.

Title: Water Hyacinth Paper Project

Project Overview

Our company XYZ Eco-vision is engaged in the manufacture of products which are of natural origin and are environmentally friendly. Water Hyacinth Paper Project has originated out of a research project conducted by our company where water hyacinth harvested out of water is used to make a high grade of paper. The hyacinth which has a high growth rate is a weed and is grown in certain tanks under controlled conditions. This plant is basically a weed and often it is cleared out of water bodies as it posses a threat for boats and swimmers who may get entangled in the hyacinth. The hyacinth's enormous growth rate and ability to absorb certain organics make it an ideal raw material for paper making.

Project Details

In a plant that is stationed around an artificial water body, which can be used to treat urban waste. The hyacinth itself, acts as an absorbing variant. The plant is harvested after it reaches a certain age. Then, it is dried out with powerful solar reflectors and is then fed into the paper plant. Here the regular paper manufacturing process is followed and output of paper amounting to 2 tons a month is derived.Currently, we are selling off the paper to different and varied sources as the situation demands. However, we wish to propose the sale of paper to your company. We also propose to launch a new product in the market in collaboration with your company which has a very powerful sales network for stationery sales.We propose to convey over the paper to you on a monthly basis upon which the procedure of turning it into a product and a selling it under your brand name would be done by your company. XYZ Eco-Vision would contract to take a positron of the revenue from these sales.

Evaluation

Attached is a cost sheet that plans out the entire cost apportionment and estimations for the cost of paper that would be delivered to you.

Appendices

Safety and quality standard certifications from 18 different institutes, authorities and bodies that depict the features of the paper have been affixed. A regular business report of the project has also been included.

Simple Business Proposal Ideas

There are a number of ideas for business proposals which can get your business ticking and first of all get you a good loan for the same! Along with these also take a look at business proposal format to get a better understanding of how a business proposal works.

— Internet related anything—article directory, video website, gaming, e-commerce. Any of these is one of the simplest and most lucrative business proposals and business plans. With a little bit of adroitness and business sense these can recover the money you had invested in setting up the business in no time. Plus, Internet and networking is the in thing.

— Stimulate and rediscover the arty side of you by a business proposal involving arts and crafts. If it clicks, nothing like it as hand made products are received well by potential customers. The money too is great in this business idea for 2010.

— Normally, regarding business proposal ideas, the person with the proposal just gives a written proposal. So to make a better impression on those who are in business financing or even to do something different you can go for visual business proposal. It can be made into one of those really creative business proposal ideas by adding pictures, videos, voice overs and the like to support your proposal. But here in this you have to be really well prepared and up for anything which can come up about the project. You cannot just give the file and leave the rest for the financier to evaluate. The equipment you use for the presentation will have to be set up properly prior to the presentation and you have to be absolutely thorough with it.

— Business proposal ideas can be put across through a business proposal template if you do not have a clue about what a business proposal looks like. Even through these templates you can get proposal ideas for a business. A business proposal for offering services like educational consultant or even marriage, psychiatrist and clinical counselor too can work as a business proposal idea.

— Speaking is a very effective form of communication and just by the way you speak, you can get your business proposal in the fast track. One of the business proposal ideas would be to make a verbal presentation. Akin to the presentation with visual aid, here you have to be clear and absolutely concise as to what you are going to say. There is hardly any scope for mistakes and goof ups there because the computer is not there for your help. Written handouts will have to back the verbal presentation, which has to be to the point and neither too long nor too short. Check out how to write a business proposal for further information about business proposal.

Writing Sponsorship Proposal

There are quite some definitions of sponsorship. The simplest way to put this business arrangement in words goes as 'the act of supporting an event, a person, organisation, business or a group of people, financially or by the contribution of goods, products, services, manpower, etc'. The object of writing a sponsorship proposal is to get such a support. In the following paragraphs, some important conventions and conceptions of such an arrangement have been discussed, along with a sponsorship proposal sample. You may also read about fundraising.

The support (in cash or kind), is known as a 'sponsorship'. The person or organisation which provides the sponsorship is known as the 'sponsor' or in some cases 'sponsor'. The person or entity that has been sponsored may be called as a 'sponsored' party, though in some cases, the word 'beneficiary' or 'patronage beneficiary' has also been used. Sponsorship is often said to have originated from the concept of patronage. Indeed the initial sponsorships were of the nature, where sportsmen, artisans and musicians were sponsored.

The age of advertising however bought in a new meaning for the concept of sponsorship. In today's era, businesses, events, programmes and individuals are sponsored by companies for advertisements. You will find banners in stadiums and at rock concerts of the sponsorship providers. Sportsmen also wear clothing that carry the brand tag of their sponsor. One of the best aspects of advertising through sponsorship is that the targeted customers are bound to notice and consider the advertisement. Advertisement of sportswear by a sponsor at a football match accelerates the purchase probability. Sponsorship within advertising sector has become a deep component of all segments of any said national economy. It is marketing in a smart manner of marketing. Often business sponsorship gains the status of a regular business proposal leading to a venture.

Writing a sponsorship proposal is not that difficult a task and getting a sponsorship is also not that difficult due to the fact if the sponsoring party sees a good scope of advertising, the funds or kind is granted without hesitation, after all what sells better than a good image and some publicity. One of the first things that you will have to decide is whether the kind of sponsorship is for an event or a regular corporate. The event sponsorship proposal, is basically written for an event, but a corporate sponsorship proposal is written to establish long term business relations. The corporate proposal is a bit difficult to write and is usually formatted as per the situation. Here is a small sponsorship proposal sample written to get the sponsorship from music record label for a rock concert.

Sponsorship Proposal Sample

To,
The Manager,
Public Relations,
XYZ music.

Subject: sponsorship proposal of DEF alternative music festival.

Dear Sir,

TUV events, a prominent event management company, has organised a 4 hour DEF alternative music festival, to cater to the alternative music demand that has erupted in the city in the past couple of years. Demographics indicate that more than 70% of the

50,000 plus students demand alternative music. Music sellers and download sites indicate that more than 20,000 alternative songs are purchased, listened, viewed, or downloaded by the youth from this locality in every 24 hours. The concert will have 4 bands playing, which have of course won national acclaim as alternative musicians. The venue is capable of holding an audience of 750.

We propose to you to sponsor the sound system, in both financial support as well as provisions of sound engineers. The venue will have 56 spaces for official advertisements plus a scope of further advertising in the form of informal souvenir advertising is also seen. Your company shall hold the sole right to advertisement. Apart from that out of the 4 bands, 3 artists are already in deep association with your company. We hope that your recording studio and label finds the terms and conditions reasonable. A cost sheet depicting the different requirements and a detailed fact sheet of the event has been attached with this letter.

Our representatives are always available for any kind of any help, negotiation and discussion that you might want to initiate.

Yours,

Addresss

Business Report Writing

Each one of you, at some point in your life, has or will have to perform business report writing. You should be prepared for writing business reports and should acquaint yourself with business report writing techniques and formats. One of the most important parts of business writing is the report writing for business. So let us first see the structure of business report writing.

Business Report Writing—Structure

1. TITLE PAGE:
   - Title of the Report
   - Your Name
   - Submission Date
2. EXECUTIVE SUMMARY:
   - General summary of subject matter

- Methodology used for analysis
- Findings
- Recommendations

3. TABLE OF CONTENTS: List of numbered sections in report along with their page numbers.
4. INTRODUCTION:
   1. Terms of reference
   2. Outline of report's structure
5. BODY: Body of a business report consists of headings and sub-headings which reflect the contents of each section. Try to include information on method of data collection (if applicable), the findings of the report and discussion of findings in light of theory.
6. CONCLUSION: In this part of business report writing, you must state the major inferences that can be drawn from the discussion and try to add your own recommendations.
7. REFERENCE LIST: Make a list of reference material you made use of, during research for your business report writing.
8. APPENDIX: Appendix consists of all the information that supports your analysis does not need an explanation necessarily.

Steps in Business Report Writing

Business report writing is basically made for clarity in communication in a business so as to assist the management of a business in the decision making process. Some of the business reports are prepared to provide solutions to business problems or as business solutions proposal or the client while other business reports are made to assist in problem solving process. In business report writing, you need to consider a few steps that if followed thoroughly can yield you the best business report. The first step includes planning the business report. Following are all the steps that are required in business report writing in that order:

1. Planning and preparing a business report
2. Analysing the scope of writing business reports
3. Understanding the real readers

4. Collecting Data and composing it into useful information
5. Organising and arranging the information in the report
6. Writing references/bibliography

Tips for Business Report Writing

Planning is the first step as well as first tip for business report writing. Make sure you plan your business report well before time. You must plan your research that is required for business report writing and make use of Internet and other technologies to speed up your research. Searching exact phrases and keywords and making proper use of tools like bookmarking will help in winning the battle!

Once you are done with the research that is essential for business report writing, you should start planning what information should be compiled in the business report. You must also analyse the scope of the business report writing that you are considering because it is important to decide what kind of topics and subjects should be included in your business reports. You must also determine what is not necessary to add in the business report as it will make your business report look more specific and focused. Contemporary business report writing is expected to be full of expected information in length.

When you are carrying out the process of finding who the real readers of your business reports are going to be, you must ask yourself few questions. Questions like who will be using this business report and what a reader would expect from a report like this? The demographic data of the expected readers should also be analysed by the makers of business report as it will help in deciding how much technical information should be given in detail in the business report.

Often business report writing needs data collection and if you have gone through that process to prepare your business report, you must clearly mention the methodologies of data collection that you have used while writing business report. At the end of the business report, you must give your solutions and recommendations. Add diagrams, graphical charts and pie diagrams in while carrying out business report writing and include that in the report. Graphical representation of the collected data must be included in business report writing.

Word Choice for Business Writing

Choosing the right words helps you produce business communication that works to achieve a goal. This section presents five items of advice about word choice, as follows:

— Use short, familiar, and descriptive words.

— Avoid slang, jargon, and buzzwords.

— Avoid abbreviations and acronyms unless you're sure the receiver knows them.

— Do not misuse apostrophe-*s*.

— Use the correct word.

Now study the explanations and examples for each of these suggestions.

Use Short, Familiar, and Descriptive Words

The English language contains hundreds of thousands of words. It has been described as the richest language in the world, because many words have very similar meanings. In business, your goal is to quickly convince, describe, or report. It makes sense, therefore, to use words that are most familiar to most people. Creative writers may use rich, unique words. Business writers, on the other hand, succeed when they find the simplest, most common words. Another way to suggest the use of common words is to use plain English.

Study the following pairs of words. The first word in each pair is longer and may be more abstract; the second is shorter and more common. Generally, your writing will achieve its purpose more successfully when you use the shorter, more common word.

currently	now
initiate	start or begin
indicate	show
inquire	ask
provide	give
assist	help
endeavour	try
obtain	get

Compare the following pairs of sentences, each labelled (a) and (b). Which sentence of each pair is easier to read quickly?

a. Employees should endeavour to provide assistance to shoppers who seem confused.

   b. Employees should try to help shoppers who seem confused.

a. Inquire at the office about obtaining health and life insurance.

   b. Ask at the office about getting health and life insurance.

Most people would agree that the (b) sentence of each pair is more direct and easier to read. Unlike writing meant for publication or scholarship, business writing does not need to be sophisticated. The purpose of business writing is to communicate information clearly and quickly. You are more likely to achieve this when you keep your words short, familiar, and descriptive.

Avoid Slang, Jargon, and Buzzwords

Slang is too casual to be used in business writing. Slang varies by age, gender, and culture, so the meaning of a slang word may not be clear to a large or international audience. Because some slang is used frequently in speech, it may be hard to recognise as something to avoid in writing. Slang is inappropriate in business writing, even though you may find such words defined in a dictionary. In the following examples, a slang word is replaced by one that is more acceptable:

— *Ace*

Jack Bowman is an ace salesperson.

Jack Bowman is a very good salesperson.

— *Awesome*

Ms. Wright has an awesome idea for getting more clients.

Ms. Wright has an excellent idea for getting more clients.

— *Call*

The director made a good call about this quarter's profits.

The director made a good prediction about this quarter's profits.

— *Glitch*

The programme has a glitch.

The programme has a defect.

— *Intense*

The meeting was intense.

The meeting was serious.

— *Hyper*

The clerk doesn't need to get hyper.

The clerk doesn't need to get overly excited or overly concerned.

— *Cool*

This is a cool place to work.

This is a good place to work.

— *Sharp*

He's sharp.

He's intelligent.

Jargon is vocabulary with special meaning to people in a trade or profession. A special vocabulary exists for most professions and trades. To people outside of an area of expertise, however, the jargon can be misunderstood or meaningless. For example, for most people the word *motion* is a simple word meaning *movement*. In the legal profession, however, *motion* can mean an application to a judge. Likewise, to a person in the film or television industry, the term *storyboard* is useful, as it refers to a series of panels that show changes in scenes. To anyone else, however, it is jargon. Use jargon only if you are certain your readers are familiar with the meaning. To make sure your message is clear, it's best to define a jargon word the first time you use it.

Similarly, a buzzword is a word or phrase that usually sounds important and is used primarily to impress people outside a particular group. An example is the term *green technology,* which is used to describe environmentally sound methods for energy production. The word *veggie* is a food industry buzzword that means a dish prepared with no meat or fish.

Good business writers avoid using slang, jargon, and buzzwords because their readers may not understand the words. Moreover, the use of such words reflects poorly on the writer. Readers generally do not appreciate trendy words or phrases when straightforward vocabulary will do.

Avoid Abbreviations and Acronyms

As a business writer, consider whether your audience is familiar with an abbreviation or acronym. If an abbreviation is common and familiar, you can leave it as is. Common abbreviations include *Mr.* for *Mister,* and *Ave.* for *Avenue.* State and territory abbreviations are familiar to people in those places, but may be unfamiliar to people elsewhere.

An acronym may or may not be pronounceable as a word; in fact, most are not. Some acronyms have become words that now appear in the dictionary: for example, *radar* and *laser.* The fact that these words were originally formed by combining the initial letters of a long term is no longer important. Indeed, spelling out the original term would distract the reader. (For example, *radar* was formed from the words *radio detecting and ranging; laser* from the words *light amplification by stimulated emission of radiation.*) Many acronyms stand for the name of an entity: for example, *WHO* for the World Health Organisation and *AFB* for the American Foundation for the Blind. Others stand for a position or a procedure. If you think your reader may be puzzled by an acronym, spell it out the first time it appears. The following is a list of some acronyms:

— *GNP* for *gross national product*

— *CEO* for *chief executive officer*

— *EU* for *European Union*

— *aka* for the phrase "also known as"

A relatively new phenomenon that occurs in email and on Internet Web sites is the use of acronyms for common phrases. People tend to make these up as they write. Be aware that most of these short-cuts have no place in proper business writing. A short list of examples follows:

— *imo* for "in my opinion"

— *bbl* for "be back later"

— *btw* for "by the way"

Do not Misuse Apostrophe-*s*

A frequent mistake is using apostrophe-*s* when you mean to use the plural form of a word. To avoid making this error, check whether the word has any indication of belonging, or the possessive form. If not, except in some rare cases, you do not use an apostrophe. The best way to practice this is to become aware of mistakes. The following incorrect uses are followed by corrections. Assume these are signs you might see or write yourself for a business.

— "Potato's, $2.99 for a 5 lb. bag"

The plural form of *potato* is *potatoes.* Do not use apostrophe-*s*.

— "Remove your shoe's before entering."

The plural form of *shoe* is *shoes.* Do not use apostrophe-*s*.

— "Pick up your ticket's at the counter."

The plural form of *ticket* is *tickets.* Do not use apostrophe-*s*.

It is clear that none of the words with apostrophes in the previous examples convey a sense of belonging, or the possessive. Therefore, no apostrophe is needed, and the word should appear in its plural form.

An occasional exception to this rule exists. Usually, when a word is used as a word, as in the example that follows, you use an apostrophe. Note that words used as words are typically italicised:

— "Avoid using two *not*'s in a sentence."

Use the Correct Word

Many words in English are easily confused with one another. In order to avoid using the wrong word, know the precise meaning of every word that you use. In addition, a spelling mistake can result in a homonym. A homonym is another word that sounds the same as the intended one but has a different meaning. This section lists pairs of words that many people confuse. Study these carefully so that you do not misuse words in your writing.

Affect versus Effect

Most often, you will use *affect* as a verb and *effect* as a noun. To affect something is to have an influence on it. For example,

— "The new programme affects only the clerical staff."

Remember this clue: *affect* is an action word. *Affect* and *action* both begin with the letter *a*.

An effect is a result or outcome. For example,

— "One effect of the new programme is that workers are happier."

Remember this clue: *effect* represents the *end result. Effect* and *end* both begin with the letter *e*.

The use of *affect* as a noun and *effect* as a verb is less common. For most business writing needs, remember to use *affect* as an action verb and *effect* as a noun that represents an end result.

It's versus Its; Who's versus Whose

It's, with an apostrophe, is a contraction, meaning "it is." For example,

— "It's vital that profits keep growing."

Its, without an apostrophe, is the possessive form of *it,* just like *his* and *hers* are the possessive forms of *he* and *she.* For example,

— "Its profits grow year after year."

Remember this clue: if you can replace the word with "it is," use an apostrophe. If you cannot replace the word with "it is," do not use an apostrophe.

Similarly, *who's,* with an apostrophe, is the contraction of "who is" or "who has" while *whose,* w-h-o-s-e, is the possessive form of *who.* Use the same clue as you did previously: if you cannot replace the word with "who is" or "who has," then the word should be *whose,* w-h-o-s-e. Study the following sentences:

— "The CEO, whose [w-h-o-s-e] tie had a stain on it, left the room to change."

— "The person who's [w-h-o-apostrophe-s] responsible for the raise in salary is the CEO."

Principal versus Principle

Principal, ending in *p-a-l,* is an adjective meaning "most important." For example,

— "Our principal problem is a lack of cash."

The hint for this word is if it's an adjective, the correct word ends with *p-a-l.*

The noun *principal,* ending in *p-a-l,* refers to a chief school administrator or the main sum of money. Remember, when the concept of "most important" or "main" fits the word, it ends with *p-a-l.*

Principle, ending in *p-l-e,* is a noun meaning "guiding rule." For example,

— "Our principle is to use our own money rather than to borrow."

Imply versus Infer

Imply means to suggest indirectly. For example,

— "In his speech, the president implied that the company needs to sell one of its divisions."

Infer means to draw meaning out of something. For example,

— "When reading the president's report, people infer that the company needs to sell one of its divisions."

Remember, a speaker or writer implies, a listener or reader infers.

Foreword versus Forward

A foreword [f-o-r-e-w-o-r-d] is text that comes near the front of a book. *Foreword* is actually a compound word composed of *fore,* meaning "near the front," and *word.*

Forward [forwar-d] means to move ahead in a direction. For example,

— "The soldiers marched forward."

If you're careful with the spelling of these homonyms, you will not mix them up.

Into versus In To

Into is a preposition. It answers a question, usually Where? or What? For example,

— "They walked into the house."

— "She got into the top math class."

— "Five goes into ten two times."

When the individual words *in* and *to* happen to fall next to one another, they must be separate. Usually the word *to* precedes a verb, for example,

— "Rachel ran in to get her gloves."

The best way to check whether you've used *into* and *in to* correctly is to read your sentence out loud, pausing between *in* and *to.* If the pause sounds wrong, use *into,* one word.

Amount versus Number; Less versus Fewer

Use the word *amount* when referring to something that cannot be counted, for example,

— "The amount of dust on our desks is creating an unhealthy work environment."

Use *number* when the entities can be counted. For example, use *number,* not *amount,* in the following sentence:

— "A large number of desks in this office are dusty."

Similarly, use *fewer* when you can count the entities and *less* when the thing you are referring to is in bulk. For example,

— "Place fewer napkins on each cafeteria table."

— "Use less ammonia when cleaning the tiles."

One of the most frequent misuses of these words occurs with the word *people.* Use *fewer*, not *less,* in the following example because you can count people:

— "Fewer people attended the fair this year."

This short section included a few common word errors. Always check the precise meaning and spelling of words to avoid using the wrong word in your writing.

Importance of Tone

Your relationship with the recipient and the subject of the message determine the tone of your writing. The tone of a written message affects the reader just as the tone of a person's voice affects a listener. You reveal the tone mainly by your word choice. As you become a more experienced business writer, you'll adjust your language to the situation just as you do in speech. This section presents the following four items of advice about writing tone:

— Use the active voice and avoid the passive voice.

— Focus on your readers.

— Rephrase the negative, leave out anger, and deliver bad news smoothly.

— Make sure your writing is unbiased.

Now study the explanations and examples for each of these suggestions.

Use the Active Voice and Avoid the Passive Voice

The active voice emphasised who or what is doing something. By stressing the doer of the action, writers can create messages that are concise and direct. Read the following examples of sentences in the active voice:

— Mr. Smith ordered fifty cases of potato chips on July 12.

— The company chose three employees to receive awards.

— John Bower wrote the report.

The passive voice tells the reader what was done. Sometimes, it is not clear who or what did the action. Other times, the use of the passive voice buries the doer at the end of the sentence. Sentences in the passive voice typically include the words *be, am, is, was, were,* or *been* and tend to be longer than sentences in the active voice. Read the following examples of sentences in the passive voice:

— Fifty cases of potato chips were ordered on July 12.

— Three employees will be chosen to receive awards.

— The report was written by John Bower.

The passive voice tends to create very wordy text. Reports filled with sentences in the passive voice often bore the reader, and therefore do not easily achieve a purpose. To improve your writing, find the passive voice and revise it. To practice turning sentences from the passive voice into the active voice, follow these steps:

— Determine the doer of the action, or the subject. State that name or object first.

— Decide on the action, or the verb. Write that next.

— Finally, most sentences need a word or phrase to complete the sentence. Place that after the verb.

The following example shows how to change a passive sentence into an active one:

Passive voice:

An inventory was completed by Pamela.

Doer of the action: Pamela

Action: completed

Necessary end of sentence: an inventory

Active voice:

Pamela completed an inventory.

Different types of writing require different approaches. Sometimes you do need to use the passive voice. For example, you may not know the doer of the action or for business reasons, would rather not name the person. In general, however, you'll have the most success if you get to the point quickly by using the active voice.

Focus on Your Readers

One of the main objectives of business communication is to achieve a result. Most often, you want your reader to take action after reading your correspondence. Consider that when you speak, you choose words and expressions depending on your audience. For example, you use a different vocabulary and speaking tone depending on whether you're talking to children or adults, a police officer or a grocery check-out clerk, a new manager or your cousin. In the same way, you adjust your writing to appeal to the person or people who read it. Doing so makes it more likely they will respond as you would like. The following three suggestions lead to focusing your writing on your reader. Read the suggestions and the explanations that follow each.

Identify Your Reader's Motivations

If you are aware that your supervisor is concerned about saving money, which of the following sentences would you use?

a. This month I ordered Tasty Corn Chips at $45.00 a carton.

b. At $45.00 a carton, Tasty Corn Chips are less expensive than the chips we served last month.

Sentence (b) appeals more to a reader who is interested in saving money.

Assume you are writing a memo to encourage more people to eat at the cafeteria. Read the next two examples. Sentence (a) focuses on readers whose motivation is a hearty meal. Sentence (b) focuses on readers who appreciate convenience.

a. Every day we serve tasty soups, nutritious main dishes, and luscious desserts.

b. If you're a busy person who wants a good lunch, our new design lets you choose your items and pay without waiting, even at the busiest time.

Target Your Reader's Personality

According to behavioural research, a few basic personality types exist. When writing a letter, email, or memo, it makes sense to choose words that directly appeal to your reader's personality. One of the clues to a reader's personality is his or her job. This is because people tend to hold jobs that suit their personality. Those in positions of authority tend to be forceful, competitive, and decisive. Sales people have to be outgoing and optimistic. Nurses, instructors, and executive assistants are usually friendly, stable, and eager to please. Engineers and computer programmers tend to be self-controlled, cautious, and analytical rather than emotional. Of course, these examples are very broad generalisations. Remember also that most people exhibit a mixture of personalities in different situations.

Assume that you want to recommend a policy of recognising employees who have worked for more than five years. Each of the following sentences targets a specific personality.

To a person who is forceful and competitive,

— "An employee recognition policy would inspire others to excel and maintain a high degree of excellence over longer periods."

To a person who is outgoing and optimistic,

— "An employee recognition event with cake and beverages would be wonderful for raising everyone's enthusiasm about staying long-term with such a great group of employees."

To a person who is stable and eager to please,

— "People like to be recognised for their long-term contributions to the place where they work."

To a person who is cautious and analytical,

— "Our plan for an employee recognition policy can be modelled on the state employee plan, which provides specific guidelines for awarding recognition."

When you target readers' personalities, you assure them that you are sensitive to their interests. You also gain their attention and cooperation. You'll achieve better results if you include a sentence tailored to each recipient's personality type.

Recognise Your Relationship with Your Reader

In your work life, you communicate with supervisors, coworkers, and outside people, such as sales people, clients, and consumers. Each person deserves to be addressed appropriately in business communications. Your relationship with your reader also depends on whether you've met the person.

For example, when you are writing to your supervisor, even if you sometimes chat with him or her around the water cooler, you take care to explain issues or decisions thoroughly. Assume you're planning a vacation. The following examples illustrate how to tailor a message about your absence to people who have various relationships with you. One is an email to your supervisor. Another is a notice to your coworkers. And a third is the text of an auto-reply message, which is a programmed response to email messages sent during your absence.

To Your Supervisor

As of March 20, I will have accumulated four days of vacation. I am requesting two days' vacation on April 18 and 19. Please let me know whether you approve.

To Your Coworkers

I'm off to the lake April 18 and 19. Have a great long weekend!

Response to Incoming Email

I will be away from the office April 18 and 19. I will respond to your message when I return. If you need an immediate response, use the email address below this paragraph.

Note that you show respect for your immediate supervisor by asking for his or her approval. You make it easier for your supervisor to respond by providing all the facts about the amount of vacation time you have. You can be less formal with your coworkers. To people who send you email while you are away, you prepare a courteous message that allows them to decide whether to wait for your return or contact someone else.

This example was quite simple. Consider other types of associations a business writer may have. For example, you would be prudent and cautious writing to a government agency. When writing to a person in an industry or endeavour similar to yours, you would be able to use technical terms without defining them. When writing to support staff, or people who report to you, it's best to use language that is not dictatorial. For a board of directors, you would use the most formal language and provide as much detail as possible.

Some business writers think that using humour in a message helps develop a relationship with the recipient. Humour, however, is very subjective, and often results in either puzzlement or outright insult. If you know your recipient very well, go ahead and use a joke, but in general, it's best to avoid attempts at humour in business correspondence.

Rephrase the Negative Tone

Businesspeople, especially when under the stress of a project, respond better when written communication is presented in a positive, courteous style. This is true even if the content includes criticism or bad news. The following paragraphs suggest ways to rephrase the negative, remove evidence of anger, and present bad news indirectly.

Negative words and phrases such as *not, never,* and *you don't* tend to make readers feel discouraged or defensive. In such a frame of mind, it is less likely they will comply with your request or cooperate with you. Other words with negative implications include *bad, poor, fault,* and *ridiculous*. Find alternatives to negative words and phrases.

For example, assume you purchased a new tool for repairing machines. The tool is defective and needs to be returned for repair or replacement. Example (a) uses negative words, while Example (b) presents the situation in a more positive way.

a. "The new tool you sent us doesn't work well at all. The points are uneven, so it slips off the wires and cables. You must not have checked it very carefully before sending it out."

b. "Although the new tool has good handles and seems to be designed well for the task, the points are uneven, so it slips off the wires and cables. I am sending the tool to you for repair or replacement."

Anger is a part of human behavior and emotion. It is best, however, to keep these feelings out of business correspondence. When you are annoyed or upset with a reader or a situation, try to be objective. If you are too upset to keep your personal feelings out of your writing, wait for a few hours until you can. If you have time, draft the correspondence and then leave it until the next day. You'll find it easier to be objective after a day has passed.

For example, suppose you promised your supervisor that twenty machines would be checked and repaired, if necessary, by the end of the week. On Thursday, you learn that only eight have been checked by your team, and it is unlikely that you will meet the promised goal. You send a memo to your team. Example (a) exhibits an unfortunate amount of anger and directly criticised the recipients. Example (b) presents the situation objectively.

a. You have not serviced the machines on schedule. Only eight machines have been serviced so far this week. I had promised that our team finish twenty. Apparently you are not working fast enough. We'll have a talk with management about this.

b. The recent increase in problems with the machines means that fewer have been serviced than we promised. I will talk with the management about a more realistic schedule for service.

People don't like to read bad news. When you have to write a letter or memo that includes bad news, first highlight a good aspect. Then use words like *unfortunately* or *sadly,* which smooth the delivery of the bad news.

For example, assume that you manage a cafeteria in a large office building. One of your staff members has requested vacation time during a week when a large conference will take place, so you cannot approve. Example (a) presents the bad news directly. Example (b) smooths the delivery by writing something positive first, and answering tactfully.

a. I have reviewed your request to take a vacation. No employee can take vacation time during a conference week.

b. Thank you for following the proper vacation request procedure. Vacations can be scheduled in advance for weeks in which no large conferences take place in the offices we serve. Unfortunately, the week you requested falls during A-Right Company's annual conference. Therefore, I am asking you to postpone your personal vacation to another week.

Note that it is generally more difficult to avoid negative terms and control emotions when using email than when preparing a printed communication such as a business letter. Some people write email as if they were speaking face-to-face with the recipient. In business, it's best to write email messages with the same care and courtesy that you use for printed correspondence.

Review the words of your email carefully for a negative tone, and use the strategies presented in this section for revising it, if needed. If you are angry or upset, control your emotions before you press Send. One of the best ways to make sure you've composed your message carefully is to create it first in a word processor or off-line. After a while, reread your draft and make adjustments before entering the text into the message box and sending it.

Make sure Your Writing Unbiased

Today's social awareness makes it very important to identify and revise writing that is sexist, racist, or inconsiderate of people with disabilities. Think about the ways language can insult or downgrade certain groups. Common sense and some specific strategies can help you avoid unintentionally offending your reader.

Practice recognising stereotypes and generalities in your writing. For example, what is wrong with the following sentence?

— "Our training programme is designed to help your office assistant increase her computer skills."

The sentence assumes that all office assistants are women. The male office assistant who reads this sentence would be offended. It is better to use gender-neutral language. The following revision is more fair:

— "Our training programme is designed to help your office assistant increase his or her computer skills."

Modern writing aims to be gender neutral. One obvious way to achieve this, as in the previous example, is to use both masculine and feminine pronouns: "he or she," "him or her," and "his or hers." Sometimes, however, these constructions become wordy and awkward. When that happens, try using plural words rather than singular words. For example, the following sentence is biased:

— "A manager may call a meeting with his workers."

Revise it by using the plural form, as follows:

— "Managers may call meetings with their workers."

Another way to avoid gender bias is to replace a pronoun (*his* or *her*) with an article (*a, an,* or *the*). For example, the following biased sentence,

— "Every waiter should keep his apron clean."

Can be revised using a gender-neutral article, as follows:

— "Every waiter should have a clean apron."

When it is necessary to refer to a disability, give the person ownership of the condition rather than labelling that person. Read the following examples and the suggested revisions:

Labelling: "The deaf volunteer requested an interpreter."

Respectful: "The volunteer who is deaf requested an interpreter."

Labelling: "The amputee is taking the elevator."

Respectful: "The man who uses a wheelchair is taking the elevator."

Certainly, if it is unnecessary to mention a person's disability, gender, or ethnic or racial background, avoid such descriptions altogether.

Avoid any language that can be read as offensive to any group of people, including women, men, persons with disabilities, persons belonging to minorities, senior citizens, and so on. Keep in mind that English usage varies among English-speaking countries. Usage also changes over time. Words that were acceptable twenty years ago may no longer be neutral. If you're not certain of the correct terminology, consult with someone knowledgeable. Then revise your message.

The following list includes a few words and phrases to avoid, and suggested replacements:

handicapped people	people with disabilities
mongoloid child	a child with Down syndrome
a black American woman	an African-American woman
a drunk	an intoxicated person
the poor	low-income residents

Occupation titles that are gender specific, such as *poetess*, *woman doctor, cleaning lady, policeman, congressman,* and *chairman* are certainly outdated, since they suggest that only a person of one gender would do the job. You can usually replace such terms with a gender-neutral form: *poet, doctor, cleaner, police officer, representative* or *senator,* and *chair* or *chairperson.*

Designing Business Documents

The importance of effective written communication cannot be stressed enough. Written documents plays a major role, especially in the corporate world. The guidelines for designing good business documents are given below.

Use Effective Typography

Typography is designing with type in order to communicate a message. Desktop publishing (DTP) offers you the facilities to use type in many sizes and styles to achieve a professional look. You might easily be tempted to 'jazz-up' your documents with all the special effects you can muster—if you do this, you may end up having more fun than your readers. Restraint is essential, so that the content of documents is clearly understood. Typography should not call attention to itself—its purpose is to make work easier for the reader.

When designing, you should put yourself in the reader's place. Try to think through everything you do from the reader's point of view. You cannot force anyone to read anything, but you can make a document clear, accessible, and adaptable, to help readers navigate their way around the text for any purpose. There are certain principles of legibility and perception which should be followed to help achieve this.

Readers will have preconceptions about the size and general layout of a company report, or even an official letter, based on their past experience with that kind of document. Before reading at a 'word' level, they may have started reading on a global level, flicking through and picking up structural cues and features. Apart from novels, users rarely read documents from beginning to end: they have their own purposes and tasks, which the document must accommodate.

Readers will quickly pick up the 'norm' in a document. In reports and proposals, this is likely to be continuous text. Therefore any graphic feature that is different from this norm will be taken as significant, giving the designer the opportunity to emphasise elements and attract attention, with headings of different sizes and styles, or charts and tables. Even in correspondence, like letters, memos, and faxes, where there cannot be much deviation from the norm, simple graphic features can mark out different kinds of information.

Planning

Budget

If you are producing a report, the budget can affect the length of the document, how many are produced, and the way it is produced. Will you produce multiple copies by photocopying pages output on your laser printer, or have them professionally printed from the high-resolution output of a typesetting machine? Budget will also affect how the report is bound.

If you cannot afford pre-printed headed notepaper for letters, you may want to set up a template design on screen, with a letterhead that works in black and white, and is printed with each letter.

Schedule

A production schedule should be worked backwards from the deadline for delivery, taking into account the schedules of other people involved, such as suppliers and printers. Make certain you allow for several stages of proofing, and remember to keep frequent backup copies of your work.

Assess Your Capabilities

The design of a text must cater for the content: if there are three levels of heading, the design must cater for them; if there are likely to be illustrations and captions, they must be catered for; and so on.

However, the design must be geared to what you can do with your software—it's no good planning a multi-column document if you don't have the software to produce one. And at the other extreme, you should avoid the temptation to design documents that show off the different facilities of your software, such as text running around illustrations, just because you have them-they may not be appropriate to your document.

Matching Software to Document Preparation Tasks

There are three different classes of desktop publishing software: word-processing, drawing, and page make-up software.

You will probably use word-processing software for correspondence, and page make-up software for the more complex layout of a report: before page make-up, you should still use word-processing software to finalise the text, so that you are not distracted by problems of page layout when trying to concentrate on writing.

Your choice of software may depend on the nature of your document. If your report is simple, you may only need a word processor. If you are preparing a poster or chart that combines pictures with small amounts of text, it may make sense to type your text directly into page make-up software. A complex table may be best treated like a drawing, and produced with drawing software, which allows you to move the different elements relatively easily.

If you are combining software, check carefully for compatibility: make sure your page make-up software will take in text and illustrations from your word-processing and drawing software.

Testing out Your Design Work

Remember you are producing paper documents, so be sure to test out your design work on paper, rather than just looking at it on your computer screen, where its appearance will be very different.

The appearance of documents will alter considerably with changes in resolution. For example, type and rules have sharper definition at higher resolution, and the contrast between bold and plain text is more distinct. So if your document is to be typeset, rather than laser-printed, ask your typesetters to produce a sample page, so you can see how it looks at high resolution.

Remember, too, that your readers will be using documents they can hold, with pages they can flick through, rather than the flat pages you produce, or look at on screen. So make up sample documents that match the look and feel of final copies. These should help you check things such as whether there is a wide enough back margin for binding, whether page numbers and running heads will be clearly visible, and so on.

Checking

You should check the text of your document as often as possible. If you have been working on a text for some time, it is a good idea to have someone else proofread it, as you can easily overlook errors in a text you are accustomed to.

When you have finalised the page-layout of a report, print out all the pages and stick them together so that they resemble the finished document. The following list should jog your memory for things to check:

— Is the text correct? Is spelling, punctuation, and use of the 'house-style' consistent? Don't forget to check headings, captions, footnotes, text in illustrations, running heads, contents lists, and indexes, as well as the main text.

— Have the correct headings been given for the text? And the correct running heads? Do the headings in the text match the headings given in the contents list? And are the page numbers in the contents list correct?

— Is the content of the illustrations correct? Are they the right size, the right way around, has the correct part of the illustration been used? Do the illustrations match the captions? Is the numbering of illustrations correct?

— Are the cross-references within the text and between text and illustrations correct?

— Are the page numbers in the index correct?

Content and Structure

Consider what your readers need from a particular document. Often they will want to find out quickly what it's about, and then read the text, or sections of it, in detail. They will perform these reading tasks by using the document's access structure.

Access Structure

This refers to the contents list, headings, and other things that help people to find out what a document is about or who it is from. Even official correspondence will benefit from subheadings, simply to divide it into manageable chunks. In longer documents, try to relate all the elements of the access structure to one another—so they make sense to someone flicking through the report. Notice how the contents list and headings have been designed to help you access information in this booklet.

Numbering Systems

All documents that are more than a couple of pages long should have page numbers, and a contents list linking page numbers to sections of the text. Long letters, memos, or faxes will also need page numbers.

In reports, you may also need numbering systems for sections and subsections within the text, illustrations, and footnotes. Try to keep the systems distinct from one another: for example, if you are using numbers for headings, consider using letters for illustrations (though not if you have more than 26 illustrations). Avoid roman numerals (xxiii, xxiv, xxv), especially for long series, as many people find them difficult to understand.

Numbered sections will also provide quick access when you are discussing the report with somebody, who may ask you to look at a specific section.

Remember that the page numbers you use while originating your text and illustrations may not be the same as the final page numbers in your assembled document. If you make cross-references to page numbers, it may be best to give them a temporary place-marker (such as '00'), filling in the real page number when the document has been assembled after page make-up. When you think you have filled them all in, run a search for the marker: it's easy to miss one or two.

Using Styles and Tags to Format Text

You can save a huge amount of time when you come to format text if you use the style facilities in word processors and page make-up programmes. These allow you to store all the style attributes (such as typeface name, type size, space between lines, line length, indents, and tabs) for individual elements of text (headings, main text, footnotes) under a short name, called a tag. Then you can apply the styles quickly and consistently to appropriate parts of the text by calling up the relevant style names. If you need to change some attribute of a style then you can do so after you have created it, and all the parts of the text tagged with that style name will automatically be altered to fit the new style.

You can tag text with style names as you write, without thinking about what the styles are. Then, as you assemble the document, you can give the style names the attributes planned when the document was designed, and the text will take on its intended appearance. You can copy styles between documents produced with the same software, and so maintain consistent formatting across a series of documents. In most page make-up programmes you can take in styles, along with text and illustrations, from word-processing and drawing programmes. So once text has been tagged it can keep its tag throughout production, unless you decide to change it.

Principles of Legibility

Typeface

Typefaces can be divided into seriffed and sans serif. Serifs are the small strokes at the end of main strokes of characters, which give a horizontal emphasis to a line of type. Seriffed typefaces are therefore best for large amounts of continuous text. Sans serif type-faces have characters which tend to look similar to each other and are best reserved for headings, captions, and short pieces of text.

Type Size, Line Length, and Leading

These three factors are interrelated. If you increase the type size, for example, you might also have to increase the space between lines to maintain legibility. The rules of thumb are these: space between letters should be less than word space, and word space less than the space between lines.

In text designed for continuous reading, lines should be between 50 and 70 characters in length (including letters, numerals, spaces, and punctuation). If there are fewer than that, there may be too many awkward linebreaks; if there are more, it can get difficult for the reader to find the beginning of the next line.

For the main text of a report, a type size of 10 or 11 point is a good starting size. Try 12 or 13 point 'leading' (interline spacing)—but if your lines are more than 70 characters long, more leading might be needed. If you are using two columns, your type size can be smaller, to correspond to the shorter line length. You can therefore reduce the leading.

Do not be tempted to use a very large type size for continuous text to fill out long lines with the 50-70 characters—you don't have to make your lines fill the page width. Research shows that type sizes between 9 and 11 point are most comfortable for sustained reading. However, don't rely on these figures—different typefaces may vary in visible appearing size at the same 'point' size.

You should make trials with samples of your text, tuning the type size, line length, and leading so that the text is comfortable to read, in the circumstances in which it is likely to be read.

Text Alignment and Hyphenation

There are two main alignments to choose from for text: justified and ranged left.

Justified Text

Justified text has straight left-hand and right-hand edges. Because readers may be familiar with seeing justified text in books (and newspapers), the assumption is that this gives a formal appearance to text. It does not improve legibility, however, and it is difficult to achieve a satisfactory result: for justified text to look good, words at line endings may have to be hyphenated and the spaces between words controlled.

If you accept the default 'hyphenation and justification' (h&j) settings in many page make-up programmes, few or no hyphenation breaks are made, and the system will often spread out the words on a line to fill a column, by varying the width of word spaces and even by putting extra space between letters, which ruins the evenness of the text. You should do some trials to achieve good-looking text, allowing hyphenation, and controlling the minimum and maximum word spaces. If possible, specify zero letter-spacing. You should aim for an even appearance to each line of text.

Do not use justified setting for your letters, memos, and faxes. Whatever the style of your letterhead, it is not worth making the text justified, as the brevity of correspondence, often made up of short paragraphs, does not sufficiently define a straight right-hand edge. More importantly, some word-processing programmes do not allow you to alter the default settings for word spaces and hyphenation, which may result in justified text with an uneven appearance.

Ranged Left Text

Ranged left (or 'flush left') text has a ragged right-hand edge. This is a safer option than justified text and legibility is not impaired: it may even be improved, since word spaces are kept constant. In page make-up programmes, if you have the hyphenation option switched off, very ragged line endings may result, so you may want to accept some hyphenation.

Space between lines should appear greater than word space: this preserves horizontal cohesion and assists the 'flow' of reading. In all DTP programmes, the default word space is usually large, but in page make-up programmes you can reduce the word space throughout. Word-processing programmes do not allow you to change these settings, so you may try to compensate for this by increasing the leading: for 10 point type try 14, 15, and 16 point leading.

Ranged Right and Centred Text

Your DTP programme also offers you these other choices for text alignment. They are both fine for short items such as titles but they make longer passages of text difficult to read. Ranged right is useful for captions to tables or graphs, and for side-headings appearing in the left-hand margin.

Paragraphs

There are two common ways of indicating the start of a new paragraph: by indenting the first line or inserting extra space above the first line. If you insert extra space, it should be at least half of your normal line space: so with 10 point leading, add an extra 5 points between paragraphs (making 15 points in all). If you use this method, be aware that a paragraph end may not be clear at the bottom of a page.

If you indent the first line, a rule of thumb is to set the indent to the same value as your type size. If you have a short line length, a smaller indent may look better. Indenting first lines is the better option if you want to save space.

Office Practice versus Printing Practice

When all office documents were typewritten, the conventions of typing were appropriate for the details of text: the typewriter typeface conveyed a certain level of formality, and the limited flexibility of the typewriter was acceptable. There are usually imitation typewriter typefaces available on most systems, and some people prefer to use them for correspondence to preserve the impression of a document less formal than, for example, a bound report. Using typewriter typefaces will also save time because you will not need to worry about the typographic details necessary when you use the professional typefaces available on DTP systems. However, if you do choose to use more formal typefaces traditionally only available from typesetters, you should use typesetters', not typists', conventions.

Aspects of Typographic Style

Certain basic features of typing style have never been current in professional typesetting and should be avoided in your documents:

— Do not use a double word space after full stops, only use one.

— Straight inch marks (") and feet marks (') should not be used for true 'curly' quotation marks.

— For the character combinations fi and fl, use ligatures.

— Use proper en and em dashes when appropriate.

— Don't underline type. In DTP, you can use italic or bold for emphasis. Italic is most often used to distinguish titles of publications.

These are basic features; you may also wish to define a 'house-style' so that you ensure consistency of spelling, capitalisation, punctuation, etc. in your organisation.

Designing Reports and Proposals

'Reports and proposals' covers a wide range of documents used in business and other organisations, including:

— Sales reports

— Progress reports

— Grant proposals

— Procurement proposals

— Position papers

— Procedural manuals.

Page Size

There may already be some restrictions on the page size you choose depending on your method of production and distribution. If you aim to output pages on a desktop printer and produce multiple copies by photocopying, then a standard size like A4 (297 x 210 mm) or US letter (11 x 8V$_2$ inches) is advisable. If you are having your report professionally printed, any page size is possible, although it will be cheaper and easier for printers to work with standard sizes. You may also be restricted to a standard size by the envelopes you will use to send the report to your readers.

Given that most company reports are A4 or US letter (and this is an expected 'norm'), it would be hard to find a good reason for using an irregular page size. You should therefore accept this constraint, so that you can concentrate on more important issues.

Margins

Most DTP programmes start by asking you to define your margins, the area between the text and the edge of the page. Most reports will be bound using the sort of office binding that can take up quite a bit of page space, so you should treat the inner 35 mm (1y$_2$ inches), the back margin, as out of bounds. Your minimum margin for the outside edge of the page is dictated by the limits of your laser printer (usually about 5 mm or *Vt* inch), but for comfortable handling, you should leave at least 12 mm (7$_2$ inch) and considerably more if you are using a single column layout on A4 paper (otherwise your line length will be too long. Remember that by defining your margins you are effectively defining your line length. It may be easier to work backwards: decide a suitable line length and then calculate what the margins need to be.

A Page Grid

A grid is the framework of guidelines (made visible on your screen in page make-up programmes) to assist page layout. These guides allow you to systematically position headings, paragraphs, and pictures on a page, so that the document is consistently arranged over a series of pages. This consistency then helps readers find the information they need page after page.

The kind of grid you need depends on what you want to put in your document. Reports normally use quite simple grids. Here are three well-tried alternatives.

Document Organisation

Cover and Preliminary Material

The cover should identify what the report is about, who it is from, and the date of production. A simple cover will be most effective.

The title page usually contains the same information as the cover. In a short report it may be best combined with the contents list. The contents list must work with the headings, running heads, and other features of the report to enable easy access to information.

Headers, Footers, and Page Numbers

Page numbers should also be clear. They can go in the header or footer line, but they must go on the opposite side to the bound edge, so people can see the numbers when flicking through the report. If there is enough room, they could go in the outside margin.

You may want to repeat the title of the report on each page, so if a page is photocopied its source is still clear. This isn't information that readers need when searching through the report, so it can be quite small. You may want to put the section title and page number in the header and the publication title, and possibly the author's name, in the footer.

Section Headings

To prevent your report from looking too monotonous, and to provide visible landmarks for access, you can make a feature of section headings by using a large, bold or italic style of type, highlighted further by leaving space around it. This will make these pages stand out. If there is a limited amount of space, you may not be able to start a new page for the beginning of each section; if you can, however, it is a good idea. To make your headings stand out, you could either leave a pre-defined space after the last line of the heading, or begin the following text at a fixed 'drop', regardless of the length of the section heading. This means calculating the depth of the longest section heading, and fixing the space to the first line of text. Taken together, all your headings should form a hierarchy, with section headings as the first level.

Problems of Page Layout

Page Breaks

When you divide your report into pages, it is important to make sure that the page breaks occur at the right places—don't allow single words or lines to appear at the top of a column.

It looks better to have at least two lines of a paragraph at the top or bottom of the page. And make sure that headings don't appear as the last line of a page. They should have at least two lines following them, and more in the case of major headings.

Reports often contain lists of numbered or bullet-ed points. It's best not to break short lists (say, six or fewer lines), but to start the list on a new page.

Placing Illustrations and Tables

Although most DTP programmes allow the text to flow around illustrations (and diagrams and tables), it is best to place them between paragraphs. In a single column grid, an illustration can be placed anywhere on the page. However, if this means that only three or four lines of text would appear above or below it, you might as well align the illustration at the top or bottom. Leave at least one line space between the text and the illustration.

In a double column grid, it is always best to place illustrations at the top or bottom of the page. Although illustrations can be effective in other positions, there is always a risk of the flow of text being broken up in inappropriate ways, making it difficult for the reader to follow the text in the way you intended.

Runarounds

Most DTP programmes allow you to run text around illustrations, and you can define the distance between the text and the illustration. If you have a wide margin to your report, illustrations can go there and runarounds shouldn't be necessary. If you do use runarounds, the illustration shouldn't extend to more than halfway across the column. And be careful with justified type: the narrower column left beside the illustration could have very uneven word spacing.

Making Your Message Clear

Using Type to Show Hierarchy

Items that are bigger or bolder are seen as more important than those that are smaller or lighter. This principle allows you to create a hierarchy of headings which will help graphically express the organisation of the text.

Using Space to Show Hierarchy

Typographic distinction may not be enough to make a heading system clear in itself, so you will need to adjust the space between elements to group items together. Things that are closer together will be seen as related: a heading must be closer to the text it governs than to text at a higher level in the hierarchy.

Visual Identity

Different parts of a text can be assigned different styles which are not necessarily hierarchical. Summaries and side-notes, for example, sit outside the main argument and comment on it: they can be in a different typeface, as if they are being spoken in a different voice. Even though they may be pages apart, they will be seen as belonging to the same category of information because of their similarity.

Alternatives to Text

Certain information is often much clearer if it is not buried in the flow of a sentence. You may want the reader to follow instructions, or compare totals of research findings. for example. Lists, tables, graphs, and charts can give a more distinct representation of this kind of information, and will also add variety to the layout of your document.

Lists

Numbers, Bullets, and Sorts

It helps to list collections of related ideas. Where items are referred to individually in the following text, or when they describe a sequence of actions, they can be numbered, but otherwise it is simpler just to use bullets (•) or dashes (-). These can be found in all typefaces, but if you want to make more impact you can use the Monotype Sorts font (♦ •)

Be careful not to overuse lists: there must always be enough conventional text to lead your readers through your argument. Otherwise it's like giving them self-assembly furniture with no assembly instructions: everything they need is there, but they don't know what it's for.

Tables

DTP allows great flexibility for the design of tables, but they take a bit of skill and practice. There are several ways of setting tables: if you see tables you find particularly clear you could copy the way they are designed. However, always bear in mind that your text is different and may need special treatment. Remember to put the user first, not your own design preferences. Here one system is recommended that is easy to implement in most software and for most purposes.

Vertical and Horizontal Rules

These days vertical rules are usually left out of tables because the data in the columns is well enough aligned to allow the space between the columns to do the same job. If many of the cells are left blank, though, vertical rules might be needed. You should use horizontal rules to help people read across tables. By varying the thickness of the rules you can emphasise different sections. Vertical rules are usually more difficult to use in DTP software than horizontal ones, which can be anchored to the line of type and so don't have to be adjusted separately if the text above is edited.

Column Headings

Write short headings for tables, and abbreviate where you can. If some column headings have to be split over more than one line, align the headings at the top. But because the headings will no longer form a distinct line, it is a good idea to use a horizontal rule below them, to distinguish clearly between the heading area and the table content.

Estimating the Width of Columns

If each table has a different number of columns and perhaps different kinds of data to go in the cells, you'll have to treat each table as a separate design problem.

The good thing about DTP is that you can easily try things out on screen and quickly proof your trials on paper. Set your headings with tabs between, and then adjust the tabs until the headings all fit on the page with the same amount of space between them. Once you've entered the data in the cells of the table, you'll need to adjust it again so that there is a visual balance between the columns—the reader should see them as equally spaced even if the content varies in width.

Aligning Data with Column Headings

Where the cells have text in them, they can line up on the left with the column heading above. Where they have figures that have to be aligned on the right, you can use right tabs and decimal tabs. But you will have to align them with the column heading by eye.

Row Headings

Write short headings, if you can. If you have to go to a second line, indent it slightly, or make sure there is more space between each row heading than between the lines in a single heading.

Graphs and Charts

There are numerous specialised graphs and charts, some of which are specific to particular subject areas. But for general purposes, most people want to do one of three things: they want to show trends, compare totals, or compare proportions.

Showing Trends

A traditional graph is the best way of showing a trend over time. Time is always displayed on the 'x' axis (horizontally) and the data points are joined by straight lines. Readers can easily see if there is a trend in the data.

Comparing Totals and Proportions

Bar or column charts are the simplest way of comparing totals and proportions. Bar charts run horizontally and should only be used for comparison of single bars. Column charts run vertically and are ideal for both single columns and column clusters.

Bar and column charts allow a direct comparison between lengths that start at the same base—something the human eye is very good at. Avoid techniques that don't allow such a simple comparison - including stacked bar charts and different sized symbols. Use side-by-side bars or repeated symbols instead.

Many spreadsheet programmes offer a dazzling array of statistical graphics, including three-dimensional effects and shadows. Be ultra-critical—make sure that you really need the techniques offered and that they won't just obscure your data.

If you create your charts in a drawing programme and then import them into a page make-up programme, stretching can distort the chart (and distort the type contained in it). Sizing must be done carefully to preserve the proportions.

Designing Letters, Memos, and Faxes

Correspondence to your customers or clients will influence their everyday impression of your organisation. Now that DTP offers the opportunity to make your letters and faxes appear typeset (not typewritten) by the use of printers' typefaces, you must make sure that details of layout and text design are correspondingly professional. Even internal memos are important in communicating information to your colleagues clearly, so that business runs more smoothly.

As correspondence may be produced by many people within an organisation, it is important that a standard style is set up, so that the image of a coherent organisation is presented. You could set up a template file for each kind of document you produce. Factors that should remain constant are:

— Information about your organisation
— Typeface
— Type size
— Leading
— Text area
— House-style

With a template file, all employees can simply type in the new information without worrying about the layout. This will benefit both you and your readers: you save valuable time and your readers will be able to concentrate on the content of your correspondence rather than being diverted by unnecessary variety in its presentation.

Stationery

Because letters and faxes are everyday documents, which need a stamp of identity, you will probably have a range of pre-printed stationery. This bears the details of your organisation, sometimes with a logo or namestyle.

Page Size

Most headed paper will be of standard size (A4 or US letter): there is really no other choice, as you will have to feed the paper through your printer and probably use standard envelopes designed to accommodate these sizes.

If you are likely to use window envelopes, you should check that your letterhead conforms to the relevant standards (e.g. British Standard or US Postal Service Guide). These standards give guidelines for the areas to be left blank, so that the recipients address will be visible through a window envelope. Your letterhead may have an indication of this area to guide you in typing the address: if not, you could set up some guides on a template. It is worth sending a copy of a letter to yourself to see if the address is still visible after the rigours of the post, and to see what your letter looks like to a recipient.

If in the course of your business, you use reference numbers on your letters, it may be difficult to align a number that you are typing with an associated heading on your pre-printed stationery. A better option might be to have the heading on your template file, so that you can align the reference number with it directly.

Similarly, if your headed paper does not indicate where you should begin the text of your letter, you could define a specific point. You could mark the starting point in your template file or, if you are using a word-processing programme, adjust the page-setup parameters so that you always start typing at the correct position.

Faxes

Faxes must include the same information about you as your letterhead. For this reason, you may want to use the same headed paper and even the same standard text style. However, beware of the effects faxing has on type: some of the essential information in a letterhead may be in quite small type, which may become illegible after faxing, so you may want to set up your own separate headed paper for faxing. Try them out to make sure they are legible after transmission.

Layout

Complexities of column arrangement are not really applicable to letters. Despite the facilities offered by DTP, the conventions of letter layout still dictate a single column. If you produce a letter in two columns, it simply won't look like a letter. If you use a single column, you do not have to fill the width of the page: a moderate line length will mean that your type size can be within the desired range for text (9 to 11 point), whereas a longer line might require 12 point or more, so that the lines do not exceed 70 characters in length.

The space between the address and the text of the letter should make it clear that they are separate units. If the date immediately follows the address, it should be separated by extra space, but the space between the date and 'Dear Sir/Madam' should be greater. This will separate the information into groups, as elements close together are seen as belonging to each other.

Points of Information

It may not seem that a planned structure is necessary for correspondence, with its very common rules and conventions. But you should try to think of every possible use of the document and of anything that could go wrong along the way. If a letter or fax has more than one sheet, for example, they may get separated: so you should include the name of the sender and a page number on each page. Pre-printed headed paper, with special continuation sheets, usually contains abbreviated information. This is not so vital with faxes, as the fax machine includes the date and at least the fax number of the sender, but page numbers are especially important.

A fax might easily be sent to the wrong number. So however informal your communication, don't be tempted to leave out essential identifying information. The reader's main priority is to find out what's been said, by whom, when, and how they can reply.

An internal memorandum should feature the word 'memorandum' or 'memo' as a heading, as it needs to distinguish itself quickly from the other kinds of documents that accumulate on a desk. Identifying a memo immediately tells the reader that this is internal communication.

As a documented record of a decision or policy which needs to be registered with the appropriate personnel, a memo often needs to be sent to many people. Their names are crucial, as they might be the only instruction to a secretary about who needs a copy of the memo. You might try setting all the identifying information in a different typeface or variant (e.g. bold, italic) to that of the main text: this will give the information a visibly different status.

Tips to Improve Written Communication Skills

The importance of effective written communication skills cannot be stressed enough. Written communication plays a major role, especially in the corporate world. Hence, it is doubly important to have good written communication skills in the workplace. Business writing or any other form of written communication can be very simple for those who follow the guidelines that are given below.

— *Audience*: Keep your audience/reader in mind before you begin writing the piece. The audience is mainly what determines the content to be written. Once you have an idea about who is the intended audience, you can judge for yourself what other necessary steps need to be taken to ensure the completion of the communication cycle, which is, after all, the intention of any piece of communication.

— *Information*: The basics of communication should be covered in your piece of written communication. The 5 Ws and 1 H—Who, What, Where, When, Why and How (either completely or at least the ones that need to be) should be in your piece. This is basically almost the entire information that you wish to give the reader. However you present the data, these points need to covered, only then is it an effective way of communication.

— *Tone*: Deciding the tone of your communication depends on the audience to a large extent. You must be able to gauge what kind of tone you should use to ensure maximum comprehension and retention by your audience. For instance, you cannot use a condescending tone with a person who is at a higher post than you at work. Nor can you use an arrogant tone for something that is meant to reach a large number of people at one time. Another instance, is letter writing. If you're writing a letter to a customer to remind him (for the third time) to pay his bills, your tone will be slightly more stern than the first or second letter of notice that you must have written to him. Tones can vary from casual, semi formal to formal, depending on who you're communicating with and what you intend to communicate.

— *Language*: This forms one of the major chunks of written communication skills that one needs to develop. This does not mean that you need to have a flair for writing. It simply means that you must be well versed with the fundamentals of the language. These include grammar, spellings, figures of speech, parts of speech, punctuation, etc. Following the basics of the language is more than enough to be a decent writer. Of course, this is just the case with formal writing. In the case of creative writing like copywriting for ads or storytelling in any form, it is essential that along with the basics, you must possess a flair for writing and a creative sense as well.

— *Length*: Knowing when to stop applies to written communication skills as well. You can't just keep rambling on and on, when not required. The beauty of effective written communication can be seen in its presentation. How well and how concisely you manage to accommodate all the information that you need to give is what shows how proficient your written communication skills are. The key, as the old adage goes, is to be 'clear, concise and correct'. But this does not necessarily mean that you cut short on something that requires to be explained in detail. So, in short, you must be able to estimate how much you need to write about something. And, if you feel something's getting too long, break it up into parts. This makes it easier for you as well as the reader.

These were some pointers on how you can improve your written communication skills. These are just basic guidelines and writing tips which need to be paid attention to. There are many more intricacies involved in every style of writing, which can be mastered only with in-depth study and regular practice.

REFERENCES

Charles T. Brusaw, Gerald J. Alfred, and Walter E. Oliu. (1976). *The Business Writer's Handbook*. St. Martin's Press, New York.

Donald Pattow and William Wresch. *Communicating Technical Information: A Guide for the Electronic Age*. Blair Press, The Statler Building.

Ernst Jacobi. *Do's, Don'ts, and How to's: Writing at Work.* Ten Speed Press,Berkeley.

William Zinsser. (1976). *On Writing Well* Harper Perennial.

Elizabeth W. Adler. (1991). *Print That Works: The First Step-by-Step Guide that Integrates Writing, Design, and Marketing.* Bull Publishing Company, California.

6

Modern Technology in Business Communication

Modern business requires modern technology. Any business that expects to thrive today must have at least a basic understanding of the various innovations, programmes and devices as well as the knowledge of how to apply these technologies. The many tools and powers that technology makes available to the business owner and employees can help the business succeed in its goals after understanding how to use them properly.

Before anything else, work can be done collaborating projects and documents using such computer programmes such as Google Docs, Zoho Writer and, to a lesser extent, MS Word, which allows several users to work on a single document while placing changes/descriptions and even modifying the document in real-time. While the ideal of a "paperless office" is still a few years away, businesses can use the Internet or internal programmes to spur real-time work on projects so businesses can quickly finish what is needed to succeed.

Sometimes, businesses need to make conference calls bringing several people together and technology can help here too. Programmes such as Skype or Gizmo Project offer Voice over Internet Protocol (VoIP) services that allow individuals and businesses to call places all over the world for prices much cheaper then regular landline services.

Microsoft pointed out that a Forrester study done in 2006 showed that 17 percent of businesses made converting to VoIP a priority, with another 18 percent already using VoIP to some degree. VoIP allows businesses to be in near-constant communication with employees and others at a fraction of a cost.

Sites such as Youtube see millions of hits a day, with online video and audio becoming extremely prevalent on websites. Businesses can capitalize by making their own media. Companies can create in-house advertisements for use on websites, webinars on the use of products that can further communicate between businesses and their consumers, and provide education. These forms of media are also available nearly 24 hours a day, so think of them as day-long commercials for your business.

With the rise of social networks such as Facebook, Myspace, Digg and others, a form of crowd-based media known as social media has emerged. Businesses can take advantage of social media as another aspect of business communication, by performing such tasks as creating profiles on social networks, submitting online media to sites such as Digg, and using websites like Twitter to answer consumer questions. Many businesses have already jumped on the social media bandwagon, with some (Microsoft and Wal-Mart in particular) having experimented with their own social networks.

You can also automate certain tasks. Years ago, sending an email of a document or backing up a computer required extensive time, thus reducing productivity. Backups can be done today with a mere click of a button and automatic emails can be sent on a routine schedule with a minimum of work. A company that works automation to its fullest advantage can concentrate on more important tasks at hand, while reducing cost and increasing productivity in the workplace, as well as optimising success for the business itself.

Role of Internet

Advice on getting on the net abounds, but a review of recent publications reveals a lack of attention to such basic issues as what services the Internet actually offers, what options businesses have for using the Internet (most advice focuses only on building web sites, for example) and how businesses can use intranets as communication tools.

It is essential to think of intranets and the Internet as communication media. After all, although businesses are selling goods on the web, this selling is done by information exchange between two or more parties. Likewise, advertising products and services, or providing on-line customer support are other examples of businesses communicating information to their clients. To really understand the business potential of the Internet and the web type interface used for intranets, it is crucial that their significance as communication tools be understood. Once businesses understand the implications of new communication networks, it is then possible to determine how best to use them for their own specific purposes.

The Internet is an electronic communication medium that emerged from the ARPANET in the late 1960s and early 1970s. Originally a U.S. government sponsored research-based computer network, it was established primarily for the exchange of military and scientific information, but electronic mail (e-mail) quickly emerged as the most popular feature. By the mid 1980s, the network had been divided into separate military and research networks. The research network was supported by the National Science Foundation in the U.S. and academic institutions worldwide. Until the late 1980s, access to the Internet was available only to government employees and to people associated with academic institutions, thus commercial activities were insignificant. The Internet changed dramatically in early 1990, when commercial e-mail providers were given access to the network. Since that time, the Internet has been growing exponentially, both in terms of numbers of users and volume of traffic. In North America, the Internet is now accessible to anyone with a computer, a modem, and a phone line, who is willing to pay a monthly or hourly connection fee.

But what is on the Internet? It is often described as a network of networks linking businesses, universities, governments and individuals. The links enable sending and receipt of electronic mail, and provide access from any point on any network to any other. A wide variety of information is stored on host computers, in databases, or as text, graphics, audio or video files, accessible to either authorised users or the world at large. It is this stored information that makes up the content of the Internet, which is supplemented by real-time information exchange in forums such as IRCs (Internet Relay Channels), MUDs (multi-user dungeons, where games are played) or MUSHs (multi-user social hours). The Internet is constantly changing, as new hosts come on-line, others go off-line, and sites (locations at which host computers are found) are updated.

There are six main services or functions available to Internet users: e-mail, news and mailing lists, interactive multi-user services, file transfers, browsing via the World Wide Web, and directory services and indexing. For many users, Internet access is synonymous with e-mail. However, it is important to note that access to e-mail does not necessarily imply access to the Internet, as many corporations have their own internal e-mail systems running on local area networks (LANs). For those e-mail users who do have Internet access however, connectivity can be established to all other Internet e-mail users worldwide.

A popular service found on the Internet is Usenet news, also known simply as news. Technically speaking, "Usenet is the set of machines that exchange articles tagged with one or more universally-recognised labels, called newsgroups (or 'groups' for short)". In practical terms, Usenet is analogous to a collection of bulletin boards, on which individuals can post articles providing information, and seek or give advice. Unlike e-mail, where a message is transmitted directly between the sender and receiver(s), a Usenet article is sent to a public forum (the newsgroup), open to all readers of that group . There are thousands of newsgroups, with discussion topics ranging from food, movies, sex, jobs, Windows 95, Macintosh hardware to urban folklore . Electronic mailing lists serve a similar purpose to newsgroups, in that they unite people with a common interest. Unlike newsgroups however, information disseminated by electronic mailing list arrives in a user's e-mailbox. Users must subscribe to the mailing list, and only members of the list receive messages from it. In contrast to news and mailing lists, which send prepared storable messages, interactive multi-user services operate in real-time, exchanging conversations and advice instantaneously.

E-mail, news and mailing lists are all message-based. But as much of the traffic over the Internet arises from the direct transfer of files from site to site, file transfer mechanisms are needed. FTP is an acronym for File Transfer Protocol, used to move files from one computer to another. Various search engines are available to help users locate the files they are looking for, many of which can be downloaded on an anonymous basis. A related technology, Gopher, is a menu-driven text retrieval system, allowing the user to follow branches in the text in a non-linear (hypertext) format.

At present, the most sophisticated means of accessing the Internet is through the World Wide Web. The web, as it is commonly known, offers Internet users features not available through other access mechanisms. Using software browsers such as Netscape or Microsoft's Internet Explorer, users can access information in text, audio or visual formats, or in a multimedia combination. The web is navigated by means of hypertext links embedded within home pages, or starting points, found at each site. Web pages are stored at host sites and are easily created and updated. It is on the web that businesses are making their presence known. While growth on the Internet as a whole has been extremely quick, the web is growing exponentially. *Forbes* estimated that there were 466 home pages on the web being used by businesses in September 1994. In 1995 *Business Week* estimated there were 21,000 businesses on the Internet. The latest figures show more than 40,000 businesses are present on the web, with estimates of an additional 150 joining every day.

A year ago, businesses racing to get on the Internet were unsure as to the best interfaces they could use to reach their customers. Although the World Wide Web was gaining acceptance as the preferred interface for accessing the Internet there was uncertainty as to whether web browsers would be superseded by more advanced technology, in the same way the browsers themselves had rendered earlier stand alone Internet access mechanisms less important. Nearing the end of 1996, this issue appears to be resolved, at least temporarily. There is no doubt that browsers and the web interface will continue to emerge and change as technology advances. But for the foreseeable future, browser software that offers easy access to web sites, Gopher materials, FTP and e-mail in an integrated package operated by a simple point and click graphical user interface ensures that the web will remain the place to be for businesses on the Internet.

Intranets

The popularity and success of the web interface is seen in the rapid adoption of business intranets. Although organisations like Hewlett-

Packard have been using intranets since 1991, it is only in the past year that their use has become widespread. When investigating and implementing web sites for external users, it occurred to many businesses that the web interface offered an excellent means of disseminating information within their own organisations. In fact, many software developers, vendors and consultants are now focusing their efforts on building intranet systems. The difference between the Internet and intranets is that the Internet provides unrestricted access to any users worldwide, whereas access to an intranet is restricted by the organisation operating it. Intranets may be accessible by some suppliers and customers, in addition to employees in various locations, but an intranet cannot be accessed by the general public.

Described by *Information Week* as "arguably the hottest trend in IT", the development of intranets is booming. Intranets offer integrated databases and communication systems, e-mail and file transfer. Some experts predict intranets will eventually replace existing corporate networks. The popularity of intranets should not come as a surprise. They can be established relatively cheaply and quickly, and they enable all users in an organisation to access information in the same format, regardless of the platform used to access the network.

Importance of Communication Networks

Technological advances mean that the interfaces and networks we use to communicate with others are changing rapidly. What we know today as the Internet will likely be a very different network in a few years, or even twelve months' time. Nevertheless, it is argued that NCNs, as we currently understand them, are fundamentally different than the non-electronic means of information exchange that preceded them.

Establishing a new communication network (NCN) of some description is not a difficult undertaking. Technical help is available from a wide variety of vendors and consultants. Trade and professional journals have published a multitude of "how to get on the Internet" articles. As companies develop external web sites, they gain expertise that can be used when establishing intranets. Although intranet development is a new field, there is no shortage of written advice on how to proceed.

From a technical perspective then, it is easy to establish an NCN. But what should such a network be employed to do? NCNs can be used to share information and files, offer goods and services for sale and work collaboratively. However, just because such technology is available does not mean it should be deployed in all organisations. NCNs offer new means of communicating, and may have significant impacts upon the structure and culture of the organisations using them. In the section that follows, the features of NCNs that differentiate them from older communication mechanisms will be outlined. Once these features are identified, the implications of their use in businesses will be discussed. The importance of understanding features of networks rather than focusing on the technological interfaces should not be understated. Although interfaces may change, there are certain core features specific to a medium that distinguish it from other media.

Sproull and Kiesler argue that new computer-based communication technologies "overcome temporal and geographic barriers to the exchange of information" and "connect anyone with anyone or everyone on the same computer communication network". They go on to suggest that new communication technologies "do not simply cross space and time; they also can cross hierarchical and departmental barriers, change standard operating procedures, and reshape organisational norms". These are not trivial implications, and they support the view that new technologies are significantly different than older communication mechanisms (e.g. phone, fax). The facility by which people using new communication technologies can communicate with individuals they might otherwise never meet is a significant innovation, as it renders geographic location irrelevant. For businesses, this opportunity alone may justify the establishment of an NCN. But the rapid speed of electronic communication, coupled with its relatively low cost, also differentiate it from previous technologies, where information or documents could not be simultaneously transmitted to multiple recipients.

The essential characteristics of new electronic communication technologies are summarised by Huber, under the term "advanced information technologies". He suggests these new technologies:

— exhibit high level basic characteristics (e.g. data storage capacity, transmission capacity and processing capacity)

— facilitate individual or organisational ability to communicate both more easily and more cheaply across time and geographic space

— allow greater precision and more rapid communication with targeted groups

— enable and facilitate indexing and recording of communication events and content

— allow more selective control over participation in and access to a communication event or network.

They also permit interactivity and multidirectional information flows.

These properties are all reflected to varying degrees in the services and features of intranets and the Internet. But are these properties indicative of a changed way of communicating?

The issue of whether a new communication technology is significantly different from those it replaces or supplements is not new. Thompson considered it in 1975, offering a framework to assess the value of communication innovations. He outlines three criteria which can be used for this purpose. The first regards communications with the past. Significant new technologies adopted over the ages (Thompson lists the phonetic alphabet, papyrus, and the moveable type printing press as examples) have made it easier to access stored human experiences. Easier access (for example better indexing and retrieval mechanisms) has led to increased use of existing human experience. Secondly, significant innovations enable shared access to an information space, which is generally enlarged by the new technology. (Thompson's example here is the printed word, which enabled people to read and compare identical information.) Related to this point, significant innovations tend to increase interrupt strategies, thus enriching the communication experience. Thompson's third criteria for judging communication innovations is the ease with which the new technology can enable the dissemination of new ideas throughout society, thus encouraging the discovery and development of shared understandings, often in exciting and unexpected ways.

Given Thompson's criteria, how do electronic communication technologies measure up? To begin, it is noted that some of the properties of advanced information technologies described by Huber are consistent with Thompson's criteria. There is no doubt that the computerisation of information has made it easier to access stored or archival experiences, whether recorded in text, audio or video format. Technology enables simultaneous access to many materials, from points around the globe, (although Internet indexing systems do leave much to be desired at present). Given that it is common to discover people with shared interests through Usenet, mailing lists or web pages, electronic communication generally facilitates interruptions, that is unexpected communications that have the potential to expand a common information space. Browsing on the web or an intranet and then corresponding with people with shared interests (discovered at random or met by chance) would likely be considered an interrupt strategy by Thompson. The World Wide Web also provides a prime example of how a new communication technology can be used to share ideas and create new understandings among people. Like the Internet as a whole, the web was initially developed as a mechanism by which to exchange scientific information. It has greatly facilitated information sharing and exchange within and beyond the scientific community, exposing many people to new research and ideas. Similar opportunities for information exchange and sharing are available through corporate intranets.

Although existing electronic communication technologies and networks will be improved upon over time, according to Thompson's criteria electronic communication as it exists today is a significant innovation. One important consideration, however, is ease of access to new technologies. Technologies must be accessible in order to have utility for the general public. Related to accessibility is the probability that the innovation will actually be implemented and used in the desired manner. At present, the Internet does not score well on either of these points, thus potentially limiting its current impact as an innovative technology. For the most part, the Internet and the World Wide Web, despite attempts to simplify user interfaces and access methods, are still difficult for the average user to use, and not available to the majority of the population. Those who argue that new electronic communication technologies do not live up to the substantial hype that has been generated about them do have a significant argument in current Internet user demographics. Intranets, however, can overcome many of these difficulties, as organisations can ensure that their employees have access to the appropriate hardware, software and training required to use a corporate intranet.

The discussion of new technologies identified four features that distinguished new electronic communication technologies from existing communication technologies. These are:

— high level capacity for data storage and transmission speed, combined with easy access to stored data;

— creation of a new shared space in which communication can occur, enabling contact between individuals and groups who might otherwise have never communicated;

— capacity for widespread idea dissemination or targeted communication, combined with interactivity and multidirectional information flows; and

— improved communication abilities over time and space, rendering geographic location unimportant.

USING COMMUNICATION NETWORKS FOR BUSINESS PURPOSE

With an understanding of the unique communication features available to users of the Internet and corporate intranets, the discussion now turns to the issue of how these features can best be incorporated into business strategies and actions.

Using the Internet

In the past few years, much has been written about the Internet and how it can be used for business purposes. The focus of attention has been electronic commerce, that is any use of the Internet by businesses or individuals for commercial purposes. Many businesses have been disappointed by the results of their electronic commerce projects. Profits from electronic commerce are not yet evident, or lower than expected for many Internet marketers. Online shopping has not taken off, and the only businesses consistently making money from the Internet are technology suppliers and companies that sell advertising on web sites.

There are many possible explanations for the underwhelming success of Internet business ventures to date. Certainly, the fact that the

Internet is still not easily accessible is an important one. (Compare accessing the Internet to "accessing" television or radio. Until the Internet can be used by simply bringing home an appliance and plugging it in, without worrying about buying software, signing up with an Internet service provider and establishing a network connection, it will remain of limited appeal to a large segment of the population.) Those who do access the Internet regularly may find it congested and difficult to navigate. Furthermore, many company offerings are little more than electronic brochures, and once a site has been visited an initial time, there is no reason to go back. Businesses need to be smarter in their uses of the Internet. Some suggestions as to how this can be accomplished are outlined below.

Firstly, it is important that business web sites offer their consumers more than can be provided through traditional interfaces. For example, a product catalogue that is available on the web could use a combination of text and graphical images or video, supplemented by audio, to describe a firm's products. This is something that cannot be offered with traditional print catalogues, but that is viable over the Internet. Advantages for the business include reduction or elimination of printing costs, and the capacity to update product information whenever necessary.

If a business is committed to doing business on the web, it should ensure that all necessary transactions can be carried out in that environment. It is frustrating for consumers to find the product they want to purchase, and then be referred to a telephone number to order it. Complete service should be available on the web, from initial information gathering to purchasing to after sales service. Although many consumers are wary of providing a credit card number over the Internet, secure systems are now available to ensure that credit card numbers can be transmitted safely. The main issue for businesses is convincing consumers to use them.

A clear understanding of target markets is important to be successful on the Internet. Although the technology offers businesses a potential market of millions of Internet users, the reality is that only a small portion of that market will be looking for a specific product or service offered by any given company. And despite the fact that high volume, high speed data transfer is available, not all users have access to it.

Does this mean that businesses should ignore the opportunity to employ high end technologies in favour of ones that will not take advantage of the Internet's potential speed for handling large data volumes? Not necessarily, but it is important to understand the basic demographics of the target consumer. Bandwidth availability (the capacity of an Internet connection) will determine whether a given consumer can easily access a particular service or information source offered by a business. For many individual consumers accessing the Internet by modem, available bandwidth is insufficient to handle graphics or video files. But for corporate clients with high speed data networks bandwidth is not an issue. Recognising that different levels of bandwidth are available to different consumer groups should allow businesses to design their web pages with particular groups in mind. It may be necessary to offer a variety of options to access information (e.g. text only for users with modem access, and full graphics plus video for high speed access), or to decide to only target certain groups.

Businesses offering services on the Internet should take advantage of the possibilities for interactivity. Unlike most existing communication media, the web can be used in a dynamic way. Businesses can make searchable databases available to their customers, and allow access to query real time processes. FedEx has been a leader in this regard, allowing customers to track their parcels and packages without needing to talk to a customer service representative. Customers have embraced this technology, and FedEx's competitors quickly developed similar services.

One of the perceived advantages of the Internet is the opportunity to reach out to new consumers who would never otherwise come into contact with a particular business. Geography is rendered irrelevant, because interactions take place on the network, not in a single physical location. But these facts alone do not guarantee business success on the Internet. As has been mentioned previously, the Internet is often difficult to navigate, search engines are not reliable, and many consumers do not idly browse the web looking for new products to acquire (although no doubt some do). To take advantage of geographic irrelevance, and the opportunity to reach new customers, businesses have to intelligently target specific groups. This advice may seem paradoxical, since in targeting groups businesses are identifying potential customers, rather than letting them stumble across their offerings. But given the size and structure of the Internet, this tactic simply helps businesses to zero in on consumers who would be most likely to appreciate their services. Thus, to ensure maximum exposure for interested parties, there are several actions to take. Web sites should be properly indexed by search engines, and page titles and text must be descriptive of the products or services being offered. This will improve the chances that people looking for a specific business will be able to locate it. People who use a business's products or services should be encouraged to link the business's web pages to their own. Professional associations, student groups and clubs may be willing to do the same thing.

Finally, businesses must have a clear plan as to how their operations will be supported in various geographic regions, before people find their sites. Small operators may decide to limit activities to a local area. This is a perfectly reasonable way to use to the web, but potential customers must be aware of geographic restrictions on services. Likewise, businesses operating in the global environment must be prepared to cope with the challenges it may bring (e.g. product distribution, language of business, and currency conversion).

Using an Intranet

The recommendations discussed above have focused primarily on relationships with customers who are not initially known to a business. Although a business may target its Internet activities to certain groups of individuals or other businesses, its products or services will be available to anyone with Internet access. An organisation's own employees may also use the Internet to communicate with each other, but substantial additional benefits may be gained by adopting an intranet for internal organisational communication. There are also significant advantages to offering intranet access to specific customers, who deal with a business on an ongoing basis.

The use of an intranet to create a shared communication space can be beneficial. Although the participants in this shared space are connected to the intranet because they are associated with a specific organisation, this does not remove the benefits of such a space. In large organisations or those with global operations there will be many participants who are unknown to each other, thus the importance of a forum where people can communicate with those they would not otherwise meet remains a key benefit. In terms of using such a forum to exchange specific advice and ideas related to company business, it is expected that an intranet forum, while limited in total numbers of participants, will be more effective than an Internet one. This is because participants will already have a shared understanding of organisational goals and culture. Recent research examining the behaviours of people who contribute to intranet type forums suggests that one motivator for doing so is the sense of contributing to the organisation, by responding to specific requests for assistance. Thus, if potential contributors are motivated by a desire to help their organisation, an intranet forum is likely to be more successful than an Internet one, which does not address a specific organisation's issues. Another key benefit of using an intranet to exchange ideas and advice is that the cumulative records of discussion in such forums can be made available to all participants. This is an example of technology being used to facilitate or encourage organisational learning, a subject worthy of further research into its impacts on corporate performance.

Some of the technical issues that are important for businesses operating on the Internet are less relevant for intranet activities. Intranets do allow companies to take full advantage of the technological capacities of new communication networks, including high speed data transfer and use of full multimedia. These features can be used in intranets provided that all users have means of accessing the network at high speeds. Businesses offering services on the Internet cannot assume that common access mechanisms are available to all their potential users, but within an organisation, it is much easier to control access devices, and to design networks with an understanding of how users will access them. Even if an intranet is accessible by selected customers and clients who are external to the firm, it is still much easier to assess their technological capacities and develop the intranet with them in mind, than it is to guess the sorts of access mechanisms the general public will want to use for a specific Internet service.

The fact that new communication networks facilitate widespread dissemination of information offers companies enormous scope in redesigning internal communication systems. In the past, it was difficult and expensive to make information available to everyone who might benefit from it. It was also difficult to identify those who might find specific information useful, and often people did not ask for information because they did not know it existed. Moving to an intranet for internal communication can change the way companies make internal information available. By putting documents up on the intranet (e.g. home pages for each department) anyone anywhere else in the company can access basic information on a subject, and identify where more information can be found if desired. In addition, as web pages are very easily updated, the latest information can be stored electronically as soon as it is available, saving costs of printing multiple document updates, for example. People in organisations can get information when they want it, and no longer have to put up with reams of irrelevant paper arriving in their mailboxes daily. An intranet does not guarantee that all required information will be available at all times, or that all information available on the intranet will be of value to all users, but it does offer much more flexibility in information distribution than existing communication technologies have done.

Organisational Impacts of Communication Networks

The section above has outlined some ways organisations can deploy new communication networks. The suggestions are not exhaustive by any means. Indeed, the key to using NCNs intelligently is to understand their properties, and to develop applications that take advantage of the unique features of networked communication, while building on existing organisational strengths. Much will be learned by trial and error, but a good understanding of network features and business objectives in using the Internet or an intranet will reduce the cost of experimentation, and reduce the potential for serious misjudgment. What is also needed before adopting new communication networks is an understanding of some of the impacts they may have within an organisation. Although it is too early to understand the full organisational impacts of new communication technologies, there is ample evidence to suggest that even basic network services such as e-mail have had significant effects on organisational structure and culture.

Previous studies of the use of e-mail in organisations indicates that e-mail not only speeds up communication within organisations, it also changes the distribution of information, expanding the size and scope of organisational networks. Similar effects are expected in organisations using the Internet and/or an intranet. Expanding electronic networks have impacts beyond changing organisational information flows and gathering procedures. Zmud suggests that changing information processing behaviours will lead to real changes in individual influence and status within organisations. Hierarchical organisational forms will become less effective, as hierarchies are essentially bypassed by electronic networks. When employees have access to the Internet, and internal organisational information through their computer networks, the need for middle management as information disseminators is drastically reduced. Thus, providing internal and external information access to employees has far greater effects than might initially be anticipated.

Information technology is changing organisational structures in a variety of contexts. One consultant says "when work is carried out through networks, an organisation's structure changes whether you want it to or not. I can't find a single case where it doesn't happen". Another suggests that "information technology, after decades of unfulfilled promise, is finally creating major operating economies as well as influencing organisational structure". Morgan argues that "information technology has the capacity to transform the nature and structure of many organisations".

New communication networks have the potential to change organisational structure in ways that might not initially be anticipated. While structural changes may not have an immediate impact on how a business operates a new communication network, they will be important for longer term strategic and human resources planning, and should not be discounted.

It is also necessary to sound a cautionary note about information gathered from the new shared spaces NCNs create. Information gathered over a network does not always carry the same cues that might be found when seeking information through more traditional sources. Organisations must be careful to ensure the credibility of the information source, remembering that the trust and familiarity usually used to ensure credibility may not be present in the new networked environment.

A final issue to consider is the impact of making significant volumes of corporate information available via an intranet. The changes in managerial hierarchy and responsibility this may cause have already been identified, but there may be political implications within an organisation as well. Although information may have been readily available on demand before the introduction of an intranet, making it available in a hypertext interface makes it much more accessible. Employees no longer have to know what they're looking for to find out information on their organisation. Because of this, certain departments or areas within an organisation may resist the implementation of an intranet. Using an intranet democratised information availability, meaning that the power inherent in supplying information dissipates. Thus, even though network technology will permit the creation of an intranet, political issues may have to be overcome to ensure that the intranet can deliver on its potential as a venue for information exchange.

Recommendations for Adopting Communication Networks

This section will discuss specific actions businesses can take to assess their current usage of new communication networks, and to determine whether investments in additional network activities are desirable for their own organisations.

— *Determine reasons for using new communication networks*: Although organisations can't predict exactly how business initiatives on the Internet or an intranet will be received, they should have strong notions of why the initiatives are being undertaken. Measurable objectives should be drawn up, and regular progress assessments should be implemented. The implications of running parallel or similar services on and off the Internet should be considered before offering Internet services.

— *Identify the technologies required to enact business objectives*: What are the primary goals of the NCN initiative(s)? Should an Internet presence be established, or will an intranet suffice? The table below helps address these issues.

It is important for a business to understand what it wants to achieve, and with whom it is communicating, before making decisions as to which communication technologies are most appropriate. For those businesses whose communication needs are primarily internal, an Internet presence is not necessary, but an intranet may be invaluable. For those with limited external communication (e.g. with a select group of customers or suppliers) LANs or WANs (wide area networks) may suffice. But for those wanting to make and maintain contact with a wide base of clients and suppliers, the Internet is likely to be the medium of choice. The Internet is now a defacto public communication system, which means that it can be used for a wide variety of corporate communication tasks. The challenge for businesses is to understand the nature of their communications (e.g. one sender to one receiver, one sender to many receivers, public or private access) before selecting the communication technologies they will adopt.

— *Identify the characteristics of users in target markets for NCN activities*: If good business reasons exist to establish a web site, it is important to consider the target audience. Do the prospective customers have easy access to the web? Are target customers web users? For example, baby boomers comprise the largest segment of consumer markets but it is uncertain whether they are well-represented in the electronic community. For customers who are known to be using the Internet, is their access by modem? Will all internal users have high speed access to an intranet?

— *Assess network technologies currently in use in the organisation*: Does the business already have an Internet site? Is there an intranet in use? How effectively do these networks meet their stated objectives? What monitoring systems are in place to assess these networks? Who is in charge of the networks? If these questions cannot be answered then businesses must assess their overall information systems infrastructure and ensure that qualified employees are put in place to manage corporate information technology.

— *Match user characteristics and business objectives, revising existing network use if necessary*: If target network users are primarily individuals who access an Internet site by modem, but the site is graphics-laden and accessible only by the latest version of browser software it would not be a surprise to find that the site is ineffective. As the president of Southwest Airlines remarked recently, customers visit their web site to buy airline tickets, not to download sophisticated web browsers. This insight should be kept in mind by all businesses establishing Internet sites. It is essential to understand how consumers will be accessing a site, and to offer them options that will facilitate their use of the site. In the world of electronic commerce, one size does not fit all. In addition, services or products offered through an NCN must be more convenient to access than by conventional means, otherwise the networks will be bypassed.

— *Ensure that a network management team is in place and has the necessary skills to operate an intranet or Internet site*: A network management plan should be established to address such issues as network security, maintenance and technology upgrades. Which department will support proposed Internet services? Is the Internet function seen as a technical responsibility, or one to be handled by a sales, marketing or public relations group? Which individuals will be responsible for development and maintenance of Internet services?

— *Be prepared to deal with the structural impacts of introducing new technologies*: Management at all levels must understand the nature of new communication networks and their implications at both the technological and organisational levels. Businesses must be prepared to make structural adaptations, and to expect to undergo cultural changes if their new communication strategies are to succeed. Another factor to consider before providing Internet access to employees is employee work habits. Employers should consider the implications of allowing employees unlimited Internet access. While the Internet can increase productivity by improving information networks, employees may spend more time on-line than is necessary. Explicit monitoring of Internet use is not recommended, but employers must be aware of the time-wasting potential of the Internet.

Use of Mobile Communication in Organisations

For carrying out work, people tend to organise themselves, often for the simple reason that together they can do things that they cannot do alone. People organise themselves into groups, communities and networks of varying size and cohesion. An organisation is often defined as a group of people who work together. Organisations show much variety. They can be for instance large or small, hierarchical or flat, centralised or distributed.

There are many types of organisations. One way to analyse them is through the use of metaphors, which according to Morgan shape the way in which organisations are conceptualised and understood. The machine served as a metaphor for the hierarchical and centralised organisations of the industrial era. Later on, other metaphors emerged, reflecting changes in societal values: organisations as living systems in the 1970s, organisations as cultures in the 1980s. In the 1990s, the organisation-as-computer metaphor emerged, to be followed by the organisation-as-network metaphor current today. The shift from earlier metaphors to computers and networks is undoubtedly related to advances in information and communication technologies (ICTs).

Today, there is an array of organisational forms, among them the knowledge-based, alternately known as the knowledge-intensive or virtual, organisation. *Knowledge-based organisations* are characterised by the importance of information seeking and utilisation, as well as knowledge creation, team and project work, collaboration and competition, and the use of information and communication technologies. There are also *distributed organisations*, uniting geographically distant members or parts of the organisation by means of ICT. It is evident that such organisations need tools for communication and collaboration at a distance.

Recently, networks have received much attention as novel forms of organising for work, undoubtedly to some extent concomitant with the rise of knowledge as the crucial asset of an organisation and the advent of the Internet. Knowledge work comprises seeking existing information, creating and sharing ideas, and knowledge of products and services. Knowledge work often takes place in networks, knowledge networks, which can be seen as networks of knowledge-generating relationships between persons linked by face-to-face and electronic forms of communication. Such networks are based on human interaction and have a constant need for up-to-date information and innovative ideas.

Mobility

Mobility refers to several phenomena. People can be mobile, for instance when commuting to work and when travelling on business. Tools can be mobile; common examples are mobile phones and portable computers. Communication and work can be mobile, when people interact and collaborate at a distance through ICT.

The nature of work and the workplace is changing. Work practices are being diversified, as workers are increasingly mobile and ICT enabled. Telework, or distance work, and flexwork, which is a combination of office work and out-of-office work, are commonly practised. Two variants can be distinguished in telework and flexwork. The first variant is *wired* telework and flexwork, where landline telephones and wired computers are used as tools for working and communicating. In the second variant, *wireless* telework and flexwork, mobile devices such as mobile phones and laptop computers wirelessly connected to the Internet are used. By means of such mobile devices it is possible to collaborate with fellow employees outside the office. For instance, members of a team can collaborate even though they are geographically distributed; they can also be away from the "home base," visiting clients or travelling, and still be in contact with the other team members. Telework and flexwork with mobile tools can be called *mobile work.*

Mobile Work

Mobile work involves operating at multiple locations and travelling between them—in moving vehicles, in waiting areas, and in hotel rooms. Mobile work is made possible by communication technologies, from landline phones to current and emerging information and communication systems, such as mobile phones, and wireless and wired computers.

The emerging work practices of mobile workers have received some attention during the last few years. Churchill and Munro sum up that there are workers who themselves are mobile (moving between fixed offices equipped with stable ICT) and there are workers who carry wireless mobile technologies to be able to work in various unpredictable locations, where resources (e.g., connection to the

Internet) may or may not be available. They point out that in mobile work the entire environment where work takes place contributes to the use of mobile technologies. In other words, the interface to mobile technologies includes the environment. Therefore, the health and safety of mobile workers is an important issue. For instance, hotel rooms frequently have poor ergonomy for work.

Mobile work can be analysed from several aspects. Kakihara and his colleagues conducted a study of 60 mobile professionals in Tokyo. Among these, they chose three examples to illustrate the consequences of mobile technology in work: an independent town planning consultant, a freelance computer graphics designer, and a software entrepreneur. According to the researchers, emerging mobile professional work can be analysed from three interrelated aspects of mobility, represented to a varying degree in the professionals investigated. The three aspects are locational mobility, concerned with the workers' extensive geographical movement; operational mobility, in relation to their capability for flexible operation as an independent unit of business; and interactional mobility, associated with their intense and fluid interaction with a wide range of people.

Thus, people can be mobile; people can work or operate from anywhere; people can interact with others who also are mobile and working from anywhere via mobile tools. When interacting with each other, people constantly need to negotiate whether the interaction is desirable or disruptive. From the perspective of many workers, the flexibility of mobile communication is definitely an advantage. For instance, a plumber can take new work orders while visiting a client. On the other hand, mobile communication can also be a nuisance. If the plumber's phone continually keeps ringing, he or she can't get any work done. Thus, the plumber has to make a choice regarding the priority, or must find a balance between accessibility and undisturbed work.

In many lines of work, the possibility of arranging appointments through mobile devices and accessing the company database from a distance helps in organising and coordinating work practices. Mobile devices make it possible to negotiate with clients and fellow employees while away from the office. In fact, often an office is not needed at all. However, it appears that mobile communication is infrequently included in the information system of an organisation, even though access from mobile devices to organisational databases would be highly useful.

How do employees cope with their work in environment where both wired and wireless ICT is used? A study of workplace communication by Valtonen, based on interviews with employees working in a large Finnish machinery company with worldwide clientele, highlights two areas where changes have taken place. First, the pace of interaction with clients has increased, and second, work and spare time have fused together. Such changes can lead to higher productivity, but how do the employees feel about them? According to the interviews, the fusion of work and spare time is not regarded as a problem; the interviewees are used to it. What they especially value is the possibility of having connections with their spouse and children while at work. However, as knowledge workers can operate at an intense pace for a great many hours a day, indeed, fatigue and stress may result.

Mobile Technology

Alongside with changes in organisations and work practices, a new kind of information environment is emerging. With mobile devices, be they phones or computers, people can reach each other as well as sources of stored information, such as company documents and databases, electronic libraries, and encyclopedia. Lyytinen and Yoo refer to such an environment as a *nomadic information environment.* According to them, the main drivers for this environment are mobility, digital convergence and mass scale (meaning that digital gadgets are available for a large number of people on a global level).

Mobile phones have been used in organisations for some time already. They have become everyday communication devices in industrialised countries and they show great promise for building the communication infrastructure in developing countries. Mobile phones are extensively used both in the workplace and in the family, during travels and at home, for business and for fun. Mobile telephony is clearly a global success. It is not only a gadget or technology but also a social and cultural phenomenon. The mobile phone can be used for many purposes. Ling and Yttri distinguish three main uses: for safety or security in emergencies, for microcoordination in the logistics of everyday life and work, and for hypercoordination, using the mobile phone as a tool for self-presentation, personal expression and social interaction.

Mobile phones are a facet of information and communication technology, the technology developed for information processing. ICT has its roots in stand-alone computers, the "number-crunchers." With the advent of electronic networking, computers have gained the capacity to communicate with each other and, through them, people can communicate with each other. Thus, computers have developed into communication tools, permitting such activities as e-mail, instant messaging, videoconferencing and Internet telephony.

Mobile phones have conceptually (though not technologically) evolved from landline telephones, the traditional way for interpersonal technologically mediated communication at a distance. Currently, mobile phones are in the process of developing into hand-held computers (known as "smart phones"), permitting activities such as word processing, e-mail and browsing. Computers are increasingly mobile, too. Mobile, also known as portable and laptop, computers are getting ever more popular, often at the expense of desktop computers. With wired or wireless connections they can be used both for communication, via e-mail, chat and so on, and for accessing stored information. Clearly, computers and mobile phones are technologically converging.

One of the fears often expressed in connection with ICT is that there will be less face-to-face communication, fewer social contacts, in the future. Such fears have been manifested both in everyday life and working life. Computers and the Internet, as well as mobile phones and text messaging, often have been blamed for the experienced degeneration of close contacts and work relationships.

It is certainly possible that there may be adverse effects. In Japan, there are quite a few cases of *hikikomori*: young (usually) men socially isolating themselves from the world often by locking themselves in their rooms and immersing in the Net or computer games or both. Disturbing as this may be, to regard ICT as the cause for such behavior is unfounded. There are contributing factors other than ICT for this kind of behavior, such as general unwillingness or inability to fulfil expected social roles. The Japanese educational system as well as the society at large are extremely competitive, imposing strong demands on individuals and families. In spite of all these pressures, by far the great majority of Japanese adolescents and young adults live perfectly normal lives, with ICT playing a part—and only a part—in their lives.

Actually, both in everyday life and in work organisations there is ample evidence of mobile phones and ICT reinforcing social contacts and networks.

Research on technologically mediated communication appears to show that people use whatever means they have at hand to communicate—if they want to communicate. As Valo puts it in her study of Finnish and American students collaborating in the web:

> However, technological systems per se determined neither the type of personal relationship created nor its characteristics. In the students' experience, their relationships and interactions with their transatlantic partners were not "virtual" or "cyberspace" but a slice, though captivating, in their everyday communicative life.

In the working life, the medium used does not determine the characteristics of communicative behavior. Instead, people use the available media in ways that suit their intentions and their preferences. Technology-based theories such as media richness claim that people make rational choices matching a particular communication medium to a specific task and to the degree of richness required by that task. However, the media richness theory can be criticised for failing to take into account the social context in which media choice decisions are made in organisations. There is need for a much broader social and political framework to complement the media richness theory. Mobile phones and ICT are not simply technological devices but social and cultural phenomena as well; people and technology have a reciprocal relationship. Users shape the technology they use to fulfil their needs, and communication can be rich even when the medium is not.

The consequences of the mobile phone for organisations have been examined by Geser (The word *consequences* that he uses may not be the best word here, as there hardly exists a causal relationship). He presents, among others, the following trends, connected to mobile phones:

— Organisational communication is decentralised. Members of the organisation can use informal channels for communicating irrespective of organisational hierarchy or boundaries (which is sometimes referred to as back channel communication).

— The importance of cultural traditions and internalised norms is reduced, and the impact of particular current conditions (determined by the interaction between organisation members) is heightened. Collectives may be weakened; networks may be strengthened.

— Interaction between clients or citizens and organisations is intensified. For instance, emergency services can be alerted by passers-by.

— A shift from rigid bureaucratic organisations to "adhocracies" is facilitated, where timetables and cooperation patterns are constantly reshaped.

Even though Geser specifically examines the relationship of the mobile phone and societal phenomena, his ideas are probably valid as well for other mobile communication tools, such as wireless computers. Geser comes to a radical conclusion: "It can well be argued that cell phones have a certain 'subversive' capacity to shift the weights from dominant to less powerful individuals and from formal institutions to informal social systems."

Thus, there may be emancipatory potential in the use of mobile tools in organisations. However, the issue is not that simple. When looking in general at ICT use in organisations, there are contradictory studies, some claiming that ICT may lead to empowerment and flexibility and others that it may lead to oppression and rigidity. ICT appears to have a dual function. It can be an enabler, but the outcomes depend on how it is implemented in an organisation. It is important to realise that ICT, whether mobile or stationary, cannot be separated from an organisation's social context: line of business, mission, management, structure, and culture.

Research on Mobile Communication

Discussions about organisational communication and work often start from a simplified notion of the office. Few employees are confined to their cubicles, to be stationary for the entire duration of the working day. Employees go to meetings, visit clients, chat with colleagues, have lunch, and so on. Employees differ much in how stationary or mobile their work practices are. In an organisation, there probably is a continuum from stationary to mobile work. Besides, many workplaces are not offices, but factories, shops—or even geographically distributed knowledge-based organisations.

Consequently, the communication and work practices of employees in different organisations, in various professions, and in various lines of work should be investigated. Questions include: How do different groups of workers and employees use mobile devices for communication (e.g., knowledge workers versus those working in agriculture and forestry)? How are interaction patterns and social relationships formed in organisations where work is mobile and flexible and where mobile devices are used, as compared to more traditional organisations? How can employees be assisted in functioning efficiently in a nomadic information environment? These are but a few questions that future research needs to answer.

A nomadic information environment, where ambient information and communication technology is abundant, presents challenges to the development of information systems. Krogstie and his colleagues emphasise that information systems need to be designed for mobile use, too. Mobile wireless computers are not particularly problematic (though low connection speed may sometimes be a nuisance). A bigger question is to what extent information systems need to be customised for mobile phones.

The organisation-as-computer metaphor of organisation can be associated with the idea of organisational memory, an information system where information related to work tasks is stored. Access to the system is necessary for efficient work. Naturally, information needs to be explicit in nature, as it is codified into the information system. When organisations are viewed through the organisation-as-network metaphor, both face-to-face and ICT-enabled interaction and collaboration are highlighted. Even though information systems continue to be important for efficient work, the creation of knowledge and innovations requires that implicit and tacit information be put to use through human interaction. The relationship of these two approaches is crucially relevant for knowledge-based organisations; further studies are needed.

Research on mobile communication, mobile tools and work is carried out from the perspective of many areas of research. Recently, Kakihara has suggested a new area of research, *mobile studies*, to address the challenges. According to him, the roots of this area of research are in computer-supported cooperative work, mobile informatics, and information systems. However, such a narrow view is not at all sufficient. Alongside with such mainly technological aspects, research is needed in the social and cultural aspects of ICT-enabled mobility, with an emphasis on human interaction and the sharing and creation of knowledge.

References

Allen, T. (1977). Managing the Flow of Technology. Cambridge, MA: MIT Press.

Bishop, L. (1999). Visible and Invisible Work: The Emerging Post-Industrial Employment Relation. In B. Nardi, & Engeström, Y. (guest editors). *Journal of Computer Supported Cooperative Work*, 8, 115-126.

Castells, M. (1996). *The Rise of the Network Society*. Malden, Mass.: Blackwell Publishers.

Johnsen, T. E. (2003). The social context of the mobile phone use of Norwegian teens. In J. Katz (Ed.), *Machines that become us: The social context of communication technology*, (pp. 161–170). New Brunswick, NJ: Transaction Publishers.

Pratt, J. (1999). *Cost/benefits of teleworking to manage work/life responsibilities*. Arlington, VA: International Telework Association and Council.

Rutter, M, (1987). *Communicating by telephone.* Oxford: Pergamon Press.

Sproull, L., & Kiesler, S. (1992). *Connections : New Ways of Working in the Networked Organisation*. Cambridge: MIT Press.

Trevino, L., Lengel, R., & Daft, R. (1987). Media symbolism, media richness, and media choice in organisations: A symbolic interactionist perspective. *Communication Research*, 14, 553-574.

Wildeman, L. (1998). Alliances and Networks: The Next Generation. International *Journal of Technology Management*, 15, 96-108.

7

Effective Business Meetings

Meetings come in all shapes and sizes. There are the everyday office meetings, board meetings, seminars — all the way up to major conferences. And meetings can now be face-to-face, teleconference, videoconference, or online via the Internet. And when is the last time you heard someone say, "Gee, we need to have more meetings." There are more than enough meetings to go around these days, and for a good reason. Meetings are more important than ever. Modern workplaces are built on teams, sharing of ideas, and effective project coordination.

If communication is the lifeblood of any organisation, then meetings are the heart and mind. The place where we communicate our ideas, hash them out, share our passion for better or worse, develop new understandings and new directions. It's where deals can happen or fall apart, where strategies are articulated and debated — in short — where we engage with others. That's what it's all about, people meeting with people

Planning of Business Meetings

Say the word "meeting" and expect to hear sighs, groans, or sarcastic remarks. Yet, planning requires people to come together frequently over a period of time in a word meeting. Well-planned and facilitated meetings sustain participants' energy and allow them to contribute their best thinking to the planning endeavour.

The planning process is like a slide show that follows a logical sequence from beginning to end. Each slide represents a single meeting. The whole of the planning process will be greater than the aggregate of each meeting, but only if each meeting is orchestrated to accomplish the requisite function. Like each individual slide, the composition of a meeting is designed to convey a message or fulfil a purpose.

A large part of the planning process is accomplished in meetings because, as the saying goes, "Two heads are better than one." Each member of the planning team brings an essential perspective to the process. Elements of a plan goals or solutions to problems are not the only outcome of planning meetings. The interactive work transpiring to develop the plan is as important—if not more important—than the plan itself. Think of a time you recounted a funny story, but no one laughed. Then, you realize, "Well, I guess you had to be there to appreciate it." That's the way it is with planning: Those who must carry out the plan with energy and enthusiasm, must be there to help create the plan.

The information is presented primarily for the person who will be responsible for pulling those meetings together, leading them, and coordinating tasks in preparation for meetings and the follow-up steps in their wake. Topics cover the items on a facilitator's check list.

— Identify the purpose, or expected outcome, of the meeting.
— Make sure the right people will be there.
— Develop the agenda.
— Prepare necessary materials.
— Double check the room set up.
— Lead the meeting as a facilitator
— Agree on ground rules
— Practice facilitation skills
— Use consensus-building decision making techniques
— Be prepared to handle conflict as it surfaces
— Clarify "next steps" and assignments

Think Before You Meet

It is not unusual to spend as much time planning a meeting as running it. Preparation begins with asking these questions:

What outcome do we want to achieve by the end of this meeting?

A newspaper editorial from an irate father just after attending his daughter's college orientation session serves to illustrate the usefulness of understanding the various reasons for meetings. This man went to the meeting to learn about courses of study, relevant deadlines, tuition and expenses, financial aide, and safety precautions. "I knew I was in trouble," he said, "when I entered a room full of chairs set up in a circle." The meeting was designed, instead, to explore feelings about one's child going off to college, and to build relationships with other parents.

Whether you identify with the father who sought specific information and was sorely disappointed, or the meeting planners who offered an opportunity for consciousness raising—the point is that the purpose of the meeting must be clearly identified. The purpose drives who should attend, the agenda items, what materials or equipment to have on hand, and the direction of the next meeting.

Knowing that the purpose of the meeting is "planning" is not enough. More specifically, people meet for one of, or for a combination of these reasons:

- Information exchange (acquiring or disseminating information or both)
- Self-awareness or consciousness raising
- Learning (topics and skills)
- Creative thinking and generating ideas (brainstorming)
- Critical thinking (analysis, goal setting, problem solving, decisionmaking)
- Accomplishing tasks
- Building relationships and commitment

To achieve the desired outcome, what must we do during the meeting?

Knowing the purpose of the meeting is a first step in structuring the agenda. Having a firm idea of where you want to be by the end of the meeting suggests what must be covered during the meeting. Do we need to review last year's budget? Do we want to create a common vision of our organisation in the year 2020? If we want consensus on four short-term goals, how can we both inspire creative thinking yet maintain a sense of reality?

Each step in reaching the desired meeting outcome is thought through carefully to determine the amount of time needed.

— Establish how long the meeting is to last
— List the agenda items that need to be covered or process steps that need to occur
— Estimate how long each item will take factoring in time for dialogue
— Leave about 15 minutes minimum at the end for summary and agreement on what comes next.

If, after following the above exercise, the agenda clearly requires more time, revise accordingly. Adjust the length of the meeting (and let participants know), or cut back on what you expect to accomplish. Keep in mind that critical thinking requires more time than typically allowed for in meetings, especially if there is controversy. Opportunities to voice an opinion, ask questions, and explain reasons behind positions are key to developing and achieving consensus on a plan. Short-cuts at this point could cause looping back or gridlock farther down the line.

What idea-building processes would be useful?

Planning alternates between expanding and culling ideas. Visioning and brainstorming help participants expand their thinking. Ranking, cost-benefit analysis, and comparing related concepts help participants winnow their thinking. When critical issues must be addressed, participants might use a problem solving process, or "force field analysis." Without a sequential structure to guide thinking and dialogue, participants become bogged down or overwhelmed. Using a rational framework guides and clarifies the participants' thought process.

Who needs to attend the planning meetings?

As a general rule, planning can be accomplished by a subgroup within an organisation not everyone has to participate. Ideally, the planning group will be comprised of at least one person from each unit or each level of organisational work (i.e., staff, board, volunteer). In addition to representative participation, the planning group should have someone with authority to make decisions, someone who has responsibility for carrying out decisions, someone who knows the milieux backwards and forwards (subject matter expertise), and input from someone who uses or benefits from the service or product the organisation offers.

In addition to diversity of experience, planning teams should encompass diversity of thinking styles. The world sometimes seems to be sharply divided into two types of people big picture visionaries, and practical nuts-and-bolts people. Planning teams require both types. The big picture folks have difficulty reaching closure and won't be able to convert a vision to an action plan. Developing step-by-step procedures is what the nuts-and-bolts types like doing best.

The planning group, at some point along the way, will need to perform tasks best left to individuals i.e., one person is generally charged with a writing project. Allowing two or three individuals to take information from the group, work out an idea on paper, and bring it back to the group for feedback saves meeting time. For example, when a complex issue surfaces, a subgroup may want to meet, and bring back their recommendations to the whole planning group or organisation.

The planning group might decide to elicit public participation for a specific aspect of the planning process. There are a variety of meeting formats to enhance information exchange with the public: focus groups, charettes, open house, workshops. A "talking head" format is the least effective. Make the information flow as interactive as possible.

Occasionally, either because the organisation is small, or because trust has disintegrated, all members of the organisation may need to take part in the planning process. The answer to the question, "Why are we meeting?" should help determine who needs to be there. No one who needs to be at a meeting should be left out, and no one should have to attend an unnecessary meeting.

What should we send participants in advance?

Sending out an agenda before the meeting allows participants to ask questions about it, prepare if necessary, and in general sets a businesslike tone. If participants are going to be asked to read or edit documents, send the material in advance. Even when material has been sent ahead, time for review at the meeting might be wise.

Visual aids assist in making visionary dialogue more concrete. If the planning committee must consider capital improvements to a building, obtain floor plans or blueprints. If planning focuses on publicity for the annual arts festival, make sure participants have calendars. Use worksheets to develop action plans so participants can think in terms of implementing creative ideas.

What's the best way to set up the Space?

The ideal planning group ranges from 6 to 12 members. Most rooms will allow a group of 12 to meet around a table. For a larger group up to 24 tables placed in a U-shape work well. If planning requires participation of a very large group or public input, a face-to-face arrangement may be difficult. At the least, participants should have easy visual and spatial access to speakers, facilitators, or the area of the room where most focus is directed. If the large group will need to separate into smaller groups, try to have separate "pods" of seating already set up so participants can move to their work-group areas without having to rearrange the furniture.

What Equipment will make the Meeting run more Smoothly?

The flip chart is standard equipment in planning meetings. Make sure there is wall space nearby for posting the chart paper as the meeting progresses. In other words, flipping the paper over does not provide participants the benefit of having their work product spread out on the walls before them.

For larger groups, overhead projectors work better than flip charts, but only for presenting information. The group's work product should be recorded on flip chart paper and posted, even if not easily visible by all participants. At least the information is readily available to refer to or review before leaving the meeting.

Computers that project text onto the wall can be very useful when the group is developing a carefully worded document such as a mission statement.

Innovative ways of presenting information enhances participants' attention and inspires creativity. Facilitators, for instance, might employ video-tapes to illustrate success stories or skill methodologies. Visual aids, in the final analysis, however, do not substitute for participants rolling up their sleeves and getting to work.

It is hard to imagine a reason to tape record a planning meeting. Taping can be intimidating and stifle creative thinking. Generally tape recording is used when there is a low trust level and someone anticipates a law suit.

A word about food at meetings: Light refreshments, especially coffee or other beverages can help sustain energy levels. If the meeting is planned for the evening, serving a light meal first allows more control in starting on time. In some organisations, food is an enticement to attend the meeting.

Orchestrating the Meeting

Leadership: In the olden days, meetings were run by chairmen. Bringing in an independent facilitator, or appointing someone to that role is becoming standard planning practice. There is a danger, however, as "facilitation" moves into vogue: It looks easy, but the appearance of ease may be deceptive. The word "facilitation" means to make something easier, so while others look on and think the facilitator has an easy job, the facilitator is working very hard to make it look easy. Behind the scenes, the facilitator has taken training courses, practised, taken more training, learned the hard way from experience, and puts great effort into his or her work.

The ideal arrangement is for the chairperson and a facilitator to work closely in planning and leading the meeting. The chairperson retains the prestige and authority of leader, and provides grounding in reality. The facilitator has process expertise, serves to balance participation, and is better situated to move the group through sensitive issues, controversy, and tough problems. Sometimes groups further divide functions and ask someone other than the facilitator to record meeting notes on a flip chart. Many facilitators use the flip chart as a tool in leading (and controlling) the meeting.

Separating the titular leadership role from the meeting leadership function benefits the planning process in three ways.

- By taking care of process concerns, the facilitator frees the chairperson to contribute valuable input as a meeting participant.
- The facilitator must operate on principles of objectivity. Participation is evened-out and decisions reflect joint thinking. Ideas of the more forceful participants are tempered by the facilitator's probing questions, and if those ideas are adopted, it is because others view them as worthy.
- The facilitator brings an understanding of group process and decisionmaking so that he or she can interject steps and techniques (such as those described in the attachments) to move the group through complex information and controversial positions.

Frequently a member of the planning team must assume leadership of a meeting. On those occasions, the internal leader can serve the group well, just as the external facilitator does, by adopting the following operating objectives:

- Help the group improve the way it solves problems and makes decisions
- Ensure that the group accomplishes its identified outcomes in a timely manner
- Foster within the group an enhanced sense of commitment to one another and to the achievement of goals
- See that group members share and understand all information relevant to an issue, and seek new information when necessary
- Buffer the group from internal and/or external manipulation or coercion

Key Meeting Facilitation Skills: Effective meeting facilitation requires skill in three capacities:

- Analysis
  - Separating content work from process work
  - Identifying interests
  - Framing problems
- Communication
  - choice of words

    — ability to listen, summarise and reframe
    — using questions to stimulate thinking
— Familiarity with process models
    — leadership
    — decisionmaking and consensus building
    — techniques to keep the meeting on track and moving

Analysis. A community leadership group received $2,000 gift for youth programmes from a wealthy individual. No one stepped forward to design and oversee a programme. In the meeting to plan next year's activities, the gift was overlooked. Eventually the president asked what the group wanted to do with the funds. All sorts of suggestions poured forth, always with the same conclusion: The kids wouldn't come anyway. What the group needed to do was decide a process issue before launching into content. They needed to evaluate options of how to deal with the funds (not what programme to implement). The choices were:

— give it back;
— give it to someone who would do something with it;
— use up the funds on a one-time event for youth; or
— implement the programme as envisioned when the gift was made.

After discussing the pros and cons of each option, the group agreed to implement a youth programme. Until they decided that question, they could not focus or commit to any specific plan of action on the content. This story illustrates how a facilitator needs to separate the process issue, prompt the group to take care of that issue, and then move on to the goal or content issue.

The other useful analytic ability is to spot an underlying interest, and bring it out in the open so it can be discussed and negotiated. The president of the school board does not want to incorporate public participation into the district's strategic planning process, claiming it is unnecessary and a drain on time. His underlying interest, however, is that he does not want to be chastised for low student test scores. The facilitator must recognise the validity of the president's reluctance, yet push forward with the requirement: "How can we involve the citizens of the district without the meeting turning into a gripe and blame session?" Once structures were in place to prevent wholesale attack on individual board members, he was quite willing to involve the public.

Problems must be stated without imparting judgment or implying a solution. The problem statement has to be worded so that participants with differing viewpoints accept that description. For example, an arts organisation holds a theme fair to raise funds for its operation. One of the planning committee members raises the concern that a vendor sells items that do not conform to the theme. Note the difference in how the dilemma is stated: "Should we let Henry sell his items next time?" Or, "How do we ensure items are congruent with the theme?" Or, "We're here to discuss sexual harassment," vs. "We're here to agree upon appropriate conduct in the work place."

Communication skills: The facilitator primarily relies on listening and asking questions. Listening enables the facilitator to remember the content, relate the content to the discussion, capture its essence on the flip chart, note reactions of others to what is said, and make a judgment call about sticking with the topic or moving on to the next speaker or agenda item. By summarising the speaker's point, or by recording the idea on the flip chart, the facilitator affirms to the speaker that he or she has been heard and understood.

Facilitators ask questions to control the process and to spark thinking. A question signals progress we are moving on with our agenda: "Shall we begin?" "What did you hope to walk away with by the end of the meeting?" Questions bring the discussion back on track: "Shall we add that topic to the agenda for next time?" "Do we need to make sure we cover the other items before we run out of time?" Or, "Do we need to decide this in order to decide that?" Questions can provide closure: "Is there anything else before we move on?" "What are our next steps?"

Questions also stimulate thinking, and rethinking. Statements can be perceived as, or actually are, challenges provoking a counter challenge or assertion of a superior idea. Questions, on the other hand, create a temporary vacuum a time for reflection. The facilitator, by posing questions, eliminates much of the superfluous posturing and banter. Questions maintain an air of openness, an attitude of, "Let me hear more before I decide." Examples: "If you do this, what will happen?" "Could you describe the process of communication you currently use?" "If you could change one thing about the design, what would it be?" In other words, questions, rather than directives or advice, are the most potent way to encourage the group to focus on something, rethink a course of action, or evaluate options.

"Reframing" combines skill in communication with an ability to analyse what's happening on the spot. Reframing is a way to "launder language." The facilitator extracts inflammatory or negative impact from a statement, and crystalised the legitimate underlying motivation for that statement. For example, a board member emphatically states, "There's no use in going forward with this planning process. What we need is a new executive director!" The facilitator quickly reframes the remark to highlight a valid concern: "You want to make sure staff can carry out the board's policy directives." Reframing a statement so the language is palatable to others does carry the risk of the speaker admonishing the facilitator for not summarising the statement accurately, as originally stated. If that happens, the facilitator would have to rework the wording more to the speaker's liking. On the other hand, the speaker may be relieved to see that there is a more constructive way to present the concern and feel affirmed that someone has taken the concern seriously.

Decisionmaking by vote: Traditionally, groups made decisions by voting, and allowed the "majority to rule." Voting makes sense when:

— Many people are involved
— The population is diverse
— Moving forward is more important than settlement
— Before votes are cast there is ample time for dialogue
— The dialogue includes looking at and evaluating a number of options

The disadvantage of voting is that it leads to an all or nothing, win/lose outcome. What happens to those who voted "nay" and were outnumbered? How committed are they to supporting the outcome? And, what happens to the concerns driving the no-vote. Were those concerns addressed, or will they come back to haunt the yea-sayers? Ample discussion with analysis of alternative courses of action can counteract the disadvantages of voting. Even then, voting might be reserved as a last resort. Clearly, in a small group convened for the purpose of planning, consensus is possible and more desirable.

Decisionmaking by Consensus: Over the past 15 years, making decisions by consensus has gained acceptance, yet a number of misconceptions remain. Consensus is the cooperative development of a decision that is acceptable enough so that all members of the group agree to support the decision. Consensus means that each and every person involved in decisionmaking has veto power. Keep in mind, though, that members of the planning group are team members, not adversaries. Responsible team members use power only to achieve the best results vis a vis the group's purpose, not for their own personal gain. In other words, if a team member objects, it behooves the others to find out why and give considerable thought to the concerns expressed by the dissenting member.

The remarkable result of giving individuals veto power is that they rarely use it! If participants are reassured nothing can go forward without their approval, they tend to relax, contributing more to the content and worrying less about procedural matters.

Consensus does not mean there is an absence of conflict. It does mean there is a commitment of time and energy to work through the conflict. Consensus requires taking all concerns into consideration and attempting to find the most universal decision possible. Groups able to make decisions by consensus usually demonstrate:

— Unity of purpose, a basic agreement shared by all in the group regarding goals and purpose of the group
— Commitment to the group, a belief that the group needs have priority over individual needs
— Participation, ideally no formal hierarchy equal access to
— power and to some degree, the group's autonomy from
— external hierarchic structures
— Recognition that process is as important as outcome
— Underlying attitudes of cooperation, support, trust, respect, and good communication
— Understanding and tolerance of differences, acceptance of conflicting views

— TIME willingness and capability to devote time to the process

Factors working against consensus include: competition, individualism, passivity and solution-orientation

There are many techniques to facilitating consensus:

— Frame the dilemma so participants see the big picture and recognise their interdependence: What decision do we need to make and why do we need to make it?"

— Remove insecurity and make sure all participants have the same key information and have the opportunity to discuss that information together.

— *Build little agreements along the way*: "So we agree that this is a good way to state the problem we are trying to solve." Or, "At least you do all agree that something has to be done, that things are unacceptable as they are now."

— Motivate creativity by asking "Isn't there anything else you can suggest?" and then allow for a long pregnant pause.

— *Summarise and fractionate*: "This is what we agree on, and this is still in question. What are the specific causes for concern?" Or, "How can we get the benefit from doing this, but not the detriment?"

— *Refer to the mission and purpose of the group for guidance*: "If we do this, are we in line with what we are all about?"

— *Finally, ask*: "What will happen if we can't all agree?" Or, "Do you really need to make a decision on this issue?"

Voting and consensus are the "how" of decisionmaking. Decisions, themselves, seem to come in three shapes:

— Some decisions have to be answered "yes" or "no." Either we close the theatre for inclement weather, or we go on with the show. The outcomes are mutually exclusive and a choice is imperative for the good of the organisation.

— Other decisions require finding a solution to a problem. "How shall we solve for X?" "What shall we do about lack of attendance at our performances?" Or, reframing the problem in the affirmative: "How can we ensure record attendance?"

— A third type of decision is even more open-ended. "Which way shall we go?" Or, "What goal shall we attain?"

Try out different ways of framing the decision using the above three formats. The way in which the decision is framed sets the stage for the solutions generated. Different framing of the same topical issue elicits very different solutions. For example, a decision regarding regulation of outdoor advertising can be framed, "Who is going to control outdoor advertising local municipalities or the state?" Responses will be very different from those prompted by the question: "How can local government determine the character of its land use without eliminating outdoor advertising?"

The important rule of thumb about good decisionmaking is "Do Not Decide Prematurely." Ultimately, the thinking process for any type of decision is the same:

— Gathering and analysing relevant information
— Careful framing of the question you want answered
— Discussing values and criteria
— Envisioning various scenarios
— Evaluating consequences of those scenarios
— Making the decision
— Refining specific aspects of the decision and ensuring its implementation

Other Techniques to Make Meetings More Effective

Ground Rules: An essential task early on in planning meetings is for the group to agree on ground rules. Ground rules are logistical agreements a group makes to improve its ability to work as a group. They are the standards of operating that determine how people conduct their discussions and how they will make their decisions. The value of ground rules lies in their very creation. Any preordained rule such as, "We should respect each other" will garner minimal commitment. Only through dialogue will a rule achieve its maximum self-enforcing potential. The discussion can be initiated with the question: "What operating principles should we adopt in order to make our work more efficient and of higher quality?" Or, simply: "What are some important guidelines we should all keep in mind as we work together in these meetings?"

The discussion prompted by asking for ground rules not only elicits the rules; just as importantly, it allows potentially derailing sensitivities to surface. The facilitator can normalise strongly held values and emotional issues. The participants will feel better about themselves as group members and appreciate a greater sense of safety. Some participants may discount the importance of establishing these guidelines up front. The facilitator must be prepared to assert the value of the discussion and negotiate for the participants' indulgence. If the group has polarised around issues, spending time on establishing ground rules becomes all the more important. Ground rules generally take the form of agreements on certain topics.

Typically ground rules centre around these issues:

— The purpose of the planning meetings (what people expect to have at the end of the series of meetings)

— Significant or ambiguous definitions

— Time lines for meetings length of meetings, when they are held, and for how long

— Meeting leadership and other roles

— Participation and attendance

— How decisions will be made (consensus or voting)

— The value of expressing different perspectives how disagreements should be expressed and handled ("Discuss the undiscussable" or "How to disagree without being disagreeable")

— Communication with those outside the planning process

The facilitator can offer one or two ground rules to stimulate the participants' discussion. The faciliator can also suggest thinking about ground rules participants have overlooked. Agreement on a specific rule, however, must be made by the participants.

Flip Charts: Flip charts are an essential tool. The facilitator can use chart writing to:

— Create a record of the work product. Participants can see the notes and make corrections or ask for clarification as the conversation progresses.

— Organise thinking i.e., draft wording, pose options, connect ideas, depict consequences, narrow choices, summarise decisions, organise tasks.

— Keep the participants on track by referring to the topic on the flip chart, or specific agenda items.

The information on the flip chart must be "user friendly." Use large letters, space between concepts (so ideas can be added), alternating colours, and make sure the paper can be posted rather than just flipped over.

Bin Issues: A useful tool for moving participants through the agenda is to create a separate flip chart page for issues raised, important, but either tangential or too complex to deal with during the meeting. Noting these issues on a separate sheet, also referred to as the "parking lot," respects participants' concerns and assures them that the issues will be addressed. (Make sure they are addressed eventually, or that participants no longer want to address them; otherwise the bin issue sheet soon will lose its efficacy.

Next Steps: The facilitator should have a good sense of what is going to happen in meeting 2 when planning meeting 1. That sense is confirmed by taking about 15 minutes at the end of the meeting to ask "Where do we go from here?" or, "What do you need to do so that you can move forward in this process?" There may be a number of tasks participants must accomplish before the next meeting convenes. Make sure to summarise who is going to do what, with whom, and by when. Rough-out major agenda items for the next meeting before adjourning.

When participants reach decisions, the facilitator will need to devote time to how they will implement those decisions. Thinking they are done, euphoria sets in, and participants fail to convert the decision to an action plan. Before participants leave the meeting, the facilitator should pin down action steps: Who is responsible for taking what action by when?

Evaluation: Planning requires a willingness to look critically at how the group is performing. Honest reflection can be difficult. One way to help participants become more comfortable with self-critique in a work setting is to ask them to evaluate the meeting. "What aspect of the meeting did you particularly like? Any insights? What didn't go well? What would you do differently next time?" On a written evaluation, leave room for "suggestions." If participants offer their critique orally, the facilitator will need to encourage them to be critical, that the evaluation is an important part of the facilitator's learning and improvement.

Handling conflict in a meeting: If meetings are well-planned and orchestrated, conflict is less likely to surface. If it does, it probably needs to. The most common reaction to conflict is avoidance. Repressing conflict, pretending it doesn't exist, hoping it will go away, or admonishing participants for disagreeing are all forms of avoidance. Generally the conflict does not disappear, and often times, the situation worsens.

The facilitator is in a good position to help participants engage in constructive conflict. Understanding the nature of conflict, its sources and patterns helps the facilitator remain centred when participants begin to develop oppositional stances on goals or strategies in the planning process.

Social scientists make a distinction between objective and subjective conflict. The source of subjective conflict stems from poor relationships, personality clashes, and differences in values. This type of conflict is difficult to handle because values and preferences cannot be negotiated. Rather, participants agree implicitly or explicitly work around fundamental differences either because those differences do not interfere with getting the job done, or because getting the job done is more important than expending energy on fighting.

If relationship conflicts have been allowed to fester in an organisation, members of that organisation may not be able to work together as a planning team. The group may benefit from a team development programme, sensitivity training, or application of Myers-Briggs Personality Type Indicators to enhance their ability to interact constructively before embarking on a planning process. On the other hand, when participants come together frequently for a significant purpose and experience success on joint goals, often relationships improve. There is no litmus test to determine which of these two routes to follow. The choice may be best left to the participants themselves.

The source of objective conflict lies in the allocation of resources salaries, vacation time, office space, supplies, respect. Objective conflicts can be negotiated. The conflict is framed in the same way a problem would be framed, and the negotiations would resemble problem solving. What makes resolving conflict more difficult than solving a problem is the pervasiveness of strong emotions and lack of trust. The facilitator has to move more slowly, spending time talking with participants individually, finding out from each individual or faction what it would take to be able to work together productively again.

Here too, the planning process itself may provide the group with the opportunity to improve to rethink job descriptions, performance objectives, incentives, and working conditions. Or, the group may decide to put the planning on hold and focus on settling a specific, exacerbated conflict first. When it appears addressing a specific conflict takes precedence over planning, there are a few principles to keep in mind:

— Allocate sufficient time
— Help the participants clarify what the conflict is about
— Do not take sides
— Affirm the validity of all viewpoints
— Frame the conflict in terms of a problem to be solved
— Create space for problem solving to occur
— Help participants save face
— Discuss what happens if no agreement is reached
— Ask if the group can proceed with what they do agree on and hold back on areas of disagreement
— Keep in mind that ultimately, the participants have the responsibility to resolve the conflict

The process to resolve conflict is similar to problem solving. The most important steps, especially when viewpoints have become polarised, are the first four (below). Frequently conflict does not get resolved because the participants begin at step five. The role of the facilitator is particularly valuable to ensure that the participants do start at step one.

— The facilitator gains rapport and commitment from the parties to address the conflict. (Side meetings with individuals or factions.)
— Agreement on the scope of what you are trying to solve. "What do you need to agree on so that you can proceed with your

organisational mission and goals?" This question may sound easy, yet generally requires more time than anticipated. (First time the participants meet on the conflict.)

— Agreement on ground rules, including meeting protocols, time lines, the scope, who participates and the decision making process. (Second meeting.)
— Gathering and exchanging information on the aspects of the scope from technical data to feelings in a joint session.
— Framing the decision to be made incorporating diverse interests into the problem statement.
— Developing criteria by which to evaluate a wise decision.
— Developing options to address the problem statement.
— Negotiating over the options.
— Making decisions, fine tuning terms and implementation plan.
— Checking back to see how things are going.

Following a process structure for thinking and dialogue, sharpening facilitation skills such as listening, reframing, and asking searching questions, planning meetings ahead of time are the basics of meeting effectiveness. Two additional ingredients cannot come from a book (or a computer). The first is a mindset a mindset that: believes in the wisdom of the participants, demonstrates patience and more patience, and conveys a nonjudgmental demeanour. In general, a good facilitator is supportive, respectful, and has enough extra energy to carry a group through late afternoon slump.

The second ingredient is experience. A facilitator becomes better with age having had valuable opportunities to synthesise the theory of process models, skills, and techniques with practical experience.

Sample Forms, Tools, and Checklists

The following items follow on the heels of the previous section on meeting facilitation. You may find any or all of them to be useful tools in your efforts to conduct meetings that produce significant results:

— Storyboards
— Nominal Group Technique

— Action Planning Worksheet
— Interpretive Structural Modelling: Paired Comparisons
— Force Field Analysis
— Principles of Problem Solving
— Looking for Solutions: Steps in Problem Solving
— The Process of Reaching Consensus
— Meeting Evaluation: Sample Form
— Sources of Conflict Diagram

Story Boards

A storyboard uses the same process as brainstorming, with two advantages. First, participants think before they respond. Identifying what you want them to think about is the first step. For example, you might ask the staff of a school to think of ways to create a safe, nurturing environment where learning can take place. Or, you might be interested in learning more about the strengths of a community, and ask residents to think about all the things in the community they would miss if those things no longer existed. Second, if the items are described on post-notes, they can be grouped and combined easily giving participants the satisfaction of organising their ideas quickly.

Storyboards are useful in developing a vision for the future. For example: "If you were to host a visitor who plans to move to your community in the near future, what would you want that person to see?" Or, "If money were not a problem, describe this organisation 20 years from now."

If ideas will span across a broad spectrum, the facilitator may want to think through categories in advance and post those categories to help sort information.

Step 1: Ask the question.

Step 2: Give people five to ten minutes to respond in writing. Use standard sized paper for each item.

Step 3: Each participant posts his or her ideas.

Step 4: Participants have the opportunity to walk around the room, taking in all the ideas and gaining a visual image of what they will create.

Follow-up: The information may be used as a basis for a report or plan.

Nominal Group Technique

— *Frame the question*: this takes thought before the group assembles. What do you want the group to tell you?

  Pose the question in clear, simple language (so that it can be answered with a simple idea or sentence). Encourage participants to think for a few minutes, or write down their thoughts before speaking.

— After a few minutes of thinking individually, ask the participants — in "round robin" style — to respond to the question with one (only one response at a time) of their ideas. Give instructions that this step is accomplished by just listing the ideas, discussion will follow. The facilitator puts the ideas up on flip chart paper (alternating two colours) without numbering the items.

— After all the ideas are up on the flip chart paper, review the list by discussing each item briefly. The purpose is to clarify and understand the logic behind the idea. Unless there is direct overlap of ideas, keep items separate. After discussion, number each item.

  Encourage participants to speak in favour of an idea they believe particularly worthy — or explain why they find an idea troublesome. (This is a key part of understanding diverse points of view.)

— Ranking the items can be accomplished in a number of ways. The easiest is to use sticky dots. Give each participant five dots and instruct them to write number each dot 1, 2, 3, 4, 5. Then direct the participants to select from the list the five most significant or useful ideas.

  Tell the participants, "Now that you have selected in your own mind the five most important ideas — of those five items, give the dot with five points (the number "5") to the most significant and the dot with one point ("1") to the least significant of your five favourites.

Continue giving points according to preference (four points to next most favourite idea, three, and two respectively).

(Participants can walk up to the items listed on the flip chart paper posted on the walls, and stick the dots directly on the items.)

— Tally the totals.

— Ask for discussion on the results. Do the top ranking ideas make sense?

The process can be used with large or small groups. It should not be used to bring the group to a final decision. Action planning is often the next process step after nominal group technique surfaces concerns and priorities.

Action Planning Worksheet

Objective: You have identified xyz as a significant goal for the organisation. Outline the steps necessary to achieve that goal.

Who might share your interest in achieving this goal?

How might you enlist their involvement in helping you achieve the goal?

Who else needs to be involved in achieving this goal?

How will you get them to become involved?

Timeframe: How long it will take to achieve the goal?

When do you plan to begin?

When will you complete your work?

List specific tasks you see as necessary to achieve this goal.

1..............................

2..............................

3..............................

Feedback mechanism: How will you know you have accomplished your goal?

Interpretive Structural Modelling: Paired Comparisons

ISM is a process that forces participants to focus on the importance of one idea in light of a competing idea. The structured discussion about preferences is as much a part of the process as arriving at the end product which is a list of items in order of priority.

Preparation: In a complex, potentially conflictual situation, each item would have a one-page briefing paper to inform participants more fully about what the item encompasses. This step is not necessary for all situations, though.

Each item is written on a piece of cardboard 30" by 6" (so everyone in the room can see when the cardboard is held up by the facilitator). These items are numbered. The facilitator also prepares index cards with corresponding numbers to track the group's priorities as the process moves along.

The facilitator must also prepare a "comparison statement" — i.e., "X is of greater priority to budget for than Y" — or, "A must be accomplished before we can go on to B".

Anywhere from 10 to 20 items may be compared — experienced facilitators have used this process to sort through as many as 80 items. For larger number of items, you need two facilitators — one as a "controller" and the other as a "presenter."

Step 1: The controller picks any two items. For example, item 4 and item 7. The presenter, displaying the cardboard, asks the group, "Is 4 more important to you that 7 — and encourages someone from the group to speak on behalf of each item. Then the group votes which is of greater importance.

Step 2: The controller selects the next item to be compared — compared to the lesser preferred of the first pair. For example, 3 is compared to 7. If a majority of the group votes for 7, then 3 becomes third, so far. If 3 is voted more important than 7, the presenter will ask the group to compare 3 with 4.

For the sake of an example, the majority decides 3 is of greater importance than 4. The controller arranges the index cards in this order: [3, 4, 7].

Step 3: The controller continues to select items to be compared, always starting out the comparisons from the middle of the sequence (i.e., 4 in this example) and moving up or down, depending on the preference of the group. So, if the controller selects 8, the presenter asks the group to compare 8 with 4. If 8 is of lesser importance, then the presenter will compare it with 7. If 8 is of greater importance than 4, the presenter will ask the group to compare it to 3. If 8 turns out to be of lesser importance than 3, the display becomes: [3, 8, 4, 7].

If two items are of equal importance, the display can reflect that. For example, when the new item 1 is compared with 4, the group's vote come out even. The display of index cards is formed with 4 and 1 in line vertically:

```
        1
[3      8      4, 7]
```

Step 4: Step 3 is repeated until all items have been compared and put in order. The presenter then arranges the 30" by 6" cardboard items in the same order as the controller has displayed the index cards, giving the participants a visual sense of their priorities.

Note: This process is time consuming because it involves discussion. Discussion is a critical part of reaching consensus and should be encouraged. This activity should be planned as the last activity the group will do for the day. Participants generally take great satisfaction in both the discussion and the end product of this process.

Force Field Analysis

Force field analysis is useful in clarifying a problem, and finding solutions responsive to specific obstacles preventing goal achievement.

- Participants are asked to focus on the situation with which the group is concerned—a situation they want changed. They describe in specific terms the attributes of the current state.
- Participants then imagine what the situation will be like in five years if nothing is done — the worst scenario.
- Participants then think about what the situation would be like if something were done — what would the desired state look like?
- The next step is to identify the forces driving change and those forces restraining change.
- Participants use a problem solving process to remove or buffer the restraints.

— They identify goals based on the forces driving change.

current state desired state

<— restraining forces incentives —>

GAP

(How can we get from the current state to the desired state?)

Principals of Problem Solving

Let go of the "right/wrong" or "assigning blame" paradigm.

Convey respect for the other person.

Undertake to solve the problem together.

Focus on the problem first, then look for solutions.

Looking for Solutions: Steps in Problem Solving

Prepare in advance for the meeting gather as much useful information as possible.

Agree to meet when there is time to work through a problem.

At the meeting

— Exchange view points
— Define general characteristics a solution should have (criteria)
— Identify sources of the conflict
— Identify goals and hoped-for outcomes (Formulate a clear statement of what you—plural—want to happen)
— Identify any sub-issues that need to be resolved
— Consider many options for achieving the goals
— Weigh the good and bad of each option (What would happen if...)
— Make a decision
— Develop an implementation plan (who will do what by when)

The Process of Reaching Consensus

— Item on the agenda (advanced circulation if possible)

- Proponent introduces item, giving background, rationale, benefits and drawbacks
- Clarification of the proposal itself (keep working on problem definition)
- Open up discussion on the proposal
  - Keep discussion on course (to the subject matter)
  - Keep public record (flip chart)
  - Clarify, summarise, and record new issues
- If there are unresolved concerns, list them one at a time the person who objects should be the one to talk through those unresolved concerns

  (use silence as a strategy)
- Test for consensus again

Responses

- *Agree in Principle*: with minor revisions, with reservations
- *No Agreement*: opportunity to persuade, agree to disagree
- *Blocking*: When one or more (usually two) individuals oppose an otherwise agreed upon decision that has been developed through the consensus process outlined above. Blocking is not disagreement disagreement has been expressed throughout the consensus process. This disagreement strengthens the decision. Blocking comes after the synthesising of differing views, and is a momentous undertaking.
- Advantages of consensus:
  - Quality of the decision
  - Commitment to implementation
  - Fostering values and skills we preach but forget to practice

Meeting Evaluation: Sample Form

(date)

What aspect(s) about the meeting did you find most helpful?

What aspects were least useful to you?

Please offer any suggestions you have for improving our meetings in the future.

Are there any action items coming out of this day you would like to see pursued? If so, please describe follow-up steps.

Rules of Meeting Management

Meetings are unpopular because they take up time—usually that of many people. However, there are good meetings and there are bad meetings. Meetings can be an excellent use of time when they are well-run. Unfortunately, the converse is also true, and it seems that time-wasting, poorly run meetings are far too common.

Rule 1: *Run your meetings as you would have others run the meetings that you attend*: This is the most fundamental Golden Rule of Meeting Management. Running an effective meeting—or being a good meeting participant—is all about being considerate of others. All the other Golden Rules of meeting management flow from this principle.

Rule 2: *Be prepared and ensure that all the participants can be as well*: Distribute the meeting agenda a day before the meeting and make sure everyone has access to any relevant background materials. Participants, of course, have the obligation of reviewing the agenda and background materials and arriving at the meeting prepared. If the meeting organizer has not provided adequate information about the objectives of the meeting, the participants should take the initiative to ask. No one should arrive at a meeting not knowing why they are there—and what is supposed to be accomplished.

If there is nothing to put on the agenda, the organizer should ask him/herself whether there really needs to be a meeting.

Rule 3: *Stick to a schedule*: Start the meeting on time and end it on time (or even early). Starting on time requires discipline by the organizer and the participants. Arriving late shows a lack of consideration for all those who were on time. But if all participants know that the organizer is going to start the meeting right on time, there is a much greater likelihood that everyone else will make the effort to be punctual.

Finishing in a timely manner is also crucial. If everyone agreed that the meeting would last an hour, the meeting should not run any longer than that. Keeping the agenda realistic is important, of course. Finally, if only 20 minutes are required to accomplish the meeting objectives, the meeting should end after only 20 minutes. It would be a waste of everyone's time to let it go on any longer than that.

The time for which the meeting is scheduled is also important. Scheduling regular meetings for inconvenient times (e.g. after the end of the official work day) can have a very negative impact on morale. Emergencies are a reality for most organisations and may necessitate meetings at odd times, but routine meetings should be scheduled at a time that is reasonably convenient for the participants.

Rule 4: *Stay on topic*: Most groups have at least one person who tends to go off on a tangent or tell stories during meetings. Whether this is the organizer or one of the participants, all meeting participants have the responsibility of gently guiding the meeting back to the substantive agenda items. This should not be done at the expense of all levity, of course, as that is an important ingredient for esprit de corps. Also, storytelling can be very useful if it is being used deliberately as a coaching or teaching tool. As a rule, however, someone needs to guide the discussion back to the agenda if the meeting becomes clearly off track.

Rule 5: *Don't hold unnecessary meetings*: Carefully assess how often routine meetings really need to be held. For example, if you have daily staff meetings, how productive are they? Can they be held less frequently? Or, perhaps, can they be held standing up some place and kept to a few minutes? Staff meetings are crucial vehicles for maintaining good communication in the office, but it is important to find the right balance between good communication and productive uses of time.

Rule 6: *Wrap up meetings with a clear statement of the next steps and who is to take them*: If any decisions were made at the meeting (even if the decision was to "study the issue more") the meeting organizer should clearly summarise what needs to be done and who is going to do it. If the organizer fails to do this, one of the participants needs to speak up and request clarification of the next steps. This is crucial. If the participants leave the meeting and no one is accountable for taking action on the decisions that were made, then the meeting will have been a waste of everyone's time. These simple rules can go a long way in making meetings more productive. Implementing them is not always easy, as they require preparation and discipline, but doing so can make a huge difference to the productivity of your organisation.

Tips for Effective Meetings

The following are some tips to help you make your next meeting successful, effective and maybe even fun.

Before the Meeting

1. Define the purpose of the meeting.
2. Develop an agenda in cooperation with key participants.
3. Distribute the agenda and circulate background material, lengthy documents or articles prior to the meeting so members will be prepared and feel involved and up-to-date.
4. Choose an appropriate meeting time. Set a time limit and stick to it, if possible. Remember, members have other commitments. They will be more likely to attend meetings if you make them productive, predictable and as short as possible.
5. If possible, arrange the room so that members face each other, i.e., a circle or semi-circle. For large groups, try U-shaped rows.
6. Choose a location suitable to your group's size. Small rooms with too many people get stuffy and create tension. A larger room is more comfortable and encourages individual expression.
7. Use visual aids for interest (e.g., posters, diagrams, etc.). Post a large agenda up front to which members can refer.
8. Vary meeting places if possible to accommodate different members. Be sure everyone knows where and when the next meeting will be held.

During the Meeting

1. Greet members and make them feel welcome, even late members when appropriate.

2. If possible, serve light refreshments; they are good icebreakers and make your members feel special and comfortable.
3. Start on time. End on time.
4. Review the agenda and set priorities for the meeting.
5. Stick to the agenda
6. Encourage group discussion to get all points of view and ideas. You will have better quality decisions as well as highly motivated members; they will feel that attending meetings is worth their while.
7. Encourage feedback. Ideas, activities and commitment to the organisation improve when members see their impact on the decision making process.
8. Keep conversation focused on the topic. Feel free to ask for only constructive and non- repetitive comments. Tactfully end discussions when they are getting nowhere or becoming destructive or unproductive.
9. Keep minutes of the meeting for future reference in case a question or problem arises.
10. As a leader, be a role model by listening, showing interest, appreciation and confidence in members. Admit mistakes.
11. Summarise agreements reached and end the meeting on a unifying or positive note. For example, have members volunteer thoughts of things they feel have been good or successful or reiterate the organisation's mission.
12. Set a date, time and place for the next meeting.

After The Meeting

1. Write up and distribute minutes within 3 or 4 days. Quick action reinforces importance of meeting and reduces errors of memory.
2. Discuss any problems during the meeting with other officers; come up with ways improvements can be made.
3. Follow-up on delegation decisions. See that all members understand and carry-out their responsibilities.
4. Give recognition and appreciation to excellent and timely progress.

5. Put unfinished business on the agenda for the next meeting.
6. Conduct a periodic evaluation of the meetings. Note any areas that can be analysed and improved for more productive meetings.

Scheduling Meetings

Scheduling meetings is one of the most common tasks in the modern workplace. In earlier days, the time-consuming tasks of scheduling meetings, typing up agendas, and taking minutes was the domain of the office secretary. With the advent of computer technologies and flatter hierarchies, the task of setting up meetings is a chore for all but the highest of executives, and even they get their hands in it from time-to-time.

Democracy works great in politics most of the time, but it doesn't work well in the division of labour. So the reality is that many organisations have high-paid staff doing work that used to be done by lower paid staff. And as any good secretary will tell you, what looks easy when they do it doesn't work so easily for the rest of us.

So why aren't sensible organisations hiring more secretaries to take up this task? Part of the problem is that all of the other work that secretaries used to do has also been absorbed by the rest of us. So, we type our own letters, try to create professional agendas, and blunder our way through meeting minutes. Computer technologies have given us a false sense that we can do all things well, but each of these tasks requires specialised knowledge and skills.

Scheduling a meeting really is not as simple as it looks, even with scheduling software. A lot of judgment is involved, and there is a real sense of propriety required. In bringing any group of people together, there are so many factors to take into account. It could be that there is a certain pecking order, and some people have to work around more important peoples' schedules. Or, some people can best be contacted by phone, some by e-mail, or some through a third party such as a secretary or administrative assistant. Decisions about where the meeting is held are important as well, and very political. For some meetings, a simple announcement will do. For others, participants will need to be polled for their availability and then confirmed later.

The complexity doesn't stop there. Let's look at the kinds of situations that often arise in scheduling meetings — you'll probably recognise most of them

The following are common problems when attempting to schedule meetings:

1) A date and time is announced, only to discover that some important participants can't attend, and then another date has to be found.
2) Participants are polled about their availability for a meeting, but are given so few choices that no common date can be found.
3) A meeting is confirmed, but then needs to be changed.
4) A meeting location is specified in one message, then changed in another, and those who miss the second message end up at the wrong room.
5) So many messages fly around about a proposed meeting that there's general confusion about when and where a meeting is.
6) Someone tries to use an intranet-based scheduling which is fine for work teams, but can't invite outside participants.
7) A work team decides to use a common scheduling system, posting and updating their schedules on an intranet, only to find that after the initial enthusiasm, people get lazy about updating their schedules, or resent having to show their availability to everyone else — and eventually less and less time becomes available to meet.
8) Someone goes through all the trouble of scheduling a meeting then finds out the location they were planning on using is already booked.
9) No one sends a reminder about a meeting, and sure enough, several people forget and don't show up.
10) You get invited to a meeting but the organizer forgets to say where it is, how long it will last, or even what it's about!
11) People get so frustrated trying to set up meetings that they just stop doing it, or won't take the responsibility. It's rare to see anyone volunteering gleefully to set-up a meeting these days.

What are some of the results of this?:

— lots of time wasted
— inefficiency
— money down the drain

Worst of all, there's an opportunity cost as highly paid workers waste their time performing low skill work instead of higher value activities. But didn't we imply that setting up meetings is not such an easy task? True, but it's not rocket science, and rocket scientists shouldn't be wasting their time, and neither should secretaries

Creating a Meeting Agenda

The meeting agenda is a roadmap for the meeting. It lets participants know where they're headed so they don't get off track. Most importantly, the meeting agenda gives a sense of purpose and direction to the meeting.

All agendas should list the following:

— Meeting start time
— Meeting end time
— Meeting location
— Topic headings
— Include some topic detail for each heading
— Indicate the time each topic is expected to last
— Indicate which meeting participants are expected to be the main topic participants

Taking Minutes

These days, many of us find ourselves in the position of taking minutes without a clue of how to go about it. The following is a guide for making this task easier:

— Ensure that all of the essential elements are noted, such as type of meeting, name of the organisation, date and time, venue, name of the chair or facilitator, main topics and the time of adjournment.

For formal and corporate meetings include approval of previous minutes, and all resolutions.

— Prepare an outline based on the agenda ahead of time, and leave plenty of white space for notes. By having the topics already written down, you can jump right on to a new topic without pause.

— Prepare a list of expected attendees and check off the names as people enter the room. Or, you can pass around an attendance sheet for everyone to sign as the meeting starts.

— To be sure about who said what, make a map of the seating arrangement, and make sure to ask for introductions of unfamiliar people.

— Don't make the mistake of recording every single comment. Concentrate on getting the gist of the discussion and taking enough notes to summarise it later. Think in terms of issues discussed, major points raised and decisions taken.

— Use whatever recording method is comfortable for you, a notepad, a laptop computer, a tape recorder, a steno pad, or shorthand. It might be a good idea to make sound recordings of important meetings as a backup to your notes.

— If you are an active participant in the meeting, be prepared! Study the issues to be discussed and have your questions ready ahead of time. If you have to concentrate on grasping the issues while you are making your notes, they won't make any sense to you later.

— Don't wait too long to type up the minutes, especially while your memory is fresh. Be sure to have the minutes approved by the chair or facilitator before distributing them to the attendees.

— Don't be intimidated by the prospect of taking minutes. Concise and coherent minutes are the mark of a professional. The very process of recording minutes can give you a deeper understanding of the issues faced by your organisation along with ability to focus on what's important.

Ice Breakers

Ice breakers are a great way to begin a meeting. They help to relax participants, and that makes them more receptive to listening and contributing. An ice breaker can also serve to build a team atmosphere and to generate enthusiasm. Ice breakers can be fun, amusing, humorous, thoughtful, surprising or just plain silly. The days of one-liner jokes as ice breakers are gone, and there are many new creative ideas. The most popular are games that have participants reveal something personal about themselves, or which encourage participants to get to know each other personally. The idea is that more than just having fun, the ice breaker will truly help to create group cohesion based on trust and understanding.

One of the tricks of an icebreaker is timing. It should not be too long otherwise the serious work of the meeting will not be given enough time. It should not be so short that participants feel it was a perfunctory exercise. Timing also depends on the size of the group, the overall length of the event, and the purpose of the event. An all-day retreat might warrant a half hour ice breaker, but a one-hour meeting may merit only a minute or two. The following are some ideas compiled by category, and gathered from a variety of sources:

Games

— Have participants say 3 things about themselves—2 true and 1 lie, others guess what the lie is

— Have everyone write on a piece of paper their answers to these questions: What is your favorite food, animal, TV show, hobby, and color? Sign your name. Don't let anyone else see the answers. The leader then reads the answers to the whole group, and members try to guess whom each set of answers belongs to. Award one point for each right guess. The person with the most points wins a prize.

— Give each person is given a list of 5 to 10 traits that they must find in common with the people around them. Sample items could be: "Find someone that was born in the same month", "..someone who lives in your state", or "..drives the same model of car". A prize is awarded to the participants with the most in common.

Activities

— Write the words "agree," "disagree," "strongly agree" and "strongly disagree" on separate pieces of paper and post them on four different walls of the room. Then make a statement such as "our organisation can change the world" and have everybody move to the part of the room that matches their opinion. Have the group discuss why they chose their response.

— With everyone in a circle, have someone come up with a short story that they whisper to the person next to them, and so on. Have the last person recount the story out loud.

Simple Lead-Ins

— Ask participants to state one or two "burning questions" they hope will be answered in this session.

— Have participants describe one strategy/resource they have used successfully (relevant to the topic of the meeting/training).

— Have them state their personal definition of the topic (eg., in a marketing meeting, "Participation Marketing means...").

Evite vs. Meeting Wizard

Although Meeting Wizard is often compared to Evite.com, there are significant differences. Evite specialised in sending invitations to social events. The invitation is graphic intensive, and it takes considerably more time to create and customise an evite. There are lots of features to be sure, most of them appropriate for larger social events.

Meeting Wizard is first and foremost a scheduling tool built for the modern workplace. It is an easier and more efficient way to schedule meetings, teleconferences, online conferences or any other workplace event. It's sleek and professional. For example, its messages are sent in plain text format rather than larger and slower HTML messages. Unlike Evite, it is designed to be used in the office every day. That said, many people use Meeting Wizard for everyday social events simply because it works.

In many ways, Meeting Wizard is better compared to scheduling tools found in Microsoft Outlook or Lotus Notes, yet it takes a very different approach from those as well. Meeting Wizard combines the best of an online invitation service with a calendaring tool to give users the ability to schedule meetings and events by invitation. Users do not need to post their personal schedules for everyone else to see, and the system works for anyone with e-mail and a browser. Better yet, if I'm sending a meeting invitation to my colleagues, they do not need to have an account or even agree to use Meeting Wizard in advance. They simply receive an e-mail message with a link to a response page.

Meeting Wizard specialised in giving users the ability to propose multiple times, suggest new times, confirm times, change times, send automatic reminders and more. It is designed with all the flexibility needed in the workplace. It can be accessed on the Web no matter where you are...at work, home or on the road.

What we suggest is that you use Meeting Wizard for your every day scheduling needs, and use a service like Evite for those major social events like Christmas and birthday parties when you want to send something colorful and festive.

Team Building

A lot to ask of any individual, especially one who has not played on any team since softball in the third grade! Many businesses request a team player without knowing what that actually means. Being on a team means being inter-dependent in a relationship, being able to trust others.

But first, one must be independent. If you cannot function well on your own, an office team can turn into an outlet for all your personality flaws. An independent person knows what makes him or her tick, what's important in their lives. These are called values or ethics. These values can then be brought to any team and become part of the contributing process. People who can't be managed or trust others will have a hard time being effective on any team.

A team needs a reason to get together; a project or specific plan that requires results. Of course, it also requires that the owner/manager/supervisor is willing to support the team's success. Remember, teams are not magic bullets. So, let's get started. How do you put a team together? Here are a few suggestions to follow:

— First, the owner/manager of the business must be aware of how teams work. The team is accountable to each other, not the owner. Second, someone has to lead. Third, it requires guidelines. And fourth, the team needs values of its own. Commitment, contribution, communication and cooperation are the four values or cornerstones of the foundation of any capable team or business.

— If one is not committed to the plan and the team, nothing will work. Until there is commitment there is nothing. Being committed means being charged with a responsibility for a particular result. In this time of quicker and faster, not many take the time to do whatever it takes to get the job done. What being on a team truly implies is giving up your ideals for something greater than yourself.

— Next comes contribution, the differences that make a team exciting. Not everyone on the team needs to be alike. You must trust and be accountable to each other, not the owner.

— The owner or manager may lead the team, but allows the individuals on the team to blossom and grow. No throwing cold water over anything new or different! When various types of people are on a team, the abundance of creativity can be a windfall.

— Now, how to communicate all these ideas and values. At the beginning of any meeting, everyone should be heard briefly, without interruption. This is an opportunity to settle in, to connect with each other before the real work starts. This process continues with everyone offering information about themselves, including that sense of humor that is sometimes missing in the workplace.

— Teams can be enjoyable and fun, but no one will know that unless team members relax and lighten up.

— Cooperation means to pool all the resources and ideas of each individual. It also means to put aside your personal goals for the objective of the team. The significance of cooperation is to work together in relationship and that requires patience. Remember, everyone on the team is an equal, there are no bosses.

— A word of caution. Not everyone is a team player. People who are loners need just that, to work alone. As long as they can create results on their own, let them. People on a team have to want to be there. No one wants a person on a team that does not want to be there; they just stall any progress. So, set your plan in motion and have fun

Corporate Minutes

It is vital that all corporations keep adequate documentation in the form of minutes of shareholder and director meetings. In many jurisdictions, the absence of proper records may be a liability for the shareholders of a corporation, particularly in cases where the shareholders are directors themselves, or where they have close relationships to the corporate directors.

Most jurisdictions require corporations to hold annual shareholder's meetings to elect directors. Also, the bylaws of most corporations also require their board of directors to have an annual meeting. Although the board may delegate day-to-day operation of the business, the following actions normally require approval by the board of directors:

— Electing officers of the corporation

— Adopting business policies and plans,

— Designating committees and allocating authority to them

— Issuing and selling stock

— Approving the sale, lease, conveyance, exchange, transfer, or other disposition of all or substantially all corporate property and assets

— Approving mergers and reorganisations

— Approving the adoption of pension, profit-sharing, other employee benefit plans and stock-option plans

— Approving corporate borrowing and loans

— Entering into joint ventures

The board generally should also approve the following types of transactions:

— Designating corporate bank accounts and authorised signatories

— Changing an officer's compensation

— Entering into a major lease of premises

— Entering into any other major contractual agreement or venture

This list does not include all requirements, and some corporate actions require shareholder approval as well. Also, some jurisdictions have different requirements.

Of course, small corporations in particular often have informal "meetings" where these matters are decided. However, it is important to subsequently prepare meeting minutes or unanimous written consents (signed by all the directors in lieu of a meeting) that approve the actions.

If your corporation has not kept adequate records of shareholder and board meetings, these records with can and should be reconstructed with the aid of a legal professional.

You should obtain proper legal consultation if you think that your corporate records might not be getting the attention they should be.

Business Meeting Etiquette

Business etiquette is essentially about building relationships with colleagues, clients or customers. In the business world, it is these people that can influence your success or failure. Etiquette, and in particular business etiquette, is simply a means of maximising your business potential by presenting yourself favourably.

Business meetings are one arena in which poor etiquette can have negative effects. By improving your business meeting etiquette you automatically improve your chances of success. Comfort, trust, attentiveness and clear communication are examples of the positive results of demonstrating good etiquette.

The article will focus on a few key examples of business meeting etiquette for both formal and informal business meetings. Although these are meant as guides to etiquette in the UK they are very much applicable to other nations too.

Informal Meetings

Informal meetings are generally more relaxed affairs and may not necessarily take place in the office or meeting room. Even so a sense of professionalism and good business etiquette are still required.

There are 7 points to consider with informal meetings:

- Business etiquette demands that the person calling the meeting (henceforth 'the chair') should be the most senior or the one with the most direct or urgent interest in the topic at hand.

- The chair should decide the time, place and agenda. These details should be confirmed with everyone to make sure all are in agreement and no inconvenience is caused.
- The chair must make the purpose of the meeting clear to the attendees, how long it will last and what is expected of them, i.e. particular information or preparation of documents. Failing to relay the proper information is bad business etiquette as it could cause embarrassment.
- Punctuality is a must. Keeping people waiting is considered the height of poor etiquette as it abuses their time.
- The chair should strive to ensure the meeting stays within a set framework or agenda so that it is kept as short and effective as possible. He/she must keep circular disagreements and the like to a minimum.
- The chair should (pre-)appoint someone to record the proceedings; documenting major decisions or action points. This can later be distributed to the attendees for reference.
- If the results of the meeting have an effect on others who were not present it is considered proper business etiquette to inform them.

Formal Meetings

The business etiquette of formal meetings such as departmental meetings, management meetings, board meetings, negotiations and the like can be puzzling. Such meetings usually have a set format. For example, the chair may always be the same person, minutes, agendas or reports may be pre-distributed or voting may take place.

Here are 10 business etiquette guidelines that are applicable to any formal meeting:

- Prepare well for the meeting as your contribution may be integral to the proceedings. If you are using statistics, reports or any other information make sure it has been handed out at least three days prior to the meeting.
- Dress well and arrive in good time. Your professionalism is linked to both.
- Always remember to switch of a mobile phone.

— If there is an established seating pattern, accept it. If you are unsure, ask.
— Acknowledge any introductions or opening remarks with a brief recognition of the chair and other participants.
— When discussions are under way it is good business etiquette to allow more senior figures to contribute first.
— Never interrupt anyone—even if you disagree strongly. Note what has been said and return to it later with the chair's permission.
— When speaking, be brief and ensure what you say is relevant.
— Always address the chair unless it is clear that others are not doing so.
— It is a serious breach of business etiquette to divulge information to others about a meeting. What has been discussed should be considered as confidential.

The underlying principles of the all the above business meeting etiquette pointers are good manners, courtesy and consideration. If these principles are adhered to the chances of offense and misunderstandings are greatly reduced.

References

Barry, Bryan. (1986). *Strategic Planning Workbook for Nonprofit Organisations*. St. Paul, MN: Amherst H. Wilder Foundation.

Creighton, James. (1992). *Involving Citizens in Community Decision Making: A Guidebook*. Washington, D.C. Program for Community Problem Solving.

Doyle, Michael and Strauss, David. (1982). *How to Make Meetings Work*. New York: Jove Books.

Fisher, Roger and Ury, William. (1981). *Getting to Yes*. New York: Penguin.

Howard, V.A. and J.H. Barton. (1992). *Thinking Together: Making Meetings Work*. New York: William Morrow and company, Inc.

Kaner, Sam. (1996). *Facilitative Guide to Participatory Decisionmaking*. New Society Publisher.

Katz, Neil and Lawyer, John. (1985). *Communication and Conflict Resolution Skills*. Dubuque, IA: Kendall/Hunt Publishing Company.

Kretzmann, John and McKnight, John. (1993). *Building Communities from the Inside Out*. Evanston, IL: Centre for Urban Affairs and Policy Research, Northwestern University.

Kroehnert, Gary. (1991). *100 Training Games*. Sydney, Australia: McGraw-Hill,

Pokras, Sandy. (1989). *Team Problem Solving: Reaching Decisions Systematically*. Menlo Park, CA: Crisp Publications, Inc.

Schein, Edgar. (1992).*Organisational Cultural and Leadership*. San Francisco: Jossey-Bass Publishers.

Schwartz, Roger M. (1994).*The Skilled Facilitator*. San Francisco: Jossey-Bass.

Winer, Michael and Ray, Karen. (1994). *Collaboration Handbook*. St. Paul, MN: Amherst H. Wilder Foundation.

Bibliography

Allen, T. (1977). Managing the Flow of Technology. Cambridge, MA: MIT Press.

Argyris, Chris. (1986). Skilled Incompetence. *Harvard Business Review* 64(5):74-80.

Arnold H. Schneider et.al., (1975). *Organisational Communication,* International Student Edition, McGraw-Hill Kogakusha, Ltd.

Ashby, W. R. (1947) "Principles of the self-organizing dynamic system," *Journal of General Psychology* (37) pp. 125-128.

Autry, J. A. (2001). *The servant leader: How to build a creative team, develop great morale, and improve bottom-line performance.* Roseville, CA: Prima Publishing.

Bagozzi, R. P., F. D. Davis, and P. R. Warshaw (1992) "Development and test of a theory of technological learning and usage.," *Human Relations* (45) 7, pp. 660-686.

Bales, R. F. (1950). Interaction Process Analysis: A Method of Study for Small Groups: Addison-Wesley.

Barry, Bryan. (1986). *Strategic Planning Workbook for Nonprofit Organisations.* St. Paul, MN: Amherst H. Wilder Foundation.

Berger, C. R., and Calabrese, R. J. (1975). Some explorations in initial interaction and beyond: Toward a developmental theory of interpersonal communication. *Human Communication Theory* 1:99-112.

Bishop, L. (1999). Visible and Invisible Work: The Emerging Post-Industrial Employment Relation. In B. Nardi, & Engeström, Y. (guest editors). *Journal of Computer Supported Cooperative Work,* 8, 115-126.

Blumer, Herbert. (1972). *Symbolic Interactionism.* Englewood Cliffs, N.J.: Prentice-Hall.

Brown, R., & Gaertner, S. (eds.). 2001). *Intergroup processes.* Oxford, UK: Blackwell.

Castells, M. (1996). *The Rise of the Network Society*. Malden, Mass.: Blackwell Publishers.

Charles T. Brusaw, Gerald J. Alfred, and Walter E. Oliu. (1976). *The Business Writer's Handbook*. St. Martin's Press, New York.

Chen, G., Donahue, L. M., & Klimoski, R. J. (2004). Training Undergraduates to Work in Organisational Teams. *Academy of Management Learning & Education*, 3(1), 27-40

Churbuck, D. C. (1994). "Dial-a-catalog". *Forbes*, 10 October, 126-130.

Cohen, S. G., & Bailey, D. E. (1997). What makes teams work: Group effectiveness research from the shop floor to the executive suite. *Journal of Management, 23*, 239-290.

Conrad, C. (1994). *Strategic Organisational Communication—Toward the Twenty-First Century*. Fort Worth, TX: Harcourt Brace College Publishers.

Cooke-Davies, T., S. Cicmil, L. Crawford, and K. Richardson (2007) "We're not in Kansas anymore, Toto: Mapping the Strange Landscape of Complex Theory, and its Relationship to Project Management," *Project Management Journal* (28) 2, pp. 50-61.

Creighton, James. (1992). *Involving Citizens in Community Decision Making: A Guidebook*. Washington, D.C. Program for Community Problem Solving.

D'Aprix, R. 1996. *Communicating for Change—Connecting the Workplace with the Marketplace*. San Francisco: Jossey-Bass Publishers.

Daft, R. L. and N. B. Macintosh (1981) "A Tentative Exploration into the Amount and Equivocality of Information Processing in Organizational Work Units," *Administrative Science Quarterly* (26) 2, pp. 207-224.

Daft, R., & Lengel, R. (1984). Information richness: A new approach to managerial behaviour and organizational design. *Research in Organizational Behavior*, 6, 191-233.

Davenport, T. (1995). "Use the Power of the Web". *InformationWeek*, 16 January, 65.

Donald Pattow and William Wresch. *Communicating Technical Information: A Guide for the Electronic Age*. Blair Press, The Statler Building.

Doyle, Michael and Strauss, David. (1982). *How to Make Meetings Work.* New York: Jove Books.

Drucker, P. (1992). *Managing for the future: The 1990's and beyond.* New York: Truman Talley Books/Dutton.

Eisenberg, E. M., and Goodall, Jr., H. L. (1997). *Organisational communication: Balancing creativity and constraint.* 2nd ed. New York: St. Martin's Press.

Eisenhardt, K. M. (1989) "Building Theories from Case Study Research" *Academy of Management Review* (14) 4, pp. 532-550.

Elizabeth W. Adler. (1991). *Print That Works: The First Step-by-Step Guide that Integrates Writing, Design, and Marketing.* Bull Publishing Company, California.

Engeström, Y., Engeström, R., & Vähäaho, T. (1999): When the Centre Doesn't Hold: The Importance of Knotworking. In S. Chaiklin, Hedegaard, M., & Jensen, U. (Eds.), *Activity Theory and Social Practice: Cultural-historical Approaches.* Aarhus, Denmark: Aarhus University Press.

Ernst Jacobi. *Do's, Don'ts, and How to's: Writing at Work.* Ten Speed Press,Berkeley.

Everett-Green, R. (1996). "U.S. universities announce birth of new baby, Internet II". *Globe & Mail*, 17 October 1996, pp. E1.

Feyerabend, P. K. (1993) *Against Method,* 3 edition. London, UK and New York, NY, USA: Verso.

Filipczak, B. (1995). "An Internet of your very own?" *Training*, 32 (8), 70.

Fisher, B. A. (1985). Leadership as Medium: Treating complexity in Group Communication Research. Small Group Behavior, 16, 167-196.

Fisher, Roger and Ury, William. (1981). *Getting to Yes.* New York: Penguin.

Gillooly, C. (1996). "Blazing a Trail in Intranet Usage". *InformationWeek*, 9 September 1996, 98-102.

Gladstein, D. (1984). Groups in Context: A Model of Task Group Effectiveness. Administrative Science Quarterly, 29(4), 499-517

Hackman, J. R., Brousseau, K. R., & Weiss, J. A. (1976). The Interaction of Task Design and Group Performance Strategies in Determining Group Effectiveness. Organisational Behavior and Human Performance, 16, 350-365.

Hayes, M. (1995). "Working Online, or Wasting Time?". *InformationWeek*, May 1, 38-51.

Heath, C. and Luff, P., (1991). Disembodied Conduct: Communication through video in a multimedia environment, *Proceedings of CHI'91 Conference on Computer Human Interaction*, New York, ACM Press, 99-103,

Hevner, A., S. March, J. Park, and S. Ram (2004) "Design Science in Information Systems Research" *MIS Quarterly* (28) 1, pp. 75-105.

Howard, V.A. and J.H. Barton. (1992). *Thinking Together: Making Meetings Work.* New York: William Morrow and company, Inc.

Illich, I. (1973). *Tools for Conviviality.* New York: Harper & Row.

Jackson, S. E. (1992). Team Composition in Organisational Settings. In S. Worchel, W. Wood & J. A. Simpson (Eds.), *Group Process and Productivity* (pp. 138-173). Newbury Park, CA: Sage.

Jennings, C. G. (1996a). "Creating an Internet Presence for Your Business - Part I." *CGA Magazine* (June), 34-39, 68.

Johnsen, T. E. (2003). The social context of the mobile phone use of Norwegian teens. In J. Katz (Ed.), *Machines that become us: The social context of communication technology,* (pp. 161–170). New Brunswick, NJ: Transaction Publishers.

Johnsen, T. E. (2003). The social context of the mobile phone use of Norwegian teens. In J. Katz (Ed.), *Machines that become us: The social context of communication technology,* (pp. 161–170). New Brunswick, NJ: Transaction Publishers.

Kaestle, P. (1990). "A New Rationale for Organizational Structure." *Planning Review* (July-August), 20-22, 27.

Kamlah, W. and P. Lorenzen (1984) *Logical Propaedeutic. Pre-School of Reasonable Discourse.* Lanham, MD, USA: University Press of America.

Kaner, Sam. (1996). *Facilitative Guide to Participatory Decisionmaking.* New Society Publisher.

Katz, Neil and Lawyer, John. (1985). *Communication and Conflict Resolution Skills.* Dubuque, IA: Kendall/Hunt Publishing Company.

Knapp, M.L. (1984). *Interpersonal communication and human relationships.* Boston: Allyn & Bacon.

Kretzmann, John and McKnight, John. (1993). *Building Communities from the Inside Out.* Evanston, IL: Centre for Urban Affairs and Policy Research, Northwestern University.

Kroehnert, Gary. (1991). *100 Training Games.* Sydney, Australia: McGraw-Hill,

Land, F. (1985) "Is an information theory enough?," *The Computer Journal* (28) 3, pp. 211-215.

Levine, J. M., & Moreland, R. L. (1990). Progress in small group research. *Annual Review of Psychology, 41,* 585-634.

Malone, T. W. and K. Crowston (1994) "The interdisciplinary study of coordination," *ACM Computing Surveys* (26) 1, pp. 87-119.

Manz, C. C., &Sims, H.P. (1987). Leading workers to lead themselves: The external leadership of self-managing work teams. *Administrative Science Quarterly, 32,* 106-128.

McCroskey, J. C., & Richmond, V. P. (1996). Human communication theory and research: Traditions and models. In M. B. Salwen & D. W. Stacks

(Eds.). *An integrated approach to communication theory and research.* Mahwah, NJ: Lawrence Eribaum Publishers, 233-242.

Morley, I., and Stephenson, G. (1969). Interpersonal and interparty exchange. A laboratory simulation of an industrial negotiation at the plant level. *British Journal of Psychology*, 60, 543-545.

Nardi, B. & Engeström, Y. (1999) (guest editors). Special issue on invisible work. *Journal of Computer Supported Cooperative Work*, 8, 1-167.

Neher, W.W. (1997). *Organisational Communication—Challenges of Change, Diversity, and Continuity.* Boston: Allyn and Bacon.

Nikolopoulos, A. and R. Holten (2007) Analysis of E-Learning Implementation Cost Pools. *Proceedings of the 18th Australasian Conference of Information Systems (ACIS 2007), Toowoomba, 2007,* pp. 407-416.

O'Reilly, C. A. (1990). "The use of information in organizational decision making: A model and some propositions." In L. L. Cummings & B. M. Staw (Eds.), *Information and Cognition in Organizations*, (pp. 169-204).: JAI Press.

Olson, G., & Olson, J. (2001). Distance Matters. Forthcoming in *Human Computer Interaction.*

Operrario, D., & Fiske, S. (2001). *Stereotypes: Content, structures, processes, and context.* In R. Brown & S. Gaertner (eds). *Intergroup processes.* Oxford, UK: Blackwell.

Pearce, Barnett. (1994). *Interpersonal Communication: Making Social Worlds.* New York: HarperCollins.

Pokras, Sandy. (1989). *Team Problem Solving: Reaching Decisions Systematically.* Menlo Park, CA: Crisp Publications, Inc.

Pratt, J. (1999). *Cost/benefits of teleworking to manage work/life responsibilities.* Arlington, VA: International Telework Association and Council.

Rasmussen, J. (1996). "The Internet - The Swiss army knife of business tools." *CMA Magazine* (March), 11-13.

Richmond, V. P., & McCroskey, J. C. (1998). *Communication: Apprehension, avoidance, and effectiveness.* (5th ed.). Needham Heights, MA: Allyn and Bacon.

Rutter, M, (1987). *Communicating by telephone.* Oxford: Pergamon Press.

Sapienza, A.M. 1995. *Managing Scientists—Leadership Strategies in Research and Development.* New York: Wiley-Liss.

Sarna, D. E. Y., & Febish, G. J. (1996). "Intranets on the Runway". *Datamation*, 1 June 1996, 21-22.

Schein, Edgar. (1992).*Organisational Cultural and Leadership*. San Francisco: Jossey-Bass Publishers.

Schwartz, Roger M. (1994).*The Skilled Facilitator*. San Francisco: Jossey-Bass.

Sproull, L., & Kiesler, S. (1992). *Connections : New Ways of Working in the Networked Organisation*. Cambridge: MIT Press.

Thach, L., & Woodman, R. W. (1994). "Organizational Change and Information Technology: Managing on the Edge of Cyberspace." *Organizational Dynamics*, 30-46.

Trenhold, S., & Jensen, A. (2000). *Interpersonal communication* (4th ed.). Belmont CA: Wadsworth.

Trevino, L., Lengel, R., & Daft, R. (1987). Media symbolism, media richness, and media choice in organisations: A symbolic interactionist perspective. *Communication Research*, 14, 553-574.

Tubbs, S. (1992). *A systems approach to small group interaction*. New York: McGraw-Hill.

Tucker, Mary L., G. Dale Meyer, and James W. Westerman. 1996. Organisational Communication: Development of Internal Strategic Competitive Advantage. *The Journal of Business Communication* 33(1):51-69.

Tullar, W. L., & Kaiser, P. R. (2000). The Effect of Process Training on Process and Outcomes in Virtual Groups. *The Journal of Business Communication*, 37(4), 408-427.

Tushman, M. L. and D. A. Nadler (1978) "Information Processing as an Integrating Concept in Organizational Design," *The Academy of Management Review* (3) 3, pp. 613-624.

Udell, J. (1996). "Your Business Needs the Web". *Byte*, August, 68-80.

Verity, J. W., & Hof, R. D. (1994). "The Internet: How it will change the way you do business". *Business Week*, 14 November, 80-88.

Watts, J. (2002). Public health experts concerned about "hikikomori." *The Lancet, 259*, 1131.

Weber, R. (2003) "Still Desperately Seeking the IT Artifact," *MIS Quarterly* (27) 2, pp. iii-xi.

Weingart, L. R. (1992). Impact of Group goals, Task Component Complexity, Effort, and Planning on Group Performance. *Journal of Applied Psychology*, 77, 682-693.

White, K.W., and E.N. Chapman. 1996. *Organisational Communication—An Introduction to Communication and Human Relations Strategies*. Needham Heights, MA: Simon and Schuster Custom Publishing.

Wildeman, L. (1998). Alliances and Networks: The Next Generation. International *Journal of Technology Management*, 15, 96-108.

William Zinsser. (1976). *On Writing Well* Harper Perennial.

Winer, Michael and Ray, Karen. (1994). *Collaboration Handbook*. St. Paul, MN: Amherst H. Wilder Foundation.

Wolf, G. (1995). "The Curse of Xanadu". *Wired*, June, 137-152, 194-202.

Zipf, G. K. (1949) *Human Behavior and the Principle of Least Effort*. New York, NY, USA: Hafner.

Zmud, R. W. (1990). "Opportunities for Strategic Information Manipulation Through New Information Technology." In J. Fulk & C. W. Steinfield (Eds.), *Organizations and Communication Technology*, (pp. 95-116). Newbury Park, CA: Sage.

Index